P9-DCJ-771

The Series on Social Emotional Learning

Teachers College Press
in partnership with the Center for Social and Emotional Education and the Collaborative to Advance Social and Emotional Learning (CASEL)

Jonathan Cohen, *Series Editor*

Building Academic Success on Social and Emotional Learning:
What Does the Research Say?
JOSEPH E. ZINS, ROGER P. WEISSBERG,
MARGARET C. WANG, AND HERBERT J. WALBERG, EDITORS

How Social and Emotional Development Add Up:
Getting Results in Math and Science Education
NORRIS M. HAYNES, MICHAEL BEN-AVIE,
AND JACQUE ENSIGN, EDITORS

Higher Expectations: Promoting Social Emotional Learning
and Academic Achievement in Your School
RAYMOND J. PASI

Caring Classrooms/Intelligent Schools:
The Social Emotional Education of Young Children
JONATHAN COHEN, EDITOR

Educating Minds and Hearts:
Social Emotional Learning and the Passage into Adolescence
JONATHAN COHEN, EDITOR

Social emotional learning is now recognized as an essential aspect of children's education and a necessary feature of all successful school reform efforts. The books in this series will present perspectives and exemplary programs that foster social and emotional learning for children and adolescents in our schools, including interdisciplinary, developmental, curricular, and instructional contributions. The three levels of service that constitute social emotional learning programs will be critically presented: (1) curriculum-based programs directed to all children to enhance social and emotional competencies, (2) programs and perspectives intended for special needs children, and (3) programs and perspectives that seek to promote the social and emotional awareness and skills of educators and other school personnel.

Building Academic Success on Social and Emotional Learning

WHAT DOES THE RESEARCH SAY?

EDITED BY

Joseph E. Zins
Roger P. Weissberg
Margaret C. Wang
Herbert J. Walberg

FOREWORD BY DANIEL GOLEMAN

Teachers College, Columbia University
New York and London

Published by Teachers College Press, 1234 Amsterdam Avenue, New York, NY 10027

Library of Congress Cataloging-in-Publication Data

Building academic success on social and emotional learning : what does the research say? / edited by Joseph E. Zins . . . [et al.] ; foreword by Daniel Goleman.
p. cm. — (The series on social emotional learning)
Includes bibliographical references.
ISBN 0-8077-4440-9 (cloth : alk. paper) — ISBN 0-8077-4439-5 (pbk. : alk. paper)
1. Affective education. 2. Social learning. 3. Academic achievement. I. Zins, Joseph E. II. Series.

LB1072.B85 2004 2003063394

ISBN 0-8077-4439-5 (paper)
ISBN 0-8077-4440-9 (cloth)

Printed on acid-free paper
Manufactured in the United States of America

11 10 09 08 07 06 05 04 8 7 6 5 4 3 2 1

Contents

PART II
Effective Strategies for Enhancing Academic, Social, and Emotional Outcomes

PART III
Recommendations

Foreword

In 1995 when my book *Emotional Intelligence* was published, the field of social and emotional learning, or SEL, was just beginning to evolve. Only a handful of well-designed, school-based SEL programs could be found. In most cases schools had put those programs in place as part of a "war on . . ." a particular problem, such as reducing dropouts, substance abuse, unwanted teen pregnancies, or school violence. Some of those programs were quite effective. Others yielded disappointing results.

As a William T. Grant Foundation study revealed, the active ingredients in the programs that worked were largely the same, no matter their ostensible target problem. The best SEL programs were implemented throughout each year of schooling. They shaped the entire school climate, and they used developmentally appropriate lessons. They also taught children specific social-emotional skills like self-awareness, self-management, empathy, perspective taking, and cooperation. In short, they were lessons in emotional intelligence.

In the intervening years, scientific data demonstrating the effectiveness of SEL programs as interventions that help lower the risk of various problems young people face, and that increase their skills in addressing life's challenges, have been accumulating steadily. But along with the case for SEL as a prevention and promotion strategy, another benefit has emerged: social and emotional learning facilitates academic learning. Thus, it offers a much-needed and very timely aid to schools in fulfilling their main mission.

Why should helping students in the social and emotional realms of their lives enhance their academic learning? If we think back to our school days and remember a teacher we enjoyed, we almost certainly will bring to mind also a classroom environment where we enjoyed learning. From the perspective of neuroscience, that optimal learning environment reflects an internal brain state well attuned for learning.

Most of us have assumed that the kind of academic learning that goes on in school has little or nothing to do with one's emotions or social environment. Now neuroscience is telling us exactly the opposite. The emotional centers of the brain are intricately interwoven with the neocortical areas involved in cognitive learning. When a child trying to learn is caught up in a distressing emotion, the centers for learning are temporarily hampered. The child's attention becomes preoccupied with whatever may be the source of the trouble. Because attention is itself a limited capacity, the child has that much less ability to hear, understand, or remember what a teacher or a book is saying. In short, there is a direct link between emotions and learning.

Multiple research studies reported in this book demonstrate that social and emotional learning programs pave the way for better academic learning. They teach children social and emotional skills that are intimately linked with cognitive development. In the ideal learning environment, children are focused, fully attentive, motivated, and engaged, and enjoy their work. Such a classroom climate can be one benefit of SEL. Similarly, caring relationships with teachers and other students increase students' desire to learn. School–family partnerships help students to do better. And, students who are more confident in their abilities try harder.

In short, BUILDING ACADEMIC SUCCESS ON SOCIAL AND EMOTIONAL LEARNING presents powerful evidence of the links between SEL and academic learning. It offers schools scientific evidence and pragmatic examples of how SEL programs can enhance students' success in school and in life. At a time when so many students at so many ages are flooded with anxiety as they struggle to succeed on standardized tests, this is welcome news. Today's growing emphasis on academic success and school accountability makes SEL programs more relevant—and useful—to schools than ever before. Thus, this groundbreaking book belongs on the shelves of all who are interested in giving students essential tools to succeed.

—Daniel Goleman

Acknowledgments

This book reflects the efforts of many individuals, and we'd like to take this opportunity to acknowledge those whose contributions helped us to complete it.

Margaret C. Wang provided much of the initial vision and energy that made this book possible. Although her passing shocked many who were unaware of her illness, her contributions continue to inspire and guide educators who care about children's learning and welfare.

Initial versions of the chapters of this book were featured at a national invitational conference held at Temple University in October 2000 to stimulate thinking about social and emotional learning (SEL) and school success. The conference was part of the Laboratory for Student Success (LSS) Signature Series of national invitational conferences. The purpose of the Series is to initiate discussion and compile the latest research on educational topics of national interest. The Series gathers a variety of stakeholders and topic experts to exchange ideas and information and develop next step recommendations. The Series is part of the mission of the LSS to disseminate information in support of student success. The gathering was supported by a grant from the Institute of Education Sciences, formerly the Office of Educational Research and Improvement of the U.S. Department of Education, to the Mid-Atlantic Regional Educational Laboratory for Student Success at the Temple University Center for Research in Human Development and Education. JoAnn Manning, Executive Director of LSS, Marilyn Murphy, Director of Outreach and Dissemination, and Stephen Page, Managing Editor, coordinated the conference and assisted in the manuscript production and in a number of other ways. Their support is appreciated.

The conference was co-sponsored by the Collaborative for Academic, Social, and Emotional Learning (CASEL). This organization provides international leadership for researchers, educators, and policy makers to advance the science and practice of school-based social and emotional learning. CASEL's mission is to establish effective SEL as an essential part of education from preschool through high school. Its three priorities are to advance the science of SEL by identifying what works, how it works, and how it contributes to children's social-emotional development; to improve the quality of school-wide and district-wide SEL practice; and to foster the widespread implementation of evidence-based SEL practices. Among its activities are dissemination of information about scientifically based SEL strategies, enhancement of the professional preparation of educators so they have the tools to implement high-quality SEL instruction, and networking and collaborating with educators, scientists, policy makers, and interested citizens to increase the coordination of SEL efforts.

Our colleagues on the CASEL Leadership Team (Tim Shriver, Maurice Elias, Sheldon Berman, Patricia Caesar, Daniel Goleman, Mark Greenberg, Eileen Rockefeller Growald, Norris Haynes, Janice Jackson, Beverly Long, JoAnn Manning, Janet Patti, Terry Pickeral, and David Sluyter) and staff members Mary Utne O'Brien, Kay Ragozzino, Hank Resnick, and Linda Lantieri are owed our continuing gratitude for the stimulation, insights, leadership, and friendship they provide. We also acknowledge May Stern at the University of Illinois at Chicago who made this entire project much more manageable with her great organizational skills.

We also express our appreciation to CASEL's funders who make this work possible: the Academic Development Institute, the John E. Fetzer Institute, the Ford Foundation, the Joseph P. Kennedy, Jr. Foundation, the Mid-Atlantic Regional Educational Laboratory for Student Success at Temple University, the Surdna Foundation, the U.S. Department of Education Office of Educational Research and Improvement, the U.S. Department of Education Safe and Drug-Free Schools Office, the Illinois Governor's Office, the University of Illinois at Chicago, and the William T. Grant Foundation.

It was a true pleasure to work with the gifted contributors to this volume. The spirit of cooperation and enthusiasm that they exhibited throughout this project was inspirational. We also thank the participants at the invitational conference, as each of them contributed to this volume and many of their ideas are reflected in the final chapter.

Finally, completion of this book would not have been possible without the continued support, encouragement, and understanding of our families. In particular, Joseph Zins wishes to express his love and appreciation to Charlene R. Ponti and their children, Lauren, Michael, and Ryan Ponti-Zins, who keep him focused on what's important. Roger Weissberg expresses similar sentiments to his wonderful, loving, supportive family, Stephanie Wright, Elizabeth Weissberg, and Ted Weissberg.

PART I

The Foundations of Social and Emotional Learning

CHAPTER 1

The Scientific Base Linking Social and Emotional Learning to School Success

JOSEPH E. ZINS, MICHELLE R. BLOODWORTH, ROGER P. WEISSBERG, AND HERBERT J. WALBERG

Schools will be most successful in their educational mission when they integrate efforts to promote children's academic, social, and emotional learning (Elias et al., 1997). There is general agreement that it is important for schools to foster children's social-emotional development, but all too often educators think about this focus in a fragmented manner, either as an important end in itself or as a contributor to enhancing children's health (e.g., drug prevention), safety (e.g., violence prevention), or citizenship (e.g., service learning). Although social and emotional learning (SEL) plays important roles in influencing these nonacademic outcomes, SEL also has a critical role in improving children's academic performance and lifelong learning. This chapter and book make a compelling conceptual and empirical case for linking SEL to improved school attitudes, behavior, and performance.

Intrinsically, schools are social places and learning is a social process. Students do not learn alone but rather in collaboration with their teachers, in the company of their peers, and with the support of their families. Emotions can facilitate or hamper their learning and their ultimate success in school. Because social and emotional factors play such an important role, schools must attend to this aspect of the educational process for the benefit of all students. Indeed most do. There is a long history of schools focusing on areas such as social responsibility and moral character (e.g., Jackson, 1968), and learning and behaving responsibly in the classroom have been seen as causally related. Researchers have found that prosocial behavior in the classroom is linked with positive intellectual outcomes (e.g., DiPerna & Elliott, 1999; Feshbach & Feshbach, 1987; Haynes, Ben-Avie, & Ensign,

 ISBN 0-8077-4439-5 (pbk), ISBN 0-8077-4440-9 (cloth).

2003; Pasi, 2001) and is predictive of performance on standardized achievement tests (e.g., Cobb, 1972; Malecki & Elliott, 2002; Welsh, Park, Widaman, & O'Neil, 2001; Wentzel, 1993). Conversely, antisocial conduct often co-occurs with poor academic performance (Hawkins, Farrington, & Catalano, 1998). But, beyond such correlational findings, it is crucial to determine whether interventions can be designed to promote social and emotional learning, and if there is empirical evidence that these SEL efforts improve children's success in school and life. Thus, the focus of this book is on *interventions* that enhance academic, social, and emotional learning.

Social and emotional learning is an integral element of education in an increasing number of schools, and such instruction is consistent with teacher education standards (see Fleming & Bay, this volume). SEL is the process through which we learn to recognize and manage emotions, care about others, make good decisions, behave ethically and responsibly, develop positive relationships, and avoid negative behaviors (Elias et al., 1997). These key characteristics need to be developed for our children to be successful not only in school but in life; those who do not possess these skills are less likely to succeed. They are particularly important for children to develop because they are linked to a variety of behaviors with long-term implications. In addition, because schools have access to virtually all children and are expected to educate them to become responsible, contributing citizens, they are ideal settings in which to promote children's social-emotional as well as academic development.

The need to address the social-emotional challenges that interfere with students' connecting to and performance in school is critical. Issues such as discipline, disaffection, lack of commitment, alienation, and dropping out frequently limit success in school or even lead to failure. Related to the need for such instruction, the many new professionals entering the teaching force need training in how to address social-emotional learning to manage their classrooms more effectively, to teach their students better, and to cope successfully with students who are challenging. Moreover, such skills likely will help these teachers to manage their own stress more effectively and to engage in problem solving more skillfully in their own lives.

Adelman and Taylor (2000) argue that if schools focus only on academic instruction and school management in their efforts to help students attain academic success, they will likely fall short of their goals. As an alternative, these authors propose a model that includes a third domain, an enabling component, that is combined with the instructional and management components. This component promotes academic success and addresses barriers to learning, development, and teaching. It includes activities such as resource coordination, classroom-focused enabling, support for transitions, and home involvement in schooling. The enabling component is an essential facet of efforts to improve academic success, and SEL serves as a critical element of it by assisting students in navigating the social and emotional contexts of the classroom effectively and by helping schools create positive environments conducive to learning. This three-component model recognizes that addressing students' social and emotional development is not an additional duty charged to schools along with academic instruction, but rather is an integral and necessary aspect to helping all students succeed.

Recent years have witnessed growing pressure and much greater interest from professionals and the public in how well schools perform with respect to student achievement. The No Child Left Behind Act of 2002, with its requirements for accountability through state and district report cards and testing of children (U.S. Department of Education, 2002), is an example of such heightened emphasis. How well schools prepare students for these various high-stakes tests has become the gold standard. While most schools remain highly concerned about the social and emotional development of their students and the need for safe, supportive schools that educate socially and emotionally competent students (Learning First Alliance, 2001), they often are hesitant to engage in any activities for which they cannot predict clear, discernable benefits to students' academic progress as reflected in their test scores. Therefore, in this era of academic accountability, receptivity for SEL programming will be even greater if a strong empirical case is made connecting the enhancement of social and emotional influences to improved school behavior and academic performance. To that end, a number of analyses of school-based prevention programs conducted in recent years provide general agreement that some of these programs are effective in reducing maladaptive behaviors, including those related to school success (e.g., Durlak, 1995; Gottfredson, 2001; Institute of Medicine, 1994), a conclusion that was not as strongly supported in the past. Indeed, this level of support and the recognized need for SEL is greater than at any time in recent decades, thereby presenting an opportunity to which educators and policy makers must give serious consideration.

One problem with current efforts to promote social and emotional learning is that they are quite often fragmented. That is, there are separate programs to promote health, prevent violence and delinquency, encourage school bonding and attachment, prevent dropping out, and decrease teen pregnancy and AIDS. As a result, there simply have been too many programs introduced; schools nationally are implementing a median of 14 practices to prevent problem behavior and to promote safe environments. With this proliferation of efforts, the question must be raised about how well they can carry out so many different activities (Gottfredson & Gottfredson, 2001). It also is a mistake to address these problems in isolation instead of establishing holistic, coordinated approaches that effectively address academic performance mediators such as motivation, self-management, goal setting, engagement, and so forth (see Christensen & Havsy, this volume).

Our goal is to examine relationships between SEL and *school success*, an outcome that, to be fully understood, must be defined far more broadly than as the scores students receive on standardized tests (Elias, Wang, Weissberg, Zins, & Walberg, 2002). Success in school can be reflected in many ways, and contributors to this volume discuss a vast array of variables associated with school success that can be addressed through effective SEL practices. Examples include school *attitudes* (e.g., motivation, responsibility, attachment), school *behavior* (engagement, attendance, study habits), and school *performance* (e.g., grades, subject mastery, test performance). These are important components that can foster commitment to academics and effective school performance.

In the next section of this chapter we define SEL and high-quality SEL programming so that readers understand the scientific foundations of the field and the bases on which the other chapters are grounded. Following that discussion we review some relevant findings from the literature. We then provide an overview of the contents and conclude with some thoughts about the field.

EFFECTIVE PRACTICES FOR SOCIAL AND EMOTIONAL LEARNING

As noted earlier, we define SEL as the process through which children enhance their ability to integrate thinking, feeling, and behaving to achieve important life tasks. Those competent in SEL are able to recognize and manage their emotions, establish healthy relationships, set positive goals, meet personal and social needs, and make responsible and ethical decisions (Elias et al., 1997; Payton et al., 2000).

Person-Centered Focus

Social and emotional education involves teaching children to be self-aware, socially cognizant, able to make responsible decisions, and competent in self-management and relationship-management skills so as to foster their academic success. The framework in Figure 1.1 makes it clear that children need to be aware of themselves and others; that they need to make responsible decisions; that they need to be ethical and respectful of others; and that they need to give consideration to the situation and relevant norms. They also need to manage their emotions and behaviors and to possess behavioral so-

Figure 1.1. Framework of person-centered key SEL competencies.

Self-Awareness
Identifying and recognizing emotions
Accurate self-perception
Recognizing strengths, needs, and values
Self-efficacy
Spirituality

Social Awareness
Perspective taking
Empathy
Appreciating diversity
Respect for others

Responsible Decision Making
Problem identification and situation analysis
Problem solving
Evaluation and reflection
Personal, moral, and ethical responsibility

Self-Management
Impulse control and stress management
Self-motivation and discipline
Goal setting and organizational skills

Relationship Management
Communication, social engagement, and building relationships
Working cooperatively
Negotiation, refusal, and conflict management
Help seeking and providing

cial skills that enable them to carry out solutions effectively with others. As a result, these skills and attitudes can help students feel motivated to succeed, to believe in their success, to communicate well with teachers, to set academic goals, to organize themselves to achieve these goals, to overcome obstacles, and so forth. In sum, their attachment to school and commitment to academics can be fostered so that they lead to effective school performance.

Environmental Focus

It is not sufficient to focus only on person-centered skill development. Consequently, effective SEL interventions are provided within supportive environments, and they also are directed at enhancing the social-emotional environmental factors that influence learning so that the climate is caring, safe, supportive, and conducive to success (Hawkins, 1997; Learning First Alliance, 2001). Communication styles, high performance expectations, classroom structures and rules, school organizational climate, commitment to the academic success of all students, district policies, and openness to parental and community involvement are all important. They can build on one another and foster the development, effective application, extension, and generalization of SEL skills to multiple settings and situations, as well as remove some barriers to learning (see Christenson & Havsy and Hawkins, Smith, & Catalano, this volume, for discussion of this aspect). Schools can give students ample opportunities to develop and practice appropriate social-emotional skills and serve as bases from which to promote and reinforce SEL. Ultimately, these efforts can enable students to become knowledgeable, responsible, caring, productive, nonviolent, ethical, and contributing members of society (Elias et al., 1997).

ILLUSTRATIVE MODEL FOR SEL PROGRAMMING AND SCHOOL SUCCESS

Figure 1.2 illustrates the connection between evidence-based SEL programming and better academic performance and success in school and in life. It indicates that SEL interventions and skill development should occur within a supportive learning environment, as well as help to produce such a climate. As a result, opportunities for reward are created and SEL competencies are developed and reinforced. These enablers in turn lead to more assets and greater attachment and engagement in school. The final outcome is improved performance in school and life (Collaboration for Academic, Social, and Emotional Learning, 2003).

SEL INSTRUCTIONAL APPROACHES THAT ENABLE ACADEMIC ACHIEVEMENT

Today's most effective SEL efforts are characterized as being provided in more coordinated, sustained, and systematic ways using comprehensive, multiyear, multicomponent approaches (see Figure 1.3) (Elias et al., 1997) than was the case in the past. Brown, Roderick, Lantieri, and Aber and others, this vol-

Figure 1.2. Evidence-based SEL programming paths to success in school and in life.

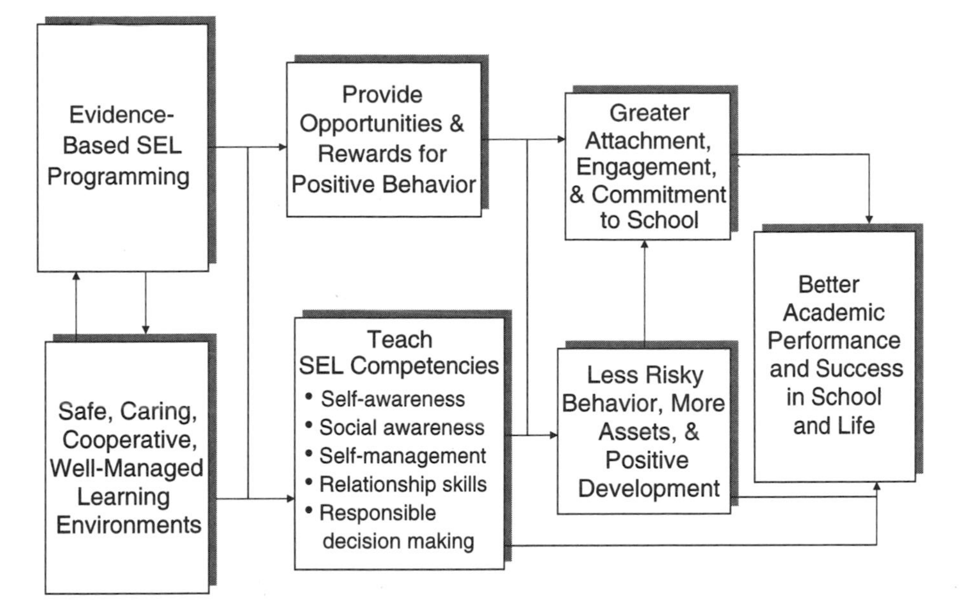

ume, present examples of such multifaceted interventions. In addition, we are learning more about the relationship of neurocognitive functioning and our emotions, and there are promising examples of how this body of knowledge can be applied to strengthen SEL instruction (see Greenberg, Kusché, & Riggs, this volume). Furthermore, the promotion of social-emotional learning goals is no longer seen as "separate" or even parallel to the academic mission of schools; rather, it is essential and can be taught and implemented in schools in a number of ways.

A number of SEL instructional approaches can be used to promote school achievement. First, there are *specific SEL curricula* (Collaborative for Academic, Social, and Emotional Learning, 2003; Osher, Dwyer, & Jackson, 2002) that address content areas such as substance abuse or bullying. Second, social-emotional skills also can be *infused into the regular academic curriculum* so that academic and SEL skills are coordinated and reinforce one another. Once students possess skills such as being able to set goals and solve problems, they can apply them to enhance their study behaviors and increase their academic engagement, or these same skills can be applied to subjects such as social studies and literacy. Schaps, Battistich, and Solomon, this volume, show how SEL can be integrated with the language arts curriculum, and Elias illustrates its infusion across the curriculum. As a result

Figure 1.3. Essential characteristics of effective SEL programming.

Carefully Planned, Theory and Research Based

- Organized systematically to address identified local needs
- Based on sound theories of child development, learning, prevention science, and empirically validated practices
- Implementation monitoring and program evaluation incorporated during planning process

Teaches SEL Skills for Application to Daily Life

- Instruction in broad range of social-emotional skills, knowledge, and attitudes provided in developmentally and socioculturally appropriate ways
- Personal and social applications encourage generalization to multiple problem areas and settings
- Helps develop positive, respectful, ethical attitudes and values about self, others, work, and citizenship
- Skills include recognizing and managing emotions, appreciating perspectives of others, setting positive goals, making responsible decisions, and handling interpersonal interactions effectively

Addresses Affective and Social Dimensions of Learning

- Builds attachment to school through caring, engaging, interactive, cooperative classroom, and school-wide practices
- Strengthens relationships among students, teachers, other school personnel, families, and community members
- Encourages and provides opportunities for participation
- Uses diverse, engaging teaching methods that motivate and involve students
- Promotes responsibility, cooperation, and commitment to learning
- Nurtures sense of security, safety, support, and belonging
- Emphasizes cultural sensitivity and respect for diversity

Leads to Coordinated, Integrated, and Unified Programming Linked to Academic Outcomes

- Offers unifying framework to promote and integrate social-emotional and academic development
- Integral aspect of formal and informal academic curriculum and daily routines (e.g., lunch, transitions, playground, extracurricular)
- Provided systematically to students over multiple years, prekindergarten through high school
- Coordinated with student support services efforts, including health, nutrition, service learning, physical education, psychology, counseling, and nursing

(*continued*)

Figure 1.3 *(cont.)*

Addresses Key Implementation Factors to Support Effective Social and Emotional Learning and Development

- Promotes a safe, caring, nurturing, cooperative, and challenging learning environment
- Monitors characteristics of the intervention, training and technical support, and environmental factors on an ongoing basis to ensure high-quality implementation
- Provides leadership, opportunities for participation in planning, and adequate resources
- Institutional policies aligned with and reflect SEL goals
- Offers well-planned professional development, supervision, coaching, support, and constructive feedback

Involves Family and Community Partnerships

- Encourages and coordinates efforts and involvement of students, peers, parents, educators, and community members
- SEL-related skills and attitudes modeled and applied at school, home, and in the community

Design Includes Continuous Improvement, Outcome Evaluation, and Dissemination Components

- Uses program evaluation results for continuous improvement to determine progress toward identified goals and needed changes
- Multifaceted evaluation undertaken to examine implementation, process, and outcome criteria
- Results shared with key stakeholders

of these efforts, materials become more relevant and engaging, and students' motivation to learn can increase.

A third approach, illustrated by Hawkins and colleagues, is to *develop a supportive learning environment* so that student learning occurs within a safe, caring atmosphere in which high expectations are expressed and there are many opportunities for reinforcement. Students thus may be more engaged, feel more attachment, and exert greater effort. Closer relationships and better communication with teachers may result, and students may be better able to seek help when they need it. These authors also describe proactive classroom management, which can lead to better discipline and a more orderly environment in which students can learn better.

Altering the instructional process to promote social-emotional skills and learning is another approach. A good example is described by Johnson and

Johnson, who review the research on cooperative learning. Within such classrooms, students not only experience the excitement of learning academic material from one another, but they also develop important skills in negotiation and conflict resolution, and a peer culture for supporting academic achievement is developed. A fifth example of how instruction can be provided is found in programming in which the *informal curriculum*, such as the learning that takes place in morning meetings, the lunchroom, on the playground, or in extracurricular activities, is used as a basis for improving behaviors so students are better able to participate in the classroom and thus become more effective learners. Schaps and colleagues illustrate this type of approach.

Partnerships between parents and teachers, as described by Christenson and Havsy, represent a sixth approach. Such efforts to create good social relationships can help make expectations clearer and also provide additional support and encouragement for student learning.

Finally, *engaging students actively and experientially in the learning process* can be highly beneficial. The best SEL approaches encourage application of SEL competencies to real-life situations, and combining SEL and service learning is an excellent way to utilize innovative instructional methodologies to engage students in the learning process. Service learning involves "teaching and learning . . . that integrates community service with academic study to enrich learning, teach civic responsibility, and strengthen communities" (National Commission on Service Learning, 2002, p. 3). The Teen Outreach program, for example, contains an explicit developmental focus aimed at reducing rates of teen pregnancy and school failure through structured service learning experiences in the community, along with classroom-based discussion of the service experiences (Allen, Philliber, Herrling, & Kuperminc, 1997). The program also incorporates classroom-based discussion of social-developmental tasks such as understanding oneself and one's values, human growth and development, and social and emotional transitions from adolescence to adulthood. Students who participated in the program reported significantly fewer pregnancies, school suspensions, and failed courses during the year compared with controls. It can be hypothesized that as an enabling component, the program's positive outcomes are in part related to the promotion and development of SEL skills such as self-awareness, empathy, problem solving, adaptive goal setting, and communication.

These examples show that SEL instruction can be provided in many different ways to promote, enhance, and support students' academic performance. Such efforts involve more than focusing on academic content; they also require addressing social-emotional or psychological aptitudes (i.e., metacognitive, cognitive, motivational, and affective), as these are among the greatest influences on school performance (Wang, Haertel, & Walberg,

1993). Further, Wang and colleagues found a number of other factors addressed by SEL programming to be linked to learning outcomes, including instructional variables (e.g., classroom management, the frequency and quality of teacher and student social interactions) and characteristics of the home environment (e.g., parents' interest in and expectations for students' success).

CHARACTERISTICS OF EFFECTIVE SEL INTERVENTIONS

Researchers from CASEL identified the essential aspects of effective SEL practice. Thirty-nine guidelines were developed based on their scientific investigations, reviews of the empirical and theoretical literature, visits to model sites throughout the country, and personal experiences in implementing and evaluating SEL practices (Elias et al., 1997). Essential characteristics of effective SEL programming are summarized in Figure 1.3, and additional discussion of the guidelines may be found in a variety of sources (e.g., CASEL, 2003; Elias et al., 1997; O'Brien, Weissberg, & Shriver, 2003; Weissberg, 2000; Zins, Elias, Greenberg, & Weissberg, 2000). The guidelines are consistent with the learner-centered psychological principles described by McCombs in this book and are supported by many of the studies cited in various other chapters.

In contrast to the guidelines outlined in Figure 1.3, the use of traditional short-term, primarily didactic, isolated (uncoordinated) efforts to promote SEL has not been shown to be as effective as long-term coordinated efforts, although these isolated approaches continue to be found in many schools. For example, negative effects on dropout, nonattendance, and several conduct problems are associated with counseling, social work, and other therapeutic preventive interventions (Wilson, Gottfredson, & Najaka, 2001). Of additional concern is the finding that many practices, including some well-designed interventions, are either not evaluated or their evaluation procedures tend to be weak (Drug Strategies, 1998). In fact, a recent review of 80 nationally available classroom programs found that only 14% provided evidence of effectiveness, as demonstrated by multiple studies documenting positive behavioral outcomes posttest, with at least one showing positive behavioral impact 1 year postintervention (CASEL, 2003).

ACADEMIC OUTCOMES ASSOCIATED WITH SEL INTERVENTIONS

SEL programs vary in the extent to which they directly address academic achievement, and in the past many researchers did not evaluate such outcomes. Nevertheless, even one of the first examinations of the research on the connections between SEL and school performance concluded that the research base was strong enough that "an important task for schools and teachers is to integrate the teaching of academic and social and emotional skills in the classroom" (Hawkins, 1997, p. 293).

Today it is becoming more common to address academic along with social-emotional issues, as well as to measure the results of such efforts. In the CASEL (2003) review of the 80 nationally available programs, 34% included methods to promote the integration of SEL with academic curricula and teaching practices. For example, some encourage students to apply SEL skills such as goal setting to improve their study habits; others emphasize integration of SEL with academic subject matter such as by providing a literature selection that requires using conflict resolution skills to resolve a disagreement between characters in the novel; and others promote teaching practices such as cooperative learning and effective classroom management. All of these approaches can have positive effects on academic performance, especially those that had teachers acquire and use more effective teaching techniques; 83% of such programs produced academic gains. In addition, 12% of the programs that did not specifically target academic performance documented an impact on academic achievement. This figure, however, might have been higher if more of these programs had assessed academic outcomes systematically, as these programs accounted for 40% of the SEL programs that yielded academic gains. These findings underscore the need to assess academic outcomes in future investigations of SEL interventions.

As you read this book, you will find what has become an impressive amount of empirical evidence documenting the connections between SEL and school success that largely reflects outcomes from the contributors' own programs. There also are many examples of relevant findings from other researchers available in the literature (e.g., Feshbach & Feshbach, 1987; Hawkins, 1997; Peisner-Feinberg et al., 2001; Ryan & Patrick, 2001; Schmitz & Skinner, 1993; Skinner, Wellborn, & Connell, 1990; Stevens & Slavin, 1995; Wentzel, 1991, 1993). These studies found a broad range of outcomes related to school success that result from SEL interventions. Additional detail about two such investigations is summarized next.

Wilson and colleagues (2001) conducted a meta-analysis of 165 published studies of the outcomes of school-based prevention programs that ranged from individually focused counseling or behavior modification programs through broad, school-wide efforts to change the way schools are managed. Among their findings are that programs focusing on SEL resulted in improved outcomes related to dropout and nonattendance, both of which are important factors in school success. Interestingly, the findings in these two areas are even stronger than those related to delinquency and substance use, the other two areas in which prevention practices appeared to be effective. Self-control or social competency promotion instruction using cognitive-behavioral and behavioral instructional methods and noninstructional programs are found consistently to be effective in reducing alcohol and drug use, dropout and nonattendance, and other conduct problems. Environmentally focused interventions (e.g., classroom management, class reorganization, school management) also have good outcomes. The intervention features associated with these outcomes correspond with those described previously.

A recent report on school-based prevention programs identified a number of them as model programs and subsequently examined them with respect to risk and protective factors related to school performance (U.S. Department of Health and Human Services, 2002). Among the specific academic outcomes were improved grades, standardized test scores, and graduation rates; increased grade point average; and improved reading, math, and writing skills. Other school performance measures found include improved attendance and fewer out-of-school suspensions, retentions, and special education referrals. The majority of these programs were comprehensive and involved school and family partnerships.

OVERVIEW OF BOOK

Contributors to the volume were commissioned by the Mid-Atlantic Regional Educational Laboratory for Student Success at the Temple University Center for Research in Human Development and Education to write papers that investigated the research on the influences of SEL on specific educational outcomes. Outcomes of interest include those that are a result of an instructional or curricular approach (e.g., cooperative learning) or a school climate change (e.g., improved behavior management), and/or that involve coordinated efforts among the constituencies who contribute to the educational process (e.g., facilitating parent–teacher partnerships). The foundation for the book is the conceptual framework developed by members of CASEL and described in several of their publications (Elias et al., 1997; Payton et al., 2000; Zins et al., 2000). The common SEL framework found across chapters that serves to unify the contents is based on this conceptualization.

In each chapter authors define the bases of their work and its relationship to SEL. They explain how much of what they do fits under the SEL umbrella and make it clear how SEL can improve opportunities for school success. Collectively, a range of developmental ages and school settings are presented. In addition, many chapters cite empirical data demonstrating the impact of SEL on school success.

Chapters in Part I describe conceptual and theoretical issues that are helpful in understanding social and emotional learning, as well as more general intervention strategies that are used in many SEL programs. Barbara

McCombs begins by discussing research-validated, learning-centered psychological principles that are relevant to most SEL programs and that can be used to integrate them into comprehensive school reform models. The principles of learning, motivation, and development help provide a solid empirical and theoretical basis for understanding learners and learning. In the next chapter, David Johnson and Roger Johnson discuss a number of facets of group social interactions and the social competencies necessary for interacting effectively. They provide extensive documentation of how schools based on cooperative community, constructive conflict resolution, and civic values create an effective and nurturing environment where children learn and develop in positive, healthy ways, and many of their ideas are reflected in the SEL interventions developed by other researchers.

Families, schools, and peers exert considerable influence on school success and are considered essential in many SEL intervention programs. Sandra Christenson and Lynne Havsy discuss Check & Connect, a program to promote student engagement in school, to build capacity within families, and to alter the culture of failure that often surrounds students. They provide a variety of empirical support for such an approach. Paulo Lopes and Peter Salovey offer several challenges to the SEL field through a series of questions about its underlying conceptual bases. They also cite evidence from the literature that SEL programs can promote children's social and emotional adaptation and bonding to school.

In the final chapter of this part, Jane Fleming and Mary Bay examine the extent to which teacher training in social and emotional learning is consistent with professional teacher preparation standards. The fact that their analysis demonstrates a high degree of congruence provides important guidance for those involved in preservice and inservice educator training, and such information may be useful to those who seek to introduce SEL into college and university educator preparation programs.

Chapters in Part II demonstrate application of many of the principles and intervention strategies contained in the first part. For example, you'll find that efforts to promote school engagement and bonding, home–school partnerships, and cooperative learning are components of most of the programs described. In addition, each of these chapters cites solid research evidence that demonstrates the effects of SEL on school success, as summarized in Figure 1.4.

The part begins with Maurice Elias providing a description of the widely used Social Decision Making and Social Problem Solving curriculum and illustrations of how it can be integrated into the overall academic curriculum. The structure for skills instruction is provided, and efforts also are directed at integrating academic instruction to promote generalization. A number of specific academic gains are described that are associated with the program.

Figure 1.4. SEL intervention outcomes related to school success.

ACADEMIC OUTCOME	INTERVENTIONS
School Attitudes	
• Stronger sense of community (bonding)	CDP
• More academic motivation and higher aspirations	CDP, Coop, SSDP
• Better understanding of consequences of behavior	SDM/SPS
• Able to cope more effectively with middle school stressors	SDM/SPS
• Positive attitudes toward school	Coop, SSDP
School Behavior	
• More prosocial behavior	C & C, CDP, Coop, PATHS, RCCP, SDM/SPS, SSDP
• Fewer absences; maintained or improved attendance	C & C, SDM/SPS
• More classroom participation	SSDP
• Greater effort to achieve	Coop
• More likely to work out own way of learning	CDP
• Reductions in aggression and disruptions; lower rate of conduct problems	Coop, PATHS, RCCP, SSDP
• Fewer hostile negotiations	CDP, Coop
• More likely to be enrolled in school/fewer dropouts	C & C
• On track to graduate	C & C
• Fewer suspensions	C & C
• Better transition to middle school	SDM/SPS
• Higher engagement	C & C, Coop, SSDP
School Performance	
• Higher in math	RCCP, SDM/SPS
• Higher in language arts and social studies	SDM/SPS
• More progress in phonological awareness	C & C
• Increases in performance over time (middle school)	CDP
• No decreases in standardized test scores	PATHS
• Improvements in reading comprehension with deaf children	PATHS
• Higher achievement test scores and/or grades	Coop, SSDP
• Better problem solving and planning	PATHS
• Use of higher-level reasoning strategies	Coop
• Improved nonverbal reasoning	PATHS
• Better learning to learn skills	SDM/SPS

Notes: "C & C" is the Check & Connect intervention (Chapter 4); "CDP" is the Child Development Project (Chapter 11); "Coop" is the cooperative learning intervention (Chapter 3); "PATHS" is the Promoting Alternative THinking Strategies curriculum (Chapter 10); "RCCP" is the Resolving Conflict Creatively Program (Chapter 9); "SDM/SPS" is the Social Decision Making/Social Problem Solving Project (Chapter 7); "SSDP" is the Seattle Social Development Project (Chapter 8).

The Seattle Social Development Project (SSDP), a universal preventive intervention in elementary schools, is described by David Hawkins, Brian Smith, and Richard Catalano in the next chapter. Using a social-developmental perspective, the program creates conditions that enable children to develop strong bonds to family, school, and community, and it increases opportunities for children to be involved in prosocial activities. A wealth of evidence is presented showing that the SSDP has a positive impact on academic performance and that these gains were still found at age 18.

Joshua Brown, Tom Roderick, Linda Lantieri, and Lawrence Aber discuss the Resolving Conflict Creatively Program (RCCP) that has been implemented widely throughout the United States. The program emphasizes professional development for teachers to support the delivery of the RCCP curriculum. Evaluations of the program show a variety of promising results. High rates of RCCP instruction were significantly related to positive changes in academic achievement, thereby reducing the risk of future school failure.

Another widely adopted curriculum, the Promoting Alternative THinking Strategies (PATHS), is the focus of the chapter by Mark Greenberg, Carol Kusché, and Nathaniel Riggs. PATHS is intended to promote skills in emotional literacy, positive peer relations, and problem solving, as well as to prevent behavioral and emotional problems in young children. It is an integrated component of the regular curriculum and also includes generalization activities. Studies have found significant positive effects on cognitive processing abilities important for school success, and that these effects had a reasonably enduring impact over time.

The final chapter in the part, by Eric Schaps, Victor Battistich, and Daniel Solomon, discusses the Child Development Project. It emphasizes helping schools become caring communities of learners so that positive relationships, norms, and values are developed. Their research shows that strengthening students' sense of community in school increased academic motivation and aspirations, that many effects persisted, and that several years later a substantial effect on academic achievement was found.

In Part III, we first summarize the most important findings in the book, along with our ideas about the future of the field. The chapter concludes with a series of recommendations for practice, research, training, and policy that were developed by participants at the invitational conference at Temple University. Among the overarching themes of the conference were a number that addressed the complexity and challenges in the research arena. For example, there is a need to employ common ideas and procedures across studies in the field so the results are more comparable. The professional preparation of educators was also a concern, and the field was challenged to include not only didactic instruction for these individuals, but also field experiences with supportive, competent supervisors that mirror effective SEL practices. Program implementation, a third general topic, is far more complex than commonly treated, and guidelines for quality implementation are needed to increase the fidelity with which the practices are implemented. The final major theme was dissemination, which was seen as a key element to introducing and maintaining SEL interventions.

CONCLUSIONS

As you read the book, we hope you are inspired by the magnitude of possible methods to address SEL and boost school success. A clear, evidence-supported case is made that SEL, as an enabling component, fosters academic learning. The contents offer educators, policy makers, university trainers, researchers, and practitioners important guidance and useful tools that can be applied to improve the lives of today's students and tomorrow's leaders. They also demonstrate that the SEL field has a solid and expanding scientific base. Our goal is to share the knowledge base regarding how SEL can improve children's academic performance, so that a similar case is made for it as already has been made regarding citizenship (Billig, 2000), health (Blum, McNeely, & Rinehart, 2002), and other important outcomes that we want for children.

The major conclusion drawn following the extensive examination of the topic reported in this book is that *there is a growing body of scientifically based research supporting the strong impact that enhanced social and emotional behaviors can have on success in school and ultimately in life*. Indeed, the research-based findings in the book are so solid that they emboldened us to introduce a new term, "social, emotional, and academic learning," or "SEAL." Our challenges now are to continue to develop the link between SEL interventions and academic achievement and to apply this knowledge more broadly to assist *all* children. By providing readers with this information, we hope to influence practice, research, training, and policy. We invite you to travel with us on the journey to learn more about the promotion of SEAL.

REFERENCES

Adelman, H. S., & Taylor, L. (2000). Moving prevention from the fringes into the fabric of school improvement. *Journal of Education and Psychological Consultation*, *11*(1), 7–36.

Allen, J. P., Philliber, S., Herrling, S., & Kuperminc, G. P. (1997). Preventing teen pregnancy and academic failure: Experimental evaluation of a developmentally based approach. *Child Development*, *64*, 729–742.

Billig, S. (2000). The impact of service learning on youth, schools, and communities: Research on K–12 school-based service learning, 1990–1999 [On-line]. Available from http://www.learningindeed.org/research/slreseaerch/slrschsy.html

Blum, R. W., McNeely, C. A., & Rinehart, P. M. (2002). *Improving the odds: The untapped power of schools to improve the health of teens.* Minneapolis: University of Minnesota, Center for Adolescent Health and Development.

Cobb, J. A. (1972). Relationship of discrete classroom behaviors to fourth-grade academic achievement. *Journal of Educational Psychology, 63*, 74–80.

Collaborative for Academic, Social, and Emotional Learning. (2003). *Safe and sound: An educational leader's guide to evidence-based social and emotional learning programs.* Chicago: Author.

DiPerna, J. C., & Elliott, S. N. (1999). The development and validation of the Academic Competence Evaluation Scales. *Journal of Psychoeducational Assessment, 17*, 207–225.

Drug Strategies. (1998). *Safe schools, safe students: A guide to violence prevention strategies.* Washington, DC: Author.

Durlak, J. A. (1995). *School-based prevention programs for children and adolescents.* Thousand Oaks, CA: Sage.

Elias, M. J., Wang, M. C., Weissberg, R .P., Zins, J. E., & Walberg, H. J. (2002). The other side of the report card: Student success depends on more than test scores. *American School Boards Journal, 189*(11), 28–31.

Elias, M. J., Zins, J. E., Weissberg, R. P., Frey, K. S., Greenberg, M. T., Haynes, N. M., Kessler, R., Schwab-Stone, M. E., & Shriver, T. P. (1997). *Promoting social and emotional learning: Guidelines for educators.* Alexandria, VA: Association for Supervision and Curriculum Development.

Feshbach, N. D., & Feshbach, S. (1987). Affective processes and academic achievement. *Child Development, 58*, 1335–1347.

Gottfredson, D. C. (2001). *Delinquency prevention in schools.* New York: Cambridge University Press.

Gottfredson, G. D., & Gottfredson, D. C. (2001). What schools do to prevent problem behaviors and promote safe environments. *Journal of Educational and Psychological Consultation, 12*, 313–344.

Hawkins, J. D. (1997). Academic performance and school success: Sources and consequences. In R. P. Weissberg, T. P. Gullotta, R. L. Hampton, B. A. Ryan, & G. R. Adams (Eds.), *Healthy children 2010: Enhancing children's wellness* (pp. 278–305). Thousand Oaks, CA: Sage.

Hawkins, J. D., Farrington, D. P., & Catalano, R. F. (1998). Reducing violence through the schools. In D. S. Eliot, B. A. Hamburg, & K. R. Williams (Eds.), *Violence in American schools: A new perspective* (pp. 188–216). Cambridge: Cambridge University Press.

Haynes, N. M, Ben-Avie, M., & Ensign, J. (Eds.). (2003). *How social and emotional development add up: Getting results in math and science education.* New York: Teachers College Press.

Institute of Medicine. (1994). *Reducing risks for mental disorders: Frontiers for preventive intervention research.* Washington, DC: National Academy Press.

Jackson, P. W. (1968). *Life in classrooms*. New York: Holt, Rinehart, & Winston.
Learning First Alliance. (2001). *Every child learning: Safe and supportive schools*. Washington, DC: Author.
Malecki, C. K., & Elliott, S. N. (2002). Children's social behaviors as predictors of academic achievement: A longitudinal analysis. *School Psychology Quarterly, 17* (1), 1–23.
National Commission on Service Learning. (2002). *The power of service learning*. Newton, MA: Author.
O'Brien, M. U., Weissberg, R. P., & Shriver, T. P. (2003). Educational leadership for academic, social, and emotional learning. In M. J. Elias, H. Arnold, & C. Steiger Hussey (Eds.), *EQ + IQ = Best leadership practices for caring and successful schools* (pp. 23–35). Thousand Oaks, CA: Corwin.
Osher, D., Dwyer, K., & Jackson, S. (2002). *Safe, supportive, and successful schools step by step*. Rockville, MD: U.S. Department of Health and Human Services, Substance Abuse and Mental Health Services Administration, Center for Mental Health Services.
Pasi, R. J. (2001). *Higher expectations: Promoting social emotional learning and academic achievement in your school*. New York: Teachers College Press.
Payton, J. W., Wardlaw, D. M., Graczyk, P. A., Bloodworth, M. R., Tompsett, C. J., & Weissberg, R. P. (2000). Social and emotional learning: A framework for promoting mental health and reducing risk behavior in children and youth. *Journal of School Health, 70*(5), 179–185.
Peisner-Feinberg, E. S., Burchinal, M. R., Clifford, R. M., Culkin, M. L., Howes, C., Kagan, S. L., & Yazejian, N. (2001). The relation of preschool child-care quality to children's cognitive and social developmental trajectories through second grade. *Child Development*, *72*, 1534–1553.
Ryan, A., & Patrick, H. (2001). The classroom social environment and changes in adolescents' motivation and engagement during middle school. *American Educational Research Journal*, *38*, 801–823.
Schmitz, B., & Skinner, E. A. (1993). Perceived control, effort, and academic performance: Interindividual, intraindividual, and multivariate time-series analyses. *Journal of Personality and Social Psychology*, *64*, 1010–1028.
Skinner, E. A., Wellborn, J. G., & Connell, J. P. (1990). What it takes to do well in school and whether I've got it: A process model of perceived control and children's engagement and achievement in school. *Journal of Educational Psychology*, *82*, 22–32.
Stevens, R. J., & Slavin, R. E. (1995). The cooperative elementary school: Effects on students' achievement, attitudes, and social relations. *American Educational Research Journal*, *32*, 321–351.
U.S. Department of Education. (2002). *What to know & where to go, parents' guide to no child left behind*. Washington, DC: Author.
U.S. Department of Health and Human Services, Substance Abuse and Mental Health Services Administration. (2002). *SAMHSA model programs: Model prevention programs supporting academic achievement*. Retrieved January 23, 2003, from http\\nidekorigrams.samhsa.gov

Wang, M. C., Haertel, G. D., & Walberg, H. J. (1993). Toward a knowledge base for school learning. *Review of Educational Research, 63*, 249–294.

Weissberg, R. P. (2000). Improving the lives of millions of school children. *American Psychologist, 55*(11), 1360–1372.

Welsh, M., Park, R. D., Widaman, K., & O'Neil, R. (2001). Linkages between children's social and academic competence: A longitudinal analysis. *Journal of School Psychology, 39*(6), 463–481.

Wentzel, K. R. (1991). Social competence at school: Relation between social responsibility and academic achievement. *Review of Educational Research, 61*, 1–24.

Wentzel, K. R. (1993). Does being good make the grade? Social behavior and academic competence in middle school. *Journal of Educational Psychology, 85*, 357–364.

Wilson, D. B., Gottfredson, D. C., & Najaka, S. S. (2001). School-based prevention of problem behaviors: A meta-analysis. *Journal of Quantitative Criminology, 17*, 247–272.

Zins, J. E., Elias, M. J., Greenberg, M. T., & Weissberg, R. P. (2000). Promoting social and emotional competence in children. In K. M. Minke & G. C. Bear (Eds.), *Preventing school problems—promoting school success: Strategies and programs that work* (pp. 71–100). Bethesda, MD: National Association of School Psychologists.

CHAPTER 2

The Learner-Centered Psychological Principles: A Framework for Balancing Academic Achievement and Social-Emotional Learning Outcomes

BARBARA L. McCOMBS

The importance of balancing the focus on high student academic achievement with a focus on students' social and emotional learning outcomes is vital. In recent years, the nation has witnessed unacceptably high rates of school violence, bullying, school dropout, youth suicide, and other negative behaviors. These negative behaviors have taken a toll on students' emotional well-being and social adjustment—documented by rising rates of childhood depression, emotion-related illnesses, and expressions of fear and hopelessness. This chapter describes how the *Learner-Centered Psychological Principles* (APA Work Group, 1997) can be used as a foundation for integrating social and emotional learning (SEL) programs into comprehensive school reform models. The research-validated principles provide a framework for balancing improved learning outcomes with enhanced social-emotional skills.

The need for a validated framework that justifies SEL programs is also vital. An issue facing programs that address nonacademic student needs is the degree to which they are integrated into comprehensive school programs. Programs focusing on affective, motivational, or social skills often are seen as secondary to the school's primary focus on academic learning and achievement. A compelling rationale is needed to demarginalize SEL programs. Two conditions have furthered progress: (1) an increased recognition of rising problem behaviors among youth, including violence, drug use, and early school withdrawal; and (2) growing research support that academic instruc-

 ISBN 0-8077-4439-5 (pbk), ISBN 0-8077-4440-9 (cloth).

tion alone is not sufficient to assist students in developing into knowledgeable, responsible, and caring learners (Payton et al., 2000).

A dilemma in integrating SEL programs into academic curricula is the view that they detract from the real mission of schools—teaching content knowledge and skills (Elias, Bruene-Butler, Blum, & Schuyler, 1997). A related concern is that SEL programs will interfere with parents' roles in teaching social and emotional skills, thus undermining their teaching of moral values and character (Palmer, 1999). Research-validated principles of learning, motivation, and development not only provide a foundation for understanding learners and learning, but also provide an empirical *and* theoretical rationale for educational systems that holistically addresses all domains of human functioning. By building on research-validated principles, a stronger case can be made than using theory and philosophical concerns alone. To develop this argument, four questions are addressed: (1) What is learning? (2) What is the purpose of education? (3) What knowledge base is needed? and (4) What are practice and policy implications?

WHAT IS LEARNING?

The past century of research has journeyed through a variety of learning theories that have focused alternately on behavioral, emotional, and/or cognitive aspects of learning. The current integrative research focus is based on growing recognition from various perspectives (e.g., neurological brain research, psychological research) that meaningful, sustained learning is a whole person phenomenon. Brain research shows that even young children have the capacity for complex thinking (e.g., Diamond & Hopson, 1998; Jensen, 1998). Brain research also shows that affect and cognition work synergistically, with emotion driving attention, learning, memory, and other mental activities. Research exists on the inseparability of intellect and emotion in learning (e.g., Elias, Zins et al., 1997; Lazarus, 2000) and the importance of emotional intelligence to human functioning and health (e.g., Seligman & Csikszentmihalyi, 2000).

Recent research also is revealing the social nature of learning. Elias, Bruene-Bulter, and colleagues (1997) discuss a number of research studies, including those in neuropsychology, demonstrating that many elements of learning are relational, that is, based on relationships. Social and emotional skills are essential for the successful development of cognitive thinking and learning skills. In addition to understanding emotional and social aspects of learning, research also confirms that learning is a natural process, inherent to living organisms (APA, 1997).

From my research and that of others who have explored differences in what learning looks like in and outside of school settings, several things become obvious (e.g., McCombs, 2001, 2003; Zimmerman & Schunk, 2001). Real-life learning is often playful, recursive and nonlinear, engaging, self-directed, and meaningful from the learner's perspective. But why are the natural processes of motivation and learning seen in real life rarely seen in most school settings? Research shows that self-motivated learning is possible only in contexts that provide for choice and control. When students have choice and are allowed to control major aspects of their learning (such as what topics to pursue, how and when to study, and the outcomes they want to achieve), they are more likely to achieve self-regulation of thinking and learning processes.

In many school experiences, learning is rote, surface, or low level. Many students simply comply with mandated demands to master growing numbers of academic standards—they go through the motions but become increasingly alienated, stressed, and angry. Too many students complain that school is boring and irrelevant, and teachers don't seem to care (McCombs & Whisler, 1997). Is this what we want or intend as the purpose of education?

WHAT IS THE PURPOSE OF EDUCATION?

For those advocating SEL as a framework for quality school programs, the primary purpose of schools is seen as preparing students to become knowledgeable, responsible, and caring citizens (Payton et al., 2000; Zins, Elias, Greenberg, & Weissberg, 2000). This is consistent with a person-centered view (e.g., Combs, 1986) in which schools are concerned with creating the kinds of experiences that develop productive, healthy people. It is also consistent with Fullan's (2000) view that the purpose of education is to build learning communities—communities that bring moral purpose back into teaching and reconnect teachers with their fundamental purpose of making a difference in young people's lives and changing the quality of relationships throughout the system. For Thornburg (1999), to prepare students for today's world, education must foster life-long learners, transforming the emphasis on existing knowledge and creating networks for dialogue, reflection, and contextual applications of learning in the real world.

Palmer (1999) offers an added perspective. He discuses the spirituality of teaching and learning as a way to address the need for connectedness with one another and with the meaning and wisdom we have to share from learned information and from our own experiences. When education ignores these issues, it produces a system that alienates and bores the learner. It also ignores young people's need for mentoring in questions of greatest significance in their lives: "What is my meaning and purpose?" "What are my greatest gifts?" "How can I maintain hope?"

Educational models thus are needed to reconnect learners with others and with learning—person-centered models that also offer challenging learning experiences. School learning experiences should prepare learners to be knowledge producers, knowledge users, and socially responsible citizens. Of course, we want students to learn academic knowledge and skills, but is that sufficient? In the twenty-first-century world, subject matter content is so abundant as to make it a poor foundation for an educational system; rather, context and meaning are the scarce commodities. This alters the purpose of education to that of helping learners communicate with others, find relevant and accurate information for the task at hand, and be co-learners and knowledge producers with teachers and peers in diverse settings that go beyond the school walls.

To move toward this vision will require new concepts defining the learning process and evolving purpose of education. It also will require rethinking current directions and practices. While maintaining high standards in the learning of desired content and skills, we must not neglect the learner, learning process, and learning environment if we are to adequately prepare students for productive and healthy futures. State and national standards must be critically reevaluated in terms of what is necessary to prepare students to be knowledgeable, responsible, and caring citizens (see Fleming & Bay, this volume). Standards must move beyond knowledge conservation to knowledge creation and production, balancing the current focus on content with a focus on the holistic learning needs of individual learners in an increasingly complex and fast-changing world. To guide the process of transforming education and to inform educators about effective integrations of SEL into school reform, a knowledge base addressing learning and change in living systems is needed.

WHAT KNOWLEDGE BASE IS NEEDED?

In addition to changing notions about learning and the purpose of education, the needs of learners are changing. An issue of concern, given its relationship to problems such as school dropout, is that of youth alienation. Ryan and Deci (2000) maintain that alienation in any age population is caused by failing to provide supports for competence, autonomy, and relatedness. Meeting these motivational needs is essential to healthy development and creating contexts that engender individual commitment, effort, and high-quality performance.

Unfortunately, there are too many examples in the current educational reform agenda of punitive consequences for students, teachers, and administrators when students fail to achieve academic standards on state and national tests. To combat these trends, Kohl, founder of the Open School Movement, shares his 36 years of experience as a teacher working in poverty-ridden urban school districts (in Scherer, 1998). He emphasizes the importance of teachers projecting hope—convincing students of their worth and ability to achieve in a difficult world. A "personalized learning" model is advocated, based on caring relationships and respect for the unique way each student perceives the world and learns. This model provides quality learning and engages students in learning communities that encourage creativity and imagination.

The knowledge base needed thus must address the foregoing issues and the working definition SEL as a framework for defining quality programs.

Defining Social and Emotional Learning

The concept of SEL derives from the work of Goleman (1995) and others (e.g., Salovey & Mayer, 1990) on emotional intelligence. It generally refers to learning those skills involved in being self-confident and motivated, knowing what behaviors are expected, curbing impulses to misbehave, being able to wait, following directions, knowing how to ask for help, expressing needs, and getting along with others. In the school learning context, SEL is the process for integrating thinking, feeling, and behavior to achieve important social tasks; meet personal and social needs; and develop the skills necessary to become a productive, contributing member of society.

Payton and coauthors (2000) define SEL programs as providing "systematic classroom instruction that enhances children's capacities to recognize and manage their emotions, appreciate the perspectives of others, establish prosocial goals and solve problems, and use a variety of interpersonal skills to effectively and ethically handle developmentally relevant tasks" (p. 13). SEL programs are also concerned with establishing environments that extend instruction so that what is learned in the classroom generalizes to learning needs outside of the classroom. SEL programs thus contribute to academic success, healthy growth and development, positive relationships, and motivation to contribute to surrounding communities (Payton et al., 2000). The practices in SEL programs address the personal domain that focuses on *people* and on personal and interpersonal *relationships, beliefs, and perceptions* affected and/or supported by other domains of the educational system. These include the technical domain that focuses on content and the organizational domain that focuses on management structures and process.

As a framework for developing SEL skills, applying SEL practices, and developing academic competence, the knowledge base of research-validated principles of learning and individual differences also becomes a foundation for comprehensive school reform that focuses on meeting cognitive, social, and emotional human needs and fostering positive teacher–student relationships. The principles lead to understanding students as knowledge generators, active participants in their own learning, and co-creators of learning experiences and curricula.

The Learner-Centered Principles as a Foundational Framework

Education is one of many complex living systems that function to support particular human needs (cf. Wheatley, 1999). Such systems are unpredictable but can be understood by principles that define human needs, cognitive and motivational processes, development, and individual differences. The research-validated *Learner-Centered Psychological Principles* (APA, 1993, 1997) provide a foundation for understanding learning and motivation as natural processes that occur when the *conditions and context* of learning are supportive of individual learner needs, capacities, experiences, and interests. This foundation is essential to integrating SEL programs and practices into academic programs that attend holistically to the needs of all learners.

The Learner-Centered Psychological Principles

Beginning in 1990, the American Psychological Association (APA) appointed a special Task Force on Psychology in Education, whose members reviewed over a century of research on learning in order to surface general principles that had stood the test of time and could provide a framework for school redesign and reform. The result was a document that specified 12 fundamental principles that, taken together, provided an integrated perspective on factors influencing learning for *all* learners (APA, 1993). This document was revised in 1997 (APA, 1997) and now includes 14 principles that are essentially the same as the original 12 principles except that attention is now given to principles dealing with diversity and standards.

The 14 learner-centered principles are categorized into four research-validated domains, shown in Figure 2.1. Domains important to learning are metacognitive and cognitive, affective and motivational, developmental and social, and individual differences. These domains and the principles within them provide a framework for designing learner-centered practices at all levels of schooling. They also define a learner-centered from a research-validated perspective.

Figure 2.1. The learner-centered psychological principles.

COGNITIVE AND METACOGNITIVE FACTORS

Principle 1. Nature of the learning process. The learning of complex subject matter is most effective when it is an intentional process of constructing meaning from information and experience.

Principle 2. Goals of the learning process. The successful learner, over time and with support and instructional guidance, can create meaningful, coherent representations of knowledge.

Principle 3. Construction of knowledge. The successful learner can link new information with existing knowledge in meaningful ways.

Principle 4. Strategic thinking. The successful learner can create and use a repertoire of thinking and reasoning strategies to achieve complex learning goals.

Principle 5. Thinking about thinking. Higher-order strategies for selecting and monitoring mental operations facilitate creative and critical thinking.

Principle 6. Context of learning. Learning is influenced by environmental factors, including culture, technology, and instructional practices.

MOTIVATIONAL AND AFFECTIVE FACTORS

Principle 7. Motivational and emotional influences on learning. What and how much is learned is influenced by the learner's motivation. Motivation to learn, in turn, is influenced by the individual's emotional states, beliefs, interests and goals, and habits of thinking.

Principle 8. Intrinsic motivation to learn. The learner's creativity, higher-order thinking, and natural curiosity all contribute to motivation to learn. Intrinsic motivation is stimulated by tasks of optimal novelty and difficulty, relevant to personal interests, and providing for personal choice and control.

Principle 9. Effects of motivation on effort. Acquisition of complex knowledge and skills requires extended learner effort and guided practice. Without learners' motivation to learn, the willingness to exert this effort is unlikely without coercion.

DEVELOPMENTAL AND SOCIAL FACTORS

Principle 10. Developmental influence on learning. As individuals develop, they encounter different opportunities and experience different constraints for learning. Learning is most effective when differential development within and across physical, intellectual, emotional, and social domains is taken into account.

Principle 11. Social influences on learning. Learning is influenced by social interactions, interpersonal relations, and communication with others.

INDIVIDUAL DIFFERENCES FACTORS

Principle 12. Individual differences in learning. Learners have different strategies, approaches, and capabilities for learning that are a function of prior experience and heredity.

Principle 13. Learning and diversity. Learning is most effective when differences in learners' linguistic, cultural, and social backgrounds are taken into account.

Principle 14. Standards and assessment. Setting appropriately high and challenging standards and assessing the learner and learning progress—including diagnostic, process, and outcome assessment—are integral parts of the learning process.

Defining "Learner-Centered"

From an integrated and holistic look at the *Principles*, the following definition emerges:

> "Learner-centered" is the perspective that couples a focus on individual learners—their heredity, experiences, perspectives, backgrounds, talents, interests, capacities, and needs—with a focus on learning—the best available knowledge about learning and how it occurs and about teaching practices that are most effective in promoting the highest levels of motivation, learning, and achievement for all learners. This dual focus then informs and drives educational decision making. Learner-centered is a reflection in practice of the Learner-Centered Psychological Principles—in the programs, practices, policies, and people that support learning for all.

This definition highlights that the *Principles* apply to all learners, in and outside of school, young and old. Learner centeredness is also related to the beliefs, dispositions, and practices of teachers. When teachers derive their practices from an understanding of the *Principles*, they (a) include learners in decisions about how and what they learn and how that learning is assessed; (b) value each learner's unique perspectives; (c) respect and accommodate individual differences in learners' backgrounds, interests, abilities, and experiences; and (d) treat learners as co-creators and partners in teaching and learning.

My research with learner-centered practices and self-assessment tools based on the *Principles* for teachers and students from K–12 and college classrooms confirms that what defines learner centeredness is not solely a function of particular instructional practices or programs (McCombs & Lauer, 1997; McCombs & Whisler, 1997). Rather, it is a complex interaction of teacher qualities in combination with characteristics of instructional practices—as perceived by individual learners. Learner centeredness is a function of learner perceptions, which, in turn, are the result of each learner's prior experiences, self-beliefs, and attitudes about schools and learning as well as their current interests, values, and goals. Thus, the quality of learner centeredness does not reside in programs or practices by themselves.

When learner centeredness is defined from a research perspective, it also clarifies what is needed in order to create positive learning contexts and communities at the classroom and school levels. In addition, it increases the likelihood of success for more students and their teachers and can lead to increased clarity about the requisite dispositions and characteristics of school personnel who are in service to learners and learning. From this perspective, the learner-centered principles become foundational for determining how to use and assess the efficacy of SEL programs in providing instruction, curricula, and personnel to enhance the teaching and learning process. Research confirms that learner perceptions regarding how well programs and practices meet individual needs must be part of the assessment of ongoing learning and development.

A Research-Validated Rationale for Integrating SEL into Comprehensive School Reform

The foregoing section provides the knowledge base to support a rationale for integrating SEL concepts and programs into comprehensive school reform strategies (i.e., through the foundation of research-validated, learner-centered psychological principles). This foundation provides a means to anchor SEL in research-validated principles and to frame SEL programs in a broader definition of learning that encompasses its cognitive and affective nature.

A visual representation of this conceptualization is presented in Figure 2.2. Starting from the bottom of this figure, the learner-centered principles provide the foundation for defining learning from a research-validated perspective. This knowledge base then gives rise to the SEL framework for quality programs, which defines the curricular and instructional approaches needed to help all students succeed in mastering desired cognitive academic outcomes as well as social and emotional nonacademic outcomes. When quality teachers demonstrate that they know, care about, and respect all students' perspectives, students are encouraged to be partners in co-creating curricula and learning experiences. The result is a comprehensive school reform model that can be characterized as a caring learning community in which SEL plays a pivotal role.

As a SEL quality program framework, it meets criteria specified by Zins and co-authors (2000): comprehensive, multiyear, multicomponent, and systematic; developmentally and culturally appropriate; and integrated into and reflected in the overall curriculum, daily routines, and extracurricular activities. Programs teach a broad range of skills that have personal and social applications and that involve school, family, and community partnerships. Although research shows the positive academic effects of SEL outcomes and processes, current school practices often work against successful SEL program implementation in that there are few opportunities for collaborative planning among and adequate staff preparation for teachers, students, and families. The grounding of SEL concepts and programs in the learner-centered principles as shown in Figure 2.2 addresses these issues.

Figure 2.2. The learner-centered psychological principles as a foundation for integrating SEL programs into comprehensive school reform.

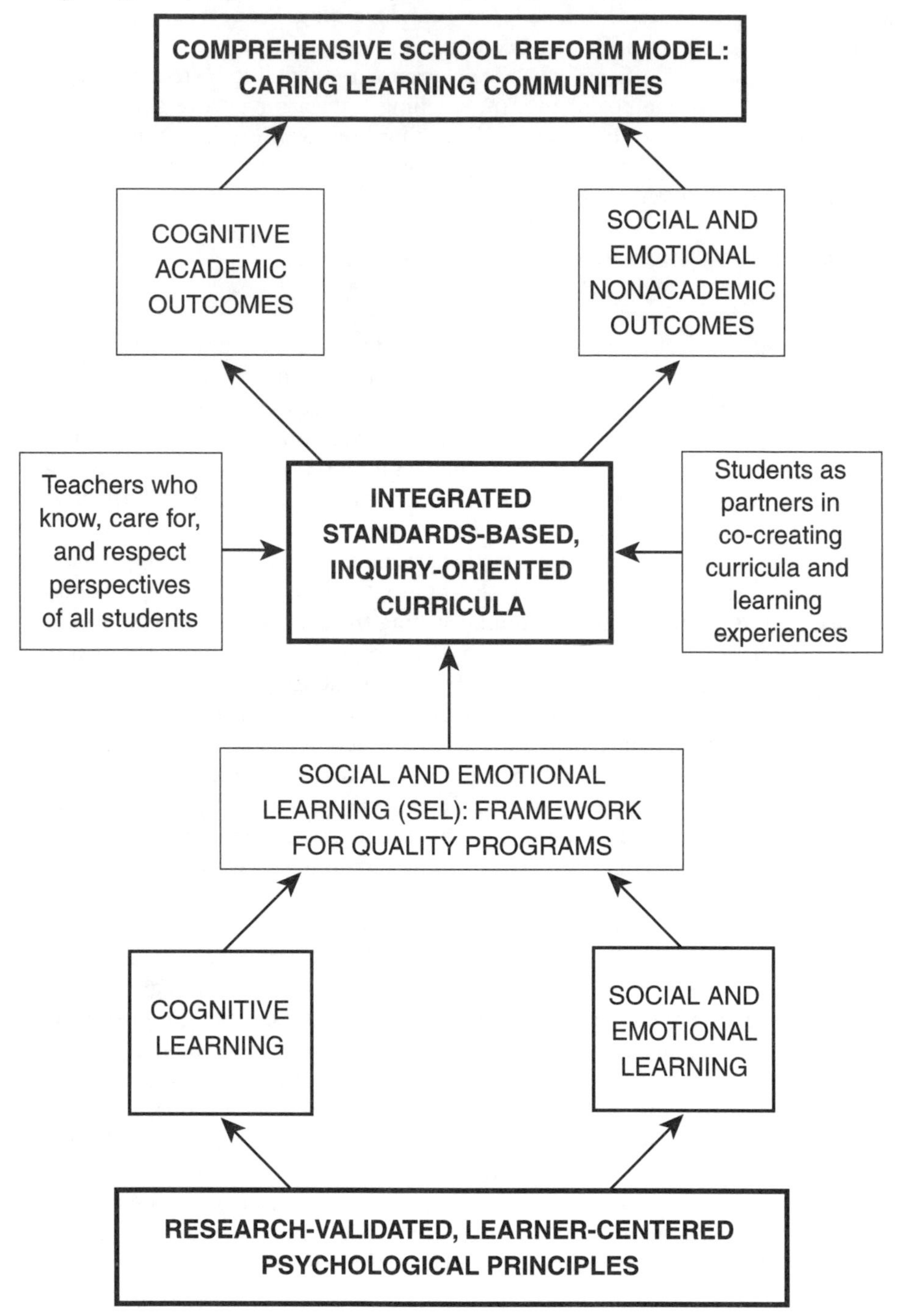

WHAT ARE THE PRACTICE AND POLICY IMPLICATIONS?

This final section presents important practice and policy implications of the learner-centered framework for integrating SEL programs into comprehensive school reform efforts.

Implications for Practice

In the areas of *practice*, a key implication is that the larger context of education must support and value individual learners as well as learning outcomes. The culture and climate must acknowledge the purpose of education as going beyond academic competence and content knowledge alone. There must be a shared vision, values, and sense of inclusive ownership among all stakeholders about the purpose of education. Restoring a sense of schools as caring communities is a fundamental way to provide social and emotional support.

Berreth and Berman (1997) emphasize the value of caring communities in nurturing empathy and self-discipline and helping students develop social skills and moral values. The practices of small schools, caring adults, community service, and parental involvement are recommended, along with processes and practices of modeling, direct instruction, experience, and continual practice. The framework of SEL and the dimensions of emotional intelligence can be used to accomplish these purposes. One guideline stressed by Elias, Zins, and colleagues (1997) is that students be active partners in creating a caring classroom climate and community.

Another critical implication for practice, then, is that attention be given to the role of student perceptions and input. As with my own research, Freiberg (1998) acknowledges that few climate measures use students as a source of feedback, but he believes that each student's perspective is critical, particularly during transitions from one school level to the next. Given the importance of this feedback, Freiberg argues that using measures that assess student perceptions and worries about school should be part of all school reform efforts. A case also is made for the importance of caring to positive development. For example, Elias, Zins, and colleagues (1997) believe that caring is central to the shaping of meaningful, supportive, rewarding, and productive relationships. Caring occurs when children believe that adults unconditionally accept and respect them, and the community believes everyone is important and has something to contribute. But can the importance of caring be acknowledged as a critical part of the current reform agenda?

Palmer (1999) argues that we need to acknowledge that teaching and learning not only involve intellect and emotion, but also involve the human spirit. He contends that teachers—regardless of their subject matter and who their students are—end up teaching *who* they are. The biggest challenge is to provide teachers with adequate time and support to reflect on questions worth asking. Time for self-reflection can renew and transform practices and ways of relating to self and others. Teachers need opportunities to learn and change their minds.

To accomplish trusting relationships among and between teachers and students, strategies for promoting school cultures of caring need to be implemented gradually and be guided by student voices. Research by Battistich, Soloman, Watson, and Schaps (1997) shows that middle school student perceptions of "sense of school as community" were consistently associated with a positive orientation toward school and learning, attraction to school, task orientation toward learning, sense of autonomy and efficacy, educational aspirations, prosocial attitudes, social skills, less involvement in delinquent behavior, and trust and respect for teachers. In caring schools that satisfy basic psychological needs, students become bonded and accept school values.

According to Schaps and Lewis (1999), the structural changes necessary to create caring school cultures are relatively simple and inexpensive to bring about. The larger issue is to achieve a fundamental attitude shift among educators, policy makers, and the public. They must be convinced that in addition to producing higher test scores, it is legitimate to develop caring people. School time spent developing trusting relationships, talking with students, and guiding them to be more competent across all domains of caring also must be deemed valuable.

Implications for Policy

In the area of *policy*, recommendations are needed to address the foregoing issues and help to balance reform efforts. Practices such as grading of schools and teachers based on student achievement misplace the responsibility for learning (cf. McCombs, 2000). Even if teachers are held responsible, *it is the student who makes the decision to learn*. Teachers *cannot make learning happen*; they can encourage learning with a variety of incentives, but teachers know well that many incentives (e.g., grades, fear of discipline) work only for some students. When teachers overly control the learning process, they may get compliance, but they won't get responsibility.

Responsibility begins with making choices. Without the opportunity to choose and face the consequences of those decisions, there is no sense of ownership. Ownership, resulting from choices, is empowering. Without empowerment and ownership, there is no responsibility or accountability—there is blaming and compliance. With ownership, learning is fun and exciting for students and teachers, and both share in the pleasures and responsibilities of control. *We own what we create*—an important implication of the learner-centered principles and framework when applied to new leadership and professional development models.

Applying a Living Systems Perspective. From a broad systems view, many agree that the current educational and social systems aren't working (e.g., Nissen, 1999; Norris, 1999; Wheatley, 1999). These systems are seen as unconnected and based on old models of human learning and development. Further, these systems often are based on principles applicable to nonliving, mechanical systems and do not match the uncertainty and complexity of living, human systems. Thus, it is time to explore a new model that includes what is needed in living systems in order to bring the overall educational system into an academic-social-emotional balance.

When successful school reform efforts are analyzed (e.g., Fullan, 1997), the critical difference is in *how* these practices are implemented and in whether there is explicit and shared attention given to individual learners and their holistic learning needs. *The critical difference is thus in whether or not they are learner-centered and focus on the people and the personal domain.* People in living systems such as education thrive when they are given more opportunities for ongoing dialogue and to be creatively involved in how their work gets done, that is, setting their own standards, organizational structures, and plans from within (Wheatley & Kellner-Rogers, 1998). In the learning and change process, research-validated principles that are agreed upon can be guides to determine what will work well in the current situation or context such that the system is designed to take care of self, others, and the place.

The spirit of vitality of learner-centered schools is that aspect of the culture committed to learning and change. Teachers' needs to be learners must be part of the culture that supports student motivation, learning, and achievement. The nature of the culture formed among teachers committed to high achievement for all learners is one that also is committed to their own ongoing learning, change, and improvement. The process that supports continuous examination and critical inquiry into ways of helping students learn better must become a normal activity that involves the whole faculty and builds community. The vision is subject to change, and the whole system maintains flexibility and openness to new learning and change.

Healthy learning communities have the further defining qualities of acceptance of, room for, and honoring of all diverse views. Individuals welcome divergent perspectives because they understand that the underlying outcome is learning and change in a context of respect and caring. Individuals also understand that successful learning communities broaden their perspectives to make room for the learning that can occur. They encompass all points of view without making anyone wrong. When different world views and beliefs are held, inclusive and respectful dialogue becomes the process for learning; relationships become the vehicle for change in beliefs and assumptions about learning, learners, and teaching. Self-organizing learning communities then meet individual needs for safety, and they encourage new relationships and ways of generating new relationships. Each learner's perspective is a valued medium of learning and a catalyst for change and improvement.

New integrated SEL programs must themselves be models of the very process and qualities they want to engender in teachers as learners. To produce quality teaching and learning, learners must experience both quality content and processes. Systems that foster quality by fear-based or punitive measures engender fear, withdrawal, and half-hearted compliance. Unfortunately, this is coloring much of today's reform agenda. Principles of respect, fairness, autonomy, intellectual challenge, social support, and security must guide the standard-setting and implementation process. Time for learning and change, to share successful practices, experiment, and continually improve must be acknowledged.

Spiritual Influences. Even with attention to a research-validated and learner-centered perspective there is perhaps still a missing piece. This piece is called *the inner edge* by Holmes-Ponder, Ponder, and Bell (1999) and refers to the spiritual condition of school leaders and teachers. The inner edge can transform education and allow *all learners to live and work successfully*. It requires a deep self-knowledge and strong connection to one's purpose for living; it also requires an awareness of spiritual influences and conditions that support or erode a sense of self and the difference one is making in the mission to support learning for all. Educators, policy makers, and researchers must reconnect the nation's teachers with feelings of empowerment and spiritual joy that originally brought them to teaching and learning. From this perspective, collaboration within caring school cultures adds *a spirit of community and success*—a process that recognizes teachers' collective and shared self.

Fullan (1997) speaks to the roles of emotion and hope during times of intense change and pressure. Barriers to learning and change must be reduced, including isolation, lack of empathy, not giving intuition and emotion a respected role, and not supporting hope as a healthy virtue. That means beginning with research-validated, learner-centered principles that confirm the foundation for best practice and give permission to slow down, reflect on the needs of all learners, establish trust, and use our collective knowledge of best practices to support optimal learning and development for all learners. We then stop looking for the quick fix and begin seeing what defines quality learning and teaching. High learning standards and quality teaching are balanced with supporting *all learners*, including those teachers committed to children and education.

CONCLUSIONS AND RECOMMENDATIONS

Here I offer a number of specific policy recommendations that underlie a framework for balancing academic achievement with social and emotional learning outcomes.

- Policies must capture individual and organizational purposes directed at continuous change and learning as a holistic process that involves intellect, emotion, and spirit.
- Policies must emphasize new leadership roles that empower teachers and students alike to take increased control over their own learning and development.
- Policies must emphasize a balance between concerns with high achievement and concerns with meeting individual learning and motivational, emotional, and social needs of diverse students.
- Policies must honor diverse talents, abilities, interests, and motivations, and seek to broaden rather than narrow the rich diversity of students that enter at preschool age and exit as young adults.
- Policies must emphasize change strategies focused on inclusive dialogue, building respectful relationships, and practices that are owned by all participants.
- Policies must value outcomes that go beyond academic achievement to emotional and social outcomes that include increased personal and social responsibility and caring.

I am hopeful that with these policies and the learner-centered research foundation, SEL concepts and programs can be integrated into comprehensive school reform models that balance concerns with learners and learning. Then we can accomplish the goals we all have—to produce academically competent, responsible, productive, and caring students and citizens.

REFERENCES

APA Task Force on Psychology in Education. (1993, January). *Learner-centered psychological principles: Guidelines for school redesign and reform.* Washington, DC: American Psychological Association & Mid-Continent Regional Educational Laboratory.

APA Work Group of the Board of Educational Affairs. (1997, November). *Learner-centered psychological principles: A framework for school reform and redesign.* Washington, DC: American Psychological Association.

Battistich, V., Solomon, D., Watson, M., & Schaps, E. (1997). Caring school communities. *Educational Psychologist, 32*(3), 137–151.

Berreth, D., & Berman, S. (1997). The moral dimensions of schools. *Educational Leadership*, *54*(8), 24–27.

Combs, A. W. (1986). What makes a good helper? A person-centered approach. *Person-Centered Review*, *1*(l), 51–61.

Diamond, M., & Hopson, J. (1998). *Magic trees of the mind*. New York: Dutton.

Elias, M. J., Bruene-Butler, L., Blum, L., & Schuyler, T. (1997). How to launch a social and emotional learning program. *Educational Leadership*, *54*(8), 15–19.

Elias, M. J., Zins, J. E., Weissberg, R. P., Frey, K. S., Greenberg, M. T., Haynes, N. M., Kessler, R., Schwab-Stone, M. E., & Shriver, T. P. (1997). *Promoting social and emotional learning: Guidelines for educators*. Alexandria, VA: Association for Supervision and Curriculum Development.

Freiberg, H. J. (1998). Measuring school climate: Let me count the ways. *Educational Leadership*, *56*(1), 22–26.

Fullan, M. (1997). Emotion and hope: Constructive concepts for complex times. In A. Hargreaves (Ed.), *Rethinking educational change with heart and mind* (pp. 216–223). Alexandria, VA: 1997 ASCD Yearbook.

Fullan, M. (2000, February). *Change forces: The sequel*. 2000 CHANGE Council Keynote Address presented at the annual meeting of the Association for Educational Communications and Technology, Long Beach, CA.

Goleman, D. (1995). *Emotional intelligence*. New York: Bantam Books.

Holmes-Ponder, K., Ponder, G., & Bell, P. (1999, Spring). Giving school leaders the inner edge. *Professional Development Newsletter*, pp. 1, 4, 6.

Jensen, E. (1998). *Teaching with the brain in mind*. Alexandria, VA: Association for Supervision and Curriculum Development.

Lazarus, R. S. (2000). Toward better research on stress and coping. *American Psychologist*, *55*(6), 665–673.

McCombs, B. L. (2000, August). Addressing the personal domain: The need for a learner-centered framework. In *Learner-centered principles in practice: Addressing the personal domain*. Symposium conducted at the annual meeting of the American Psychological Association, Washington, DC.

McCombs, B. L. (2001). Self-regulated learning and academic achievement: A phenomenological view. In B. J. Zimmerman & D. H. Schunk (Eds.), *Self-regulated learning and academic achievement: Theory, research, and practice* (2nd ed.; pp. 67–123). Mahwah, NJ: Erlbaum.

McCombs, B. L. (2003). Applying educational psychology's knowledge base in educational reform: From research to application to policy. In W. M. Reynolds & G. E. Miller (Eds.), *Comprehensive handbook of psychology: Vol. 7. Educational psychology* (pp. 583–607). New York: Wiley.

McCombs, B. L., & Lauer, P. A. (1997). Development and validation of the Learner-Centered Battery: Self-assessment tools for teacher reflection and professional development. *The Professional Educator*, *20*(1), 1–21.

McCombs, B. L., & Whisler, J. S. (1997). *The learner-centered classroom and school: Strategies for increasing student motivation and achievement*. San Francisco: Jossey-Bass.

Nissen, L. B. (1999, June). *The power of the strength approach*. Keynote presentation at the 8th Annual Rocky Mountain Regional Conference in Violence Prevention in Schools and Communities, Denver.

Norris, T. (1999, June). *Healthy communities for healthy youth*. Keynote presentation at the 8th Annual Rocky Mountain Regional Conference in Violence Prevention in Schools and Communities, Denver.

Palmer, P. J. (1999). Evoking the spirit in public education. *Educational Leadership*, *56*(4), 6–11.

Payton, J. W., Wardlaw, D. M., Graczyk, P. A., Bloodworth, M. R., Tompsett, C. J., & Weissberg, R. P. (2000). Social and emotional learning: A framework for promoting mental health and reducing risk behavior in children and youth. *Journal of School Health*, *70*(5), 179–185.

Ryan, R. M., & Deci, E. L. (2000). Self-determination theory and the facilitation of intrinsic motivation, social development, and well-being. *American Psychologist*, *55*(1), 68–78.

Salovey, P., & Mayer, J. D. (1990). Emotional intelligence. *Imagination, Cognition, and Personality*, *9*, 185–211.

Schaps, E., & Lewis, C. (1999). Perils on an essential journey: Building school community. *Phi Delta Kappan*, *81*(3), 215–218.

Scherer, M. (1998). A conversation with Herb Kohl. *Educational Leadership*, *56*(1), 8–13.

Seligman, M. E. P., & Csikszentmihalyi. M. (2000). Positive psychology: An introduction. *American Psychologist*, *55*(1), 5–14.

Thornburg, D. D. (1999, December). *Technology in K–12 education: Envisioning a new future*. White paper commissioned for the Forum on Technology in Education: Envisioning the Future, Washington, DC.

Wheatley, M. J. (1999). *Leadership and the new science: Discovering order in a chaotic world* (2nd ed.). San Francisco: Berrett-Koehler.

Wheatley, M. J., & Kellner-Rogers, M. (1998, April–May). Bringing life to organizational change. *Journal of Strategic Performance Measurement*, pp. 5–13.

Zimmerman, B. J., & Schunk, D. H. (Eds.). (2001). *Self-regulated learning and academic achievement: Theory, research, and practice* (2nd ed.). Mahwah, NJ: Erlbaum.

Zins, J. E., Elias, M. J., Greenberg, M. T., & Weissberg, R. P. (2000). Promoting social and emotional competence in children. In K. M. Minke & G. C. Bear (Eds.), *Preventing school problems—promoting school success: Strategies and programs that work* (pp. 71–100). Bethesda, MD: National Association of School Psychologists.

CHAPTER 3

The Three Cs of Promoting Social and Emotional Learning

DAVID W. JOHNSON AND ROGER T. JOHNSON

Humans are small-group beings (Johnson & F. Johnson, 2003). For over 200,000 years humans have lived in small hunting and gathering groups and in small farming communities. All day long we interact first in one group and then in another. Our family life, our leisure time, our friendships, and our careers are all filled with groups. In fact, if a person from outer space conducted a study of the people of Earth, group membership probably would be the dominant characteristic noted. As the effectiveness of our groups and interpersonal relationships go, so goes the quality of our life. The social competencies necessary for interacting effectively with others are central to the quality of family life, educational achievement, career success, psychological health, and creating a meaningful and fulfilling life. Our interpersonal and small-group skills form the basic nexus between all other people and ourselves.

Social and emotional learning may be defined as the (a) mastery and appropriate use of interpersonal and small-group skills (e.g., recognizing, managing, and appropriately expressing one's emotions), and (b) internalization of prosocial attitudes and values needed to achieve goals, solve problems, become emotionally involved in learning and work, and succeed in school and throughout life. There are many social and emotional characteristics that are important for students to develop, such as continuing motivation to learn, positive attitudes toward school and learning, prosocial attitudes and behavioral patterns, self-efficacy, and employability and success (Elias et al., 1997; Payton et al., 2000; Zins, Elias, Greenberg, & Weissberg, 2000). Two of the most important social and emotional competencies are interper-

Building Academic Success on Social and Emotional Learning: What Does the Research Say? ISBN 0-8077-4439-5 (pbk), ISBN 0-8077-4440-9 (cloth).

sonal effectiveness and actualizing one's potential (Johnson, 2003; Johnson & F. Johnson, 2003). *Interpersonal effectiveness* is the degree to which the consequences of a person's behavior in interacting with others match the person's intentions. A person's interpersonal effectiveness largely determines the quality and course of his or her life.

Self-actualization is the drive to actualize potential and take joy and a sense of fulfillment from being all that a person can be. Self-actualization is based on being aware of abilities and talents, applying them appropriately in a variety of situations, and celebrating their successful application.

There are numerous effective programs for teaching social and emotional competencies. Many of these are described in this book. Most programs are a complex mixture of elements. However, common themes throughout these programs are cooperative experiences; training in important social skills such as conflict resolution; and internalization of prosocial, civic values. One program that combines these three elements is the Three Cs Program.

THE THREE CS PROGRAM

The Three Cs (cooperative community, constructive conflict resolution, and civic values) are essential conditions for social and emotional learning. For children, adolescents, and young adults to learn and appropriately use interpersonal and small-group skills needed to establish and maintain healthy relationships and manage emotions, and internalize the prosocial attitudes and values needed to set positive goals, make responsible decisions, and solve problems, they must be members of a cooperative (as opposed to a competitive or individualistic) community, manage conflicts in constructive rather than destructive ways, and internalize civic rather than antisocial values.

The Three Cs Program is directly based on social interdependence and conflict theories, and the theories have been validated by a great deal of research on cooperation (Johnson & Johnson, 1989), constructive controversy (Johnson & Johnson, 1995a), and the Teaching Students to Be Peacemakers Program (Johnson & Johnson, 1995b, 1996a, 2000b). The Three Cs Program has been implemented in a wide variety of schools throughout North, Central, and South America, Europe, Africa, the Middle East, and Asia. It has been used with inner-city, lower-class students, with upper-class private school students, and with everyone in between. It has been used in schools in third world as well as industrialized countries. The widespread implementation of the Three Cs Program gives it a generalizability not found in most other educational programs.

THE FIRST C: COOPERATIVE COMMUNITY

Social and emotional learning begins with establishing a learning community based on faculty and staff, students, their parents, and other stakeholders in the school working together to achieve mutual goals. The heart of community is *social interdependence*, which exists when each individual's outcomes are affected by the actions of others (Deutsch, 1973; Johnson & Johnson, 1989). Social interdependence may be positive (cooperation), negative (competition), or absent (individualistic efforts). *Positive interdependence* exists when individuals work together to achieve mutual goals, and *negative interdependence* exists when individuals work against one another to achieve a goal that only one or a few may attain. *Social independence*, where the outcomes of each person are unaffected by others' actions, is characterized by individualistic actions.

Social interdependence theory assumes that the type of interdependence structured among individuals determines how they interact with each other, which in turn largely determines outcomes. Structuring situations cooperatively results in individuals promoting one another's success; structuring situations competitively results in individuals opposing one another's success; and structuring situations individualistically results in no interaction among individuals.

Benefits of Cooperation

Since 1897 over 550 experimental and 100 correlational studies have been conducted on cooperative, competitive, and individualistic efforts (see Johnson & Johnson, 1989) by a wide variety of researchers in different decades with different age subjects, in different subject areas, and in different settings. Research participants have varied as to economic class, age, sex, nationality, and cultural background. A wide variety of research tasks, ways of structuring cooperation, and measures of the dependent variables have been used. Many different researchers have conducted the research with markedly different orientations working in different settings, countries, and decades. The research on cooperation has validity and generalizability rarely found in the educational literature. The research has focused on numerous outcomes, which may be subsumed within the broad and interrelated categories of effort to achieve, quality of relationships, psychological health, and social skills (Johnson & Johnson, 1989) (see Table 3.1 and Figure 3.1). Figure 3.1 shows the relationships among the outcomes.

Effort to Achieve. From Table 3.1 it may be seen that cooperation promotes considerably greater effort to achieve than do competitive or individualistic

Table 3.1. Meta-Analysis of Social Interdependence Studies: Mean Effect Sizes

Dependent Variable	*Cooperative vs. Competitive*	*Cooperative vs. Individualistic*	*Competitive vs. Individualistic*
Achievement	0.67	0.64	0.30
Interpersonal attraction	0.67	0.60	0.08
Social support	0.62	0.70	–0.13
Self-esteem	0.58	0.44	–0.23
Time on task	0.76	1.17	0.64
Attitudes toward task	0.57	0.42	0.15
Quality of reasoning	0.93	0.97	0.13
Perspective taking	0.61	0.44	–0.13
High-quality studies			
Achievement	0.88	0.61	0.07
Interpersonal attraction	0.82	0.62	0.27
Social support	0.83	0.72	–0.13
Self-esteem	0.67	0.45	–0.25

Note: Reprinted with permission from Johnson & Johnson, 1989.

efforts. Effort exerted to achieve includes such variables as achievement and productivity, long-term retention, on-task behavior, use of higher-level reasoning strategies, generation of new ideas and solutions, transfer of what is learned within one situation to another, intrinsic motivation, achievement motivation, continuing motivation to learn, and positive attitudes toward learning and school. Overall, cooperation tends to promote higher achievement than do competitive or individualistic efforts (effect sizes = 0.67 and 0.64, respectively). The impact of cooperative learning on achievement means that if schools wish to prepare students to take proficiency tests to meet local and state standards, the use of cooperative learning should dominate instructional practice.

An important aspect of school life is engagement in learning (see Christenson & Havsy, this volume). One indication of engagement in learning is time on task. Cooperators spent considerably more time on task than did competitors (effect size = 0.76) or students working individualistically (effect size = 1.17). In addition, students working cooperatively tended to be more involved in activities and tasks, attach greater importance to success, and engage in more on-task behavior and less apathetic, off-task, disruptive behaviors. Finally, cooperative experiences, compared with competitive and

Figure 3.1. Outcomes of cooperative learning.

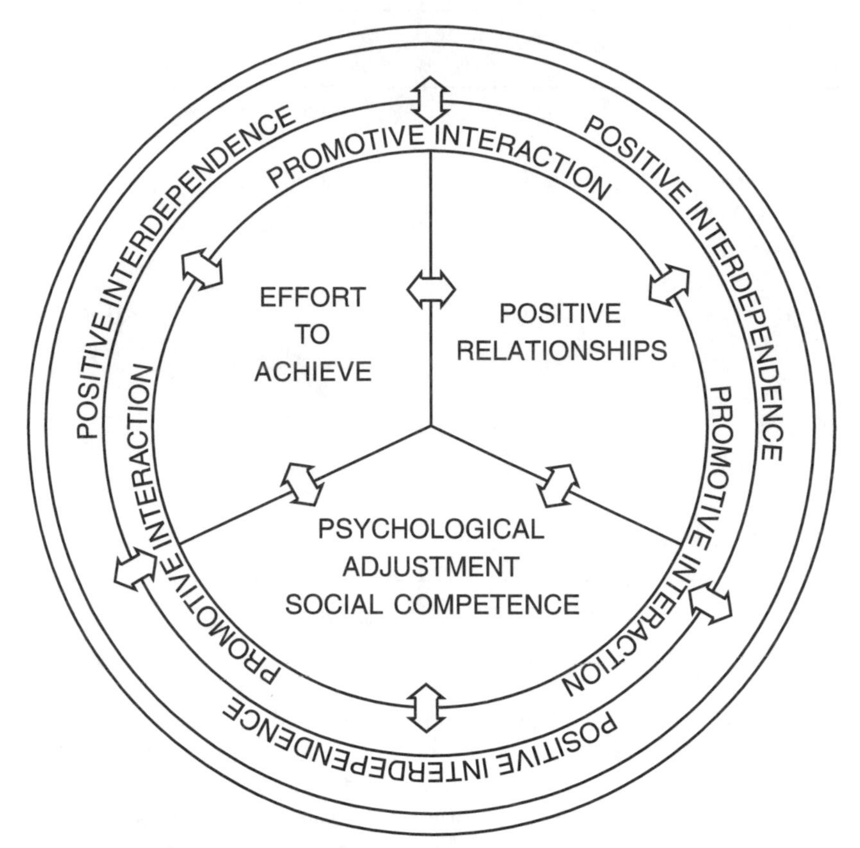

Note: Reprinted with permission from Johnson & Johnson, 1989.

individualistic ones, have been found to promote more positive attitudes toward the task and the experience of working on the task (effect sizes = 0.57 and 0.42, respectively).

Quality of Relationships. Quality of relationships includes such variables as interpersonal attraction, liking, cohesion, esprit de corps, and social support. The degree of emotional bonding that exists among students has a profound effect on students' social and emotional learning. The more positive the relationships among students and between students and faculty, the lower absenteeism and dropout rates and the greater the commitment to group goals, feelings of personal responsibility to the group, willingness to take on difficult tasks, motivation and persistence in working toward goal achievement, satisfaction and morale, willingness to endure pain and frustration on behalf of the group, willingness to defend the group against external criticism or attack, willingness to listen to and be influenced by colleagues, commitment to one another's professional growth and success, and productivity (Johnson & F. Johnson, 2003).

There are over 175 studies that have investigated the relative impact of cooperative, competitive, and individualistic efforts on quality of relationships and another 106 studies on social support (Johnson & Johnson, 1989). As Table 3.1 shows, cooperation generally promotes greater interpersonal attraction among individuals than do competitive or individualistic efforts (effect sizes = 0.67 and 0.60, respectively). Cooperative experiences tend to promote greater social support than do competitive (effect size = 0.62) or individualistic (effect size = 0.70) efforts. Stronger effects are found for peer support than for superior (teacher) support. The high-quality studies tend to have even more powerful effects.

It is difficult to overemphasize the importance of these research results. Friends are a developmental advantage (see Johnson & Johnson, 1989). There is a close association between antisocial behavior and rejection by the normal peer group. Rejected children tend to be deficient in a number of social-cognitive skills, including peer group entry, perception of peer group norms, response to provocation, and interpretation of prosocial interactions. Among children referred to child guidance clinics, 30 to 75% (depending on age) are reported by their parents to experience peer difficulties. Moreover, referred children have fewer friends and less contact with them than nonreferred children, their friendships are significantly less stable over time, and their understanding of the reciprocities and intimacies involved in friendships is less mature. Peer group acceptance and friendships may be built through the extensive use of cooperative learning.

Psychological Health. Ashley Montagu (1966) was fond of saying that with few exceptions the solitary animal in any species is an abnormal creature. Similarly, Karen Horney (1937) stated that the neurotic individual is someone who is inappropriately competitive and, therefore, unable to cooperate with others. Montagu and Horney recognized that the essence of psychological health is the ability to develop and maintain cooperative relationships. More specifically, *psychological health* is the ability (cognitive capacities, motivational orientations, and social skills) to build, maintain, and appropriately modify interdependent relationships with others to succeed in achieving goals (Johnson & Johnson, 1989). People who are unable to do so often (a) become depressed, anxious, frustrated, and lonely, (b) tend to feel afraid, inadequate, helpless, hopeless, and isolated, and (c) rigidly cling to unproductive and ineffective ways of coping with adversity.

With our students and colleagues, we have conducted a series of studies relating cooperative, competitive, and individualistic efforts and attitudes to various indices of psychological health. The samples studied included middle-class junior high students, middle-class high school seniors, high school–aged juvenile prisoners, adult prisoners, Olympic ice-hockey players, and adult step-siblings. The diversity of the samples studied and the variety of measures of psychological health provide considerable generalizability of the results of the studies. A strong relationship was found between cooperativeness and psychological health, a mixed picture was found relating competitiveness to psychological health, and a strong relationship was found between an individualistic orientation and psychological pathology.

Finally, there is evidence that cooperation promotes more frequent use of higher-level reasoning strategies than do competitive (effect size = 0.93) or individualistic (effect size = 0.97) efforts. Similarly, cooperation tends to promote more accurate perspective taking than do competitive (effect size = 0.61) or individualistic (effect size = 0.44) efforts. Thus, the more cooperative learning experiences students are involved in, the more mature their cognitive and moral decision making and the more they will tend to take other people's perspectives into account when making decisions.

Interpersonal and Small-Group Skills. An essential aspect of social and emotional learning is the mastery of the interpersonal and small-group skills needed to interact effectively with others (Johnson, 2003; Johnson & F. Johnson, 2003). A cooperative context is required for students to master interpersonal and small-group skills (Johnson & Johnson, 1989). Competitors tend not to interact in constructive ways; in individualistic situations, no interaction tends to take place. A number of studies have examined the impact of cooperative learning experiences on the mastery and use of social skills (see Johnson & Johnson, 1989). Socially isolated and withdrawn students learn more social skills and engage in them more frequently within cooperative than within individualistic situations, especially when the group is rewarded for their doing so. Emotionally disturbed adolescents who experience cooperative learning are more likely than traditionally taught students to interact appropriately with other students, and this effect is still present 5 months later. Cooperative learning enhances the appropriate interactions among emotionally disturbed students. More generally, cooperation promotes more frequent, effective, and accurate communication than do competitive and individualistic situations, and within cooperative situations communication tends to be more open, effective, and accurate, whereas in competitive situations communication is closed, ineffective, and inaccurate (Johnson, 1974).

Basic Elements of Cooperation

These outcomes tend to result only when cooperation is effectively structured to contain five basic elements (Johnson & Johnson, 1989, 1999). First, there must be a strong sense of *positive interdependence*, so individuals believe they are linked with others in such a way that they cannot succeed unless the others do (and vice versa). Positive interdependence may be structured through mutual goals, joint rewards, divided resources, complementary roles, and a shared identity. Second, each collaborator must be *individually accountable* to do his or her fair share of the work. Third, collaborators must have the opportunity to *promote one another's success* by helping, assisting, supporting, encouraging, and praising one another's efforts to achieve. Fourth, working together cooperatively requires *interpersonal and small-group skills*, such as leadership, decision-making, trust-building, communication, and conflict-management skills. Finally, cooperative groups must engage in *group processing*, which exists when group members discuss how well they are achieving their goals and maintaining effective working relationships.

Levels of Interdependence

To create a learning community, the five basic elements must be structured at all levels of the school: learning group, classroom, interclass, school, school–parent, and school–neighborhood. The learning group level is known as cooperative learning.

Cooperative learning is the instructional use of small groups so that students work together to maximize their own and one another's learning (Johnson, Johnson, & Holubec, 1998a, 1998b). Any assignment in any curriculum for any age student can be done cooperatively. Cooperative learning is usually a component of SEL programs (see Hawkins, Smith, & Catalano, this volume), as many of the social and emotional competencies can be developed only in a cooperative context. There are three types of cooperative learning—formal, informal, and cooperative base groups.

Formal cooperative learning consists of students working together, for one class period to several weeks, to achieve shared learning goals and complete specific tasks and assignments jointly (Johnson, Johnson, & Holubec, 1998b). In formal cooperative learning groups:

1. *Teachers make a number of preinstructional decisions.* They specify the objectives for the lesson (both academic and social skills) and decide on the size of groups, the method of assigning students to groups, the roles students will be assigned, the materials needed to conduct the lesson, and the way the room will be arranged.

2. *They explain the task and the positive interdependence.* A teacher clearly defines the assignment, teaches the required concepts and strategies, specifies the positive interdependence and individual accountability, gives the criteria for success, and explains the expected social skills to be used.
3. *They monitor students' learning and intervene* within the groups to provide task assistance or to increase students' interpersonal and group skills.
4. *They assess students' learning and help students process how well their groups functioned.* Students' learning is carefully assessed. Members of the learning groups then discuss how effectively they worked together and how they can improve in the future.

Informal cooperative learning consists of having students work together to achieve a joint learning goal in temporary, ad hoc groups that last from a few minutes to one class period (Johnson, Johnson, & Holubec, 1998a). During a lecture, demonstration, or film, informal cooperative learning can be used to focus student attention on the material to be learned, set a mood conducive to learning, help set expectations as to what will be covered in a class session, ensure that students cognitively process and rehearse the material being taught, summarize what was learned and precue the next session, and provide closure to an instructional session. The procedure for using informal cooperative learning during a lecture entails having 3- to 5-minute focused discussions before and after the lecture (i.e., bookends) and 2- to 3-minute interspersing pair discussions throughout the lecture.

Cooperative base groups are long-term, heterogeneous cooperative learning groups with stable membership whose primary responsibilities are to provide support, encouragement, and assistance to help students make academic progress and develop cognitively and socially in healthy ways as well as holding one another accountable for striving to learn (Johnson, Johnson, & Holubec, 1998a). Typically, cooperative base groups (a) are heterogeneous in membership, (b) meet regularly (e.g., daily or biweekly), and (c) last for the duration of the semester or year, or until all members are graduated. When students know that the base group will stay together for some time, they become committed to find ways to motivate and encourage their groupmates and solve any problems in working together.

The procedure for using base groups is to assign students to groups of three to four members, have them meet at the beginning and end of each class session (or week) to complete academic tasks such as checking one another's homework, routine tasks such as taking attendance, and personal support tasks such as listening sympathetically to personal problems or providing guidance for writing a paper.

Cooperative learning is an important part of other programs, such as the Seattle Social Development Project (see Chapter 8) and the Child Development Project (see Chapter 11).

Positive interdependence may be extended to the classroom as a whole. Class goals may be established, class rewards or celebrations may be created, class roles may be structured, class processing may take place in class meetings, and a class identity may be created through a class name, slogan, flag, or song.

Interclass interdependence may be established through organizing a set of classes into a "neighborhood" or "school within a school," classes such as science and math may be integrated, and students of different ages can become cross-class "reading buddies."

School-level positive interdependence (Johnson & Johnson, 1994) may be established through a school mission statement, faculty and staff teaching teams and study groups, school task forces to solve school problems, and ad hoc decision-making groups during faculty meetings to involve all staff members in important school decisions.

School–parent interdependence may be established through involving parents in strategic planning, producing a school newsletter, publishing the school yearbook, volunteering in classes, helping conduct special projects, and serving on school committees or the site council.

Finally, school–neighborhood interdependence may be created by eliciting local merchants to give a discount to students who have a card verifying that in the most recent grading period they achieved a "B" average or above. In return, classes could do neighborhood service projects, cleaning up a park or mowing the yards of elderly residents.

THE SECOND C: CONSTRUCTIVE CONFLICT RESOLUTION

When managed constructively, conflicts can increase (a) individuals' energy, curiosity, and motivation, (b) achievement, retention, insight, creativity, problem solving, and synthesis, (c) healthy cognitive and social development, (d) clarification of own and others' identity, commitments, and values, (e) quality of relationships, and (f) social and emotional learning (Johnson & Johnson, 1995a, 1995b). If conflicts are managed destructively, on the other hand, they destroy relationships and tear cooperative systems apart.

Managing conflicts constructively depends on (a) having clear procedures for managing conflicts, (b) community members being skilled in the use of the procedures and valuing them, and (c) having norms and values that encourage and support the use of the procedures. Faculty and staff need to teach students (and learn themselves) three procedures for managing conflicts: academic controversy, problem-solving negotiation, and peer mediation procedures.

Constructive Controversy

Constructive controversy is an important source of social and emotional learning. A *controversy* exists when one person's ideas, opinions, information, theories, or conclusions are incompatible with those of another and the two seek to reach an agreement (Johnson & Johnson, 1995a). Controversies are resolved by engaging in what Aristotle called *deliberate discourse* (i.e., the discussion of the advantages and disadvantages of proposed actions) aimed at synthesizing novel solutions (i.e., *creative problem solving*).

Teaching students how to engage in the controversy process begins with randomly assigning students to heterogeneous cooperative learning groups of four members (Johnson & Johnson, 1979, 1989, 1995a). The groups are given an issue on which to write a report and pass a test. Each cooperative group is divided into two pairs. One pair is given the conposition on the issue and the other pair is given the proposition. Each pair is given the instructional materials needed to define their position and point them toward supporting information. The cooperative goal of reaching a consensus on the issue (by synthesizing the best reasoning from both sides) and writing a quality group report is highlighted. Students then (a) research, learn, and prepare the best case possible for their assigned position, (b) present the best case for their assigned position to ensure it gets a fair and complete hearing, (c) engage in an open discussion in which there is spirited disagreement as students freely exchange information and ideas while arguing forcefully and persuasively for their position, critically analyzing and refuting the opposing position, and rebutting attacks on their position and presenting counterarguments, (d) reverse perspectives and present the best case for the opposing position, and (e) drop all advocacy and find a synthesis on which all members can agree by summarizing the best evidence and reasoning from both sides and integrating it into a joint position that is new and unique, writing a group report, and processing how well the group functioned and celebrating the group's success and hard work.

From Table 3.2 it may be seen that the research (Johnson & Johnson, 1989, 1995a) indicates that intellectual conflicts create higher achievement (characterized by higher achievement, longer retention, critical thinking, and greater creativity) than concurrence seeking (effect size = 0.68), debate (effect size = 0.40), or individualistic efforts (effect size = 0.87). Students who participate in academic controversies end up using more higher-level reasoning and metacognitive thought more frequently than students participating

Table 3.2. Meta-Analysis of Academic Controversy Studies: Mean Effect Sizes

Dependent Variable	*Controversy/ Concurrence Seeking*	*Controversy/ Debate*	*Controversy/ Individualistic Efforts*
Achievement	0.68	0.40	0.87
Cognitive reasoning	0.62	1.35	0.90
Perspective taking	0.91	0.22	0.86
Motivation	0.75	0.45	0.71
Attitudes toward task	0.58	0.81	0.64
Interpersonal attraction	0.24	0.72	0.81
Social support	0.32	0.92	1.52
Self-esteem	0.39	0.51	0.85

Note: Reprinted with permission from Johnson & Johnson, 1995b.

in concurrence seeking (effect size = 0.62), debate (effect size = 1.35), or individualistic efforts (effect size = 0.90). In addition, students in academic controversies (a) more accurately take the other's perspective than do students participating in concurrence seeking (effect size = 0.91), debate (effect size = 0.22), or individualistic efforts (effect size = 0.86), (b) have greater continuing motivation to learn than students participating in concurrence seeking (effect size = 0.75), debate (effect size = 0.45), or individualistic efforts (effect size = 0.71), (c) develop more positive attitudes toward learning than students participating in concurrence seeking (effect size = 0.58), debate (effect size = 0.81), or individualistic efforts (effect size = 0.64), (d) develop more positive interpersonal relationships than do students participating in concurrence seeking (effect size = 0.24), debate (effect size = 0.72), or individualistic efforts (effect size = 0.81), (e) experience greater social support than do students participating in concurrence seeking (effect size = 0.32), debate (effect size = 0.92), or individualistic efforts (effect size = 1.52), and (f) develop higher self-esteem than do students participating in concurrence seeking (effect size = 0.39), debate (effect size = 0.51), or individualistic efforts (effect size = 0.85). Engaging in a controversy also can be fun, enjoyable, and exciting.

Conflict Resolution Training

In addition to intellectual conflicts, conflicts may be based on individuals' differing interests within a situation. *Conflicts of interests* exist when the actions of one person attempting to maximize his or her wants and benefits prevent, block, or interfere with another person maximizing his or her wants and benefits (Deutsch, 1973). The *Teaching Students to Be Peacemakers Program* began in the 1960s (Johnson & Johnson, 1995a) to teach students how to engage in problem-solving negotiations and mediate their schoolmates' conflicts.

Conflicts of interests are resolved through negotiation and mediation. There are two ways to negotiate: *distributive*, or "win–lose" (where one person benefits only if the opponent agrees to make a concession), and *integrative*, or problem solving (where disputants work together to create an agreement that benefits everyone involved). In ongoing relationships, distributive negotiations result in destructive outcomes, and integrative negotiations lead to constructive outcomes. Using problem-solving negotiations is a six-step process:

1. *Describe what you want*, using good communication skills and defining the conflict as a small and specific mutual problem.
2. *Describe how you feel*, which requires both understanding how you feel and communicating it openly and clearly.
3. *Describe the reasons for your wants and feelings*, expressing cooperative intentions, listening carefully, separating interests from positions, and differentiating before trying to integrate the two sets of interests.
4. *Take the other's perspective, and summarize your understanding of what the other person wants, how the other person feels, and the reasons underlying both*, which requires being able to see the problem from both perspectives simultaneously.
5. *Formulate three optional plans* to resolve the conflict that maximize joint benefits and take both perspectives and sets of interests into account.
6. *Choose one of the plans, and formalize the agreement with a handshake.* The final agreement should be fair to all disputants, maximize joint benefits, strengthen disputants' ability to work together cooperatively, and strengthen disputants' ability to resolve conflicts constructively in the future. (Johnson & Johnson, 1995b)

When students are unable to negotiate a resolution to their conflict, they may request help from a mediator. A *mediator* is a neutral person who helps two or more people resolve their conflict, usually by negotiating an integrative agreement. In contrast, *arbitration* is the submission of a dispute to a disinterested third party (such as a teacher or principal) who makes a final and binding judgment as to how the conflict will be resolved. Mediation consists of the following four steps:

1. *Ending hostilities*. The mediator must ensure that the hostile encounter is ended and the disputants have cooled off sufficiently to engage in rational problem solving.
2. *Ensuring that the disputants are committed to the mediation process*. The mediator ensures that disputants are committed to the mediation process and are ready to negotiate in good faith. The mediator then introduces the process of mediation and sets the ground rules that (a) mediation is voluntary, (b) the mediator is neutral, (c) each person will have the chance to state his or her view of the conflict without interruption, and (d) each person agrees to solve the problem with no name calling or interrupting, being as honest as possible, abiding by any agreement made, and keeping anything said in mediation confidential.
3. *Helping disputants successfully negotiate with one another*. The mediator carefully takes disputants through the problem-solving negotiation steps and ensures that each disputant does each step competently.
4. *Formalizing the agreement*. The mediator solidifies the agreement into a contract and becomes "the keeper of the contract" by checking periodically with the disputants to make sure the agreement is working. If it is not, then the four steps of mediation begin again. (Johnson & Johnson, 1995b)

Each day the teacher selects two class members to serve as official mediators. Any conflicts students cannot resolve themselves are referred to the mediators. The mediators wear official T-shirts, patrol the playground and lunchroom, and are available to mediate any conflicts that occur in the classroom or elsewhere in the school. The role of mediator is rotated so that all students serve as mediators an equal amount of time. Initially, students mediate in pairs. This ensures that shy or nonverbal students get the same amount of experience as more extroverted and verbally fluent students.

If peer mediation fails, the teacher mediates the conflict. If teacher mediation fails, the teacher arbitrates by deciding who is right and who is wrong. If that fails, the principal mediates the conflict. If that fails, the principal arbitrates. Teaching all students to mediate properly results in a school-wide discipline program where students are empowered to regulate and control their own and their classmates' actions. Teachers and administrators are then free to spend more time and energy on instruction.

Between 1988 and 2000 we and our colleagues conducted 16 studies on the effectiveness of the peacemaker program in eight different schools in two different countries (Johnson & Johnson, 1996a, 2000b). Students involved were from kindergarten through ninth grade. The studies were conducted in rural, suburban, and urban settings. The benefits of teaching students the problem-solving negotiation and the peer mediation procedures are shown in Table 3.3.

First, students and faculty tend to develop a shared understanding of how conflicts should be managed and a common vocabulary to discuss conflicts. Second, students tend to learn the negotiation and mediation procedures (effect size = 2.25), retain their knowledge throughout the school year and into the following year (effect size = 3.34), apply the procedures to their and other people's conflicts (effect size = 2.16), transfer the procedures to nonclassroom settings such as the playground and lunchroom, transfer the procedures to nonschool settings such as the home, and engage in problem-solving rather than win–lose negotiations. Third, when students are involved in conflicts, trained students use more constructive strategies (effect size = 1.60) such as integrative negotiations (effect size = 0.98) than do untrained students. Fourth, students' attitudes toward conflict tend to became more positive (effect size = 1.07). Students learn to view conflicts as potentially positive, and faculty and parents view the conflict training as constructive and helpful. Fifth, students tend to resolve their conflicts without the involvement of faculty and administrators. The number of discipline problems teachers had to deal with decreased by about 60% and referrals to administrators dropped by about 90%. Sixth, the conflict resolution procedures tend to

Table 3.3. Meta-Analysis of Peacemaker Studies: Mean Effect Sizes

Dependent Variable	*Mean*	*SD*	*Number of Effects*
Academic achievement	0.88	0.09	5
Academic retention	0.70	0.31	4
Learned procedure	2.25	1.98	13
Learned procedure—Retention	3.34	4.16	9
Applied procedure	2.16	1.31	4
Application—Retention	0.46	0.16	3
Strategy constructiveness	1.60	1.70	21
Constructiveness—Retention	1.10	0.53	10
Strategy two-concerns	1.10	0.46	5
Two-concerns—Retention	0.45	0.20	2
Integrative negotiation	0.98	0.36	5
Positive attitude	1.07	0.25	5
Negative attitude	–0.61	0.37	2
Quality of solutions	0.73	0	1

Source: Johnson & Johnson, 2000a.

enhance the basic values of the classroom and school. Seventh, students generally like to engage in the procedures. A teacher stated: "They never refuse to negotiate or mediate. When there's a conflict and you say it's time for conflict resolution, you never have either one say I won't do it. There are no refusals." Finally, when integrated into academic units, the conflict resolution training tends to increase academic achievement and long-term retention of academic material (effect sizes = 0.88 and 0.70, respectively). Academic units, especially in subject areas such as literature and history, provide a setting in which to understand conflicts, practice how to resolve them, and use them to gain insight into the material being studied. There are other conflict resolution programs, such as the Resolving Conflict Creatively Program (see Chapter 9) that also have had important impacts on social and emotional learning.

THE THIRD C: CIVIC VALUES

For a community to exist and sustain itself, members must share common goals and values that define appropriate behavior and increase the quality of life within the community (Johnson & Johnson, 1996b, 2000a). A learning community cannot exist in schools dominated by (a) competition where students are taught to value striving for their personal success at the expense of others or (b) individualistic efforts where students value only their own self-interests. Rather, students need to internalize values underlying cooperation and constructive conflict.

The value systems underlying competitive, individualistic, and cooperative situations as well as constructive controversy and integrative negotiations are a hidden curriculum beneath the surface of school life. Whenever students engage in *competitive efforts*, for example, they learn the values of winning (not mastery or excellence), succeeding at other people's expense, opposing and obstructing the success of others, feeling joy and pride in one's wins and others' losses, and viewing one's worth as conditional and contingent on whether one won or lost.

The values inherently taught by *individualistic experiences*, on the other hand, include focusing on one's own self-interest, viewing success as depending on one's own efforts, taking personal pride and pleasure in succeeding, viewing other people as irrelevant, being extrinsically motivated to gain rewards, and viewing one's worth as being based on the characteristics that help one succeed.

Finally, some of the values inherently taught by *cooperative efforts* are working toward others' success (and the common good) as well as one's own, facilitating and promoting the well-being of others, taking pride and pleasure in other's success and happiness, viewing other people as potential contributors to one's success, and viewing one's worth as being unconditional.

Some of the values inherently taught by engaging in constructive controversy and integrative negotiations include improving one's conclusions by subjecting them to intellectual challenge, viewing issues from all perspectives, reaching agreements that are satisfying to all disputants, and maintaining effective and caring long-term relationships.

CONCLUSIONS AND RECOMMENDATIONS

To ensure healthy social and emotional development of all students, teachers must ensure that students master interpersonal and small-group skills and internalize prosocial attitudes and values. Perhaps the most obvious recommendation for teachers is that social skills and prosocial values cannot be inculcated when students are isolated from each other. Computer programs, individual worksheets, and curriculum materials that students use alone without interacting with classmates are of little use in and of themselves for social and emotional learning. In addition, having students compete with one another mitigates against social and emotional learning. Thus, the first recommendation for teachers interested in social and emotional learning is to ensure that students spend most of their time in cooperative learning groups. The second recommendation is to extend the levels of cooperation to the classroom, school, and neighborhood. This creates a cooperative community within which education takes place.

The long-term health of a community depends largely on how conflicts are managed. When conflicts are managed destructively (i.e., one side wins and the other loses, the relationship among disputants is damaged, and disputants are less able to deal with conflict constructively in the future), the community dissolves. There are two types of conflicts that are of special interest to educational enterprises: academic controversy or intellectual conflict and conflicts of interests. The third recommendation is for teachers to structure regular academic controversies to promote learning and retention, higher-level reasoning, and perspective taking. In addition, it teaches students how to manage intellectual conflicts to enhance problem solving and decision making. The fourth recommendation is for teachers to institute the Teaching Students to Be Peacemakers Program to teach students how to engage in problem-solving negotiations and peer mediation. Doing so will significantly increase the constructive resolution of conflicts of interests and increase achievement when the peacemaker training is integrated into academic units.

The fifth recommendation for teachers is to support the values inherently taught when students engage in cooperative activities and when students resolve conflicts constructively. Those values include a concern for others as well as oneself, a concern for the common good, empathy and the ability to see situations from others' perspectives, and maximizing joint gain.

The sixth recommendation is to promote all Three Cs (cooperative community, constructive conflict, resolution and civic values) simultaneously. Although each of the Three Cs may be discussed and implemented separately, together they represent a gestalt in which each enhances and promotes the others. Together the Three Cs are a complete program for creating effective and nurturing schools where children and youth learn and develop in positive and healthy ways.

REFERENCES

Deutsch, M. (1973). *The resolution of conflict.* New Haven, CT: Yale University Press.

Elias, M. J., Zins, J. E., Weissberg, R. P., Frey, K. S., Greenberg, M. T., Haynes, N. M., Kessler, R., Schwab-Stone, M. E., & Shriver, T. P. (1997). *Promoting social and emotional learning: Guidelines for educators.* Alexandria, VA: Association for Supervision and Curriculum Development.

Horney, K. (1937). *The neurotic personality of our time.* New York: Norton.

Johnson, D. W. (1974). Communication and the inducement of cooperative behavior in conflicts: A critical review. *Speech Monographs, 41*, 64–78.

Johnson, D. W. (2003). *Reaching out: Interpersonal effectiveness and self-actualization* (8th ed.). Boston: Allyn & Bacon.

Johnson D. W., & Johnson, F. (2003). *Joining together: Group theory and group skills* (8th ed.). Boston: Allyn & Bacon.

Johnson, D. W., & Johnson, R. (1979). Conflict in the classroom: Controversy and learning. *Review of Educational Research, 49*, 51–61.

Johnson, D. W., & Johnson, R. (1989). *Cooperation and competition: Theory and research.* Edina, MN: Interaction Book Company.

Johnson, D. W., & Johnson, R. (1994). *Leading the cooperative school* (2nd ed.). Edina, MN: Interaction Book Company.

Johnson, D. W., & Johnson, R. (1995a). *Creative controversy: Intellectual challenge in the classroom* (3rd ed.). Edina, MN: Interaction Book Company.

Johnson, D. W., & Johnson, R. (1995b). *Teaching students to be peacemakers* (3rd ed.). Edina, MN: Interaction Book Company.

Johnson, D. W., & Johnson, R. (1996a). Conflict resolution and peer mediation programs in elementary and secondary schools: A review of the research. *Review of Educational Research, 66*(4), 459–506.

Johnson, D. W., & Johnson, R. (1996b). Cooperative learning and traditional American values. *NASSP Bulletin, 80*(579), 11–18.

Johnson, D. W., & Johnson, R. (1999). *Learning together and alone: Cooperative, competitive, and individualistic learning.* Boston: Allyn & Bacon.

Johnson, D. W., & Johnson, R. (2000a). Cooperative learning, values, and culturally plural classrooms. In M. Leicester, C. Modgill, & S. Modgil (Eds.), *Values, the classroom, and cultural diversity* (pp. 15–28). London: Cassell.
Johnson, D. W., & Johnson, R. (2000b, June). *Teaching students to be peacemakers: Results of twelve years of research.* Paper presented at meeting of the Society for the Psychological Study of Social Issues, Minneapolis, MN.
Johnson, D. W., Johnson, R., & Holubec, E. (1998a). *Advanced cooperative learning* (3rd ed.). Edina, MN: Interaction Book Company.
Johnson, D. W., Johnson, R., & Holubec, E. (1998b). *Cooperation in the classroom* (6th ed.). Edina, MN: Interaction Book Company.
Montagu, A. (1966). *On being human.* New York: Hawthorn.
Payton, J. W., Wardlaw, D. M., Graczyk, P. A., Bloodworth, M. R., Tompsett, C. J., & Weissberg, R. P. (2000). Social and emotional learning: A framework for promoting mental health and reducing risk behavior in children and youth. *Journal of School Health, 70*(5), 179–185.
Zins, J. E., Elias, M. J., Greenberg, M. T., & Weissberg, R. P. (2000). Promoting social and emotional competence in children. In K. M. Minke & G. C. Bear (Eds.), *Preventing school problems—promoting school success: Strategies and programs that work* (pp. 71–100). Bethesda, MD: National Association of School Psychologists.

CHAPTER 4

Family–School–Peer Relationships: Significance for Social, Emotional, and Academic Learning

SANDRA L. CHRISTENSON AND LYNNE H. HAVSY

Who are the students in our schools? According to the National Center for Education Statistics (2003), 90,640 public schools provided instruction to 47,222,778 students during 2000–2001. Fifty-eight percent of these students were enrolled in traditional primary grades, and 62% of students were White. The number of students eligible for free or reduced price meals ranged from 23,986 in Vermont to 2,820,611 in California. Nationally, about 1 in every 13 students receives special education services.

A related but different question is: Who are the learners? Some are described as successful, others as struggling academically; some as motivated, others as unmotivated; some as involved, others as disengaged; and some as connected, others as alienated. Educators grapple with students who appear unmotivated to learn. Although the importance of motivation to learn is acknowledged, producing students who achieve good grades or test scores is the focal point of current classroom practices. And yet, when students graduate, many no longer possess the desire to learn. According to a University of California–Los Angeles survey, 40% of freshman are disengaged from educational values and pursuits. Students are "inattentive, easily bored and unwilling to work hard, especially on difficult material outside their interests" (Trout, 2000, p. A17).

There is little debate that success for all must be our standard in education, and school personnel certainly espouse this message. Success for all, however, requires attending to the physical, psychological, social, cognitive, language, and instructional needs of students. The debate highlights the intersection of social, emotional, and academic learning. Although the ABCs are essential, they seldom refer to autonomy, belonging, and competence. School success requires students to take initiative and be responsible for their learning (autonomy), have interpersonal attachments with peers and school staff (belonging), and have a sense of mastery when challenged (competence).

School completion for alienated youth provides an excellent illustration of this point. We contend that engagement at school and with learning provides a foundation for academic persistence, adjustment, and performance, especially for students at risk of educational failure. Of particular relevance is Deci's (1992) notion that interpersonal relationships that provide students with a sense of belonging may be powerful motivators of their interest in school. If our goal is to foster school success, social and emotional learning that facilitates desired academic outcomes should be addressed explicitly and effectively.

The goals of this chapter are (a) to summarize the effect of family–school–peer influences on student engagement and school success, (b) to describe Check & Connect, a social and emotional learning (SEL) intervention, and (c) to offer recommendations for future research, practice, and policy to address the needs of students at risk for educational failure.

A TROUBLING REALITY

Engaging students in school and helping them work toward graduation is a critical task for parents and educators. Current statistics indicate that the majority of states have not reached a 90% graduation rate, and for some populations the rate of graduation is significantly lower (National Center for Education Statistics, 2002). For example, students from low-income families have a graduation rate of 75%, and a disproportionate number of children who do not complete school live in families headed by a single parent; come from Hispanic, African American, and Native American backgrounds; attend large urban school districts; and are affected by disabilities. Promoting successful school completion for students is even more challenging in light of current national reform efforts to raise achievement in relation to high academic standards, end social promotion, and measure student performance using high-stakes testing.

School dropouts demonstrate the most extreme form of disengagement. They are more likely to have exhibited behavior and disciplinary problems, poor attendance, low motivation to succeed, low aspirations for educational attainment, poor self-concept, an external locus of control, and alienation from school (Hess & D'Amato, 1996; Rumberger, 1995). Significant, negative correlations between student belonging in school and frequency of absences and tardies have been reported (Goodenow, 1993b). Also, dropout rates are highest for students who are excessively absent *and* highly aggressive (Kupersmidt & Coie, 1990).

Although dropping out generally is viewed as the student's decision, it must be understood in relation to family and school support. Jordan, McPartland, and Lara (1999) categorize explanations as push or pull effects. Describing students who are unable to cope with policies and practices within the school environment, push effects (suspension) exacerbate failure and dropout. Pull effects (employment) are external factors that undermine an emphasis on schooling. Their finding that push factors are most important for predicting a student's decision to drop out is consistent with other research underscoring that the social climate of the school is a critical factor. Many dropouts report they could not get along with teachers (22.8%) or other students (14.5%), and 25% indicate they did not feel that they belonged (National Center for Education Statistics, 1993).

STUDENT ENGAGEMENT AT SCHOOL

Enhancing student engagement at school has emerged as the target variable in school completion efforts. Four terms (belonging, participation, identification, and school membership) describe aspects of engagement and illustrate social and emotional factors relevant to academic learning. Regardless of the terms used, student engagement requires psychological connections within the academic environment (e.g., positive adult–student and peer relationships) *and* active student behavior (e.g., attendance, participation, effort, prosocial behavior). For example, belonging refers to "students' sense of being accepted, valued, included and encouraged by others (teachers and peers) in the academic classroom setting and of feeling oneself to be an important part of the life and activity of the class" (Goodenow, 1993a, p. 25). McPartland (1994) suggests four broad intervention components to enhance student engagement: providing opportunities for success in schoolwork, creating a caring and supportive environment, communicating the relevance of education to future endeavors, and helping with students' personal problem.

Research on student belonging is descriptive (range of significant correlations is .10–.53); only three intervention studies were found. Correlates of belonging include motivation, self-esteem, autonomy, expectations for future success, attendance, and grades for middle and high school students of varying ethnicities (Goodenow, 1993a; Israelashvili, 1997).

Understanding the link between belonging and academic performance is critical. For example, expectations of success develop from individuals' beliefs about personal skills *and* social resources to succeed; both enable students' commitment to school and valuing of academic work (Goodenow &

Grady, 1993). Students who feel connected to and cared for by their teachers report autonomous reasons for engaging in positive school-related behaviors (Ryan, Stiller, & Lynch, 1994). It is noteworthy that students are more likely to avoid high-risk behavior (e.g., substance abuse, violence) when they feel connected to their families and schools (Resnick et al., 1997).

Engagement is a positive, significant correlate of various indicators of academic achievement (grade point averages and tests). For example, participation in the classroom and outside the regular curriculum is associated with academic performance for elementary and middle school students across race and gender (Finn, 1993) and for students with and without disabilities and across grade levels (Voelkl, 1997). Also, a negative, significant relationship between disruptive and withdrawn-inattentive behaviors and academic achievement exists (Finn, Pannozzo, & Voelkl, 1995). Finally, Finn and Rock (1997) show that participation differentiates at-risk secondary students who are academically successful and their less successful counterparts.

School completers with academic success (resilient students) engage significantly more often in a distinct set of school behaviors related directly and clearly to learning than do school completers with poor academic performance (nonresilient completers) or dropouts. Behaviors include coming to school and class on time, being prepared for and participating in class assignments, expending necessary effort to complete class assignments and homework, and avoiding being disruptive in class. Supporting these findings, Floyd (1997) identifies four protective mechanisms for high-achieving African American twelfth graders from impoverished backgrounds: supportive home environments, involvement with concerned educators, development of perseverance (willingness to work hard in the face of barriers), and optimism (belief that academic efforts would pay off).

Factors That Promote Engagement in Learning

School Policies and Practice. First, specific school policies and practices influence levels of student engagement. School practices and policies such as tracking, retention, suspension, and rigid rule structures negatively affect student engagement, whereas other practices and policies, such as smaller schools, opportunity for creativity and student choice, and highlighting the relevance of curricula to personal life goals, enhance levels of engagement (McPartland, 1994).

Caring Classroom and School Environments. Second, caring classroom and school environments enhance opportunities for student engagement by developing supportive relationships, increasing opportunities for participation in school life, and allowing for the pursuit of academic success. Evidence for this has been found for elementary and middle school students regardless of ethnicity. Schools with a committed faculty, positive teacher–student relationships, an orderly environment, and a school emphasis on academic pursuits are associated with lower rates of absenteeism and dropping out (Bryk & Thum, 1989). Baker (1998) demonstrated that a supportive social environment within the school is a significant, moderate correlate of student satisfaction with school, perception of the classroom climate, and stress. Furthermore, teaching practices that foster student autonomy, school success, and engagement influence—in expected directions—student participation, bonding to school, academic motivation, feelings of competence, and involvement in high-risk behaviors (Abbott et al., 1998; Grolnick & Ryan, 1987).

Relationships Between Students. Relationships between students play a key role in belonging. Having friends at school supports involvement in school-related activities (Berndt & Keefe, 1995). Goodenow (1993b) finds that middle school students who are more socially integrated have a significantly greater sense of belonging than those with less peer acceptance, and those with support from friends found the transition to and during ninth grade to be smoother (Isakson & Jarvis, 1999). The influence of peers for belonging may be particularly important during adolescence. Steinberg, Dornbusch, and Brown (1992) have shown that peers highly influence students' day-to-day behavior in school, such as time spent on homework and enjoyment of school. There is evidence that students who eventually drop out associate with like-minded students—those who do not feel part of the social world of school or value educational success (Hymel, Comfort, Schonert-Reichl, & McDougall, 1996).

Family Support and Involvement. Finally, family support and involvement are associated with student engagement. Statistically significant home correlates of school completion include the presence of study aids, high educational expectations and aspirations, and parental monitoring and participation (Rumberger, 1995). Students who perceived greater parental support during and after the transition to high school had significantly higher belonging (Isakson & Jarvis, 1999). Finn (1993) found that engagement was associated with discussions about school, less monitoring of homework, and greater academic resources in the home, whereas disengagement was associated with the opposite characteristics. These data suggest that motivational support for learning, specifically structuring the home environment and emphasizing children's efforts to succeed, appears to be important in facilitating academic achievement, perhaps more so than direct assistance and monitoring of homework.

FAMILY–SCHOOL–PEER INFLUENCES ON CHILDREN'S LEARNING

The descriptive empirical base for the effect of the home on children's learning is strong; many families foster values, attitudes, and behaviors that are correlated with learning at school. Home influences are correlated with *academic* (grades, test scores, homework completion, fewer placements in special education, postsecondary education), *social* (social skills, classroom participation, fewer suspensions, attendance), and *emotional* (attitudes toward school work, self-esteem, perseverance) learning outcomes for students. What parents do to support learning predicts scholastic ability better than who families are (White, 1982).

Families play different roles in motivational support for children's learning. Actions parents take to facilitate children's educational success include parental attitudes (i.e., I expect you to do well in school) and practices (i.e., I will communicate and support your learning) and have been shown to differentiate high and low achievers (Clark, 1983). Additionally, the quality of the family–school relationship cannot be ignored because it, rather than the quantity of interaction, relates to improved student achievement and behavior (Patrikakou & Weissberg, 1999) and trust between home and school (Adams & Christenson, 2000).

The social context for students' learning is receiving far greater attention than in the past. It is consistently suggested that home–school consensus about the goals of education is essential to counter information from competing sources such as television and peers, and that discontinuities between families and schools compromise the effectiveness of either system for academic socialization (Hansen, 1986). These findings corroborate the findings from recent studies, which show that gains in students' academic, social, and behavioral performance are greater when mesosystemic intervention (home and school) is used, in contrast to microsystemic intervention (classroom or parent only) (Sheridan, 1997).

Examples of the importance of the social context for academic, social, and emotional learning are illustrative. Comer's School Development Program (SDP) emphasizes relationships for children's development in six areas. Results reveal significant differences in academic achievement between randomly selected students in SDP schools and students in non-SDP control schools. Also, experimental-control studies show that SDP students experienced significantly greater positive changes in attendance, classroom behavior, attitude toward authority, group participation, perceived school competence, and self-competence when compared with non-SDP students in control schools (Comer, Haynes, Joyner, & Ben-Avie, 1996).

The Six Factors

From their review of family, school, and community influences on positive indicators of school success for elementary and secondary students, Christenson and Peterson (1998) identified six factors that reflect the complementary nature of family–school–community roles for children's school success: standards and expectations, structure, opportunity to learn, support, climate/relationships, and modeling (See Figure 4.1). They reviewed over 200 studies that reported correlations between one of the contextual influences and an indicator of positive academic, social, or emotional learning for students (i.e., teacher-desired performance). Across studies, the indicators were varied and included academic performance (tests, grades, teacher ratings), social competence (peer affiliation), and emotional development (achievement motivation, self-esteem). They found remarkable similarity in family, school, and community influences that foster engagement with learning and school success. This organization of correlational studies illustrates the notion of creating conditions for optimal student performance.

Although the significant correlations were mostly low to moderate, strength lies in the consistent direction of findings. The review did not reveal the mediating role of social and emotional factors on academic performance; however, the correlations suggest that social (e.g., teacher–peer–family support) and emotional (e.g., motivation, belonging) variables affect academic performance. For example, autonomy-supportive environments; supportive relationships with parents, teachers, and peers; and an emphasis on progress, learning, and effort have been associated with academic success, school-related interests, and pursuit of academic goals (Ames & Archer, 1988; Wentzel, 1998; Wentzel & Asher, 1995). Others have found that positive adult–student relationships have an impact on students' achievement-related beliefs, academic performance, and engagement in school (Connell, Halpern-Felsher, Clifford, Crichlow, & Usinger, 1995).

Consistent and Inconsistent Learners

Christenson and Peterson (1998) conducted focus groups that discussed the presence and importance of the factors for personal school success with consistent and inconsistent learners. Teachers nominated students using specific criteria. "Consistent learners" were characterized as working hard at school, taking school seriously, doing one's level best, and being viewed as a responsible, productive, and competent learner. In contrast, "inconsistent learners" were characterized as performing inconsistently in school, generally not taking school and assigned activities seriously, and not performing their level best.

Figure 4.1. Facilitators of children's performance across family, school, and community.

Standards and expectations—the level of expected performance held by key adults for youth. Student success in school is facilitated when parents and teachers clearly state expectations for student performance, set specific goals and standards for desired behavior and performance, discuss expectations with youth, emphasize children's effort when completing tasks, and ensure youth understand the consequences for not meeting expectations.

Structure—the overall routine and monitoring provided by key adults for youth. Students' success in school is facilitated when families and schools provide a consistent pattern of events and age-appropriate monitoring and supervision. Students perform better in school when they understand their schedule of daily activities, directions for schoolwork, rules for behavior, and so on.

Opportunity to learn—the variety of learning options available to youth in the home, at school, and within the community. Student success in school is facilitated when youth are provided with various tools for learning such as reading materials, access to clubs and organizations, varied teaching strategies, and time to practice/master new skills. Also, success is enhanced when the key adults in the youth's life communicate with each other.

Support—the guidance provided by, the communication between, and the interest shown by adults to facilitate student progress in school. Progress is facilitated when adults give frequent verbal support and praise; provide the youth with regular, explicit feedback; talk directly to youth about schoolwork and activities; and teach problem-solving and negotiation skills. It is what adults do on an ongoing basis to enhance school success.

Climate/relationships—the amount of warmth and friendliness, praise and recognition; and the degree to which the adult–youth relationships are positive and respectful. These relationships are facilitated by cooperative, accepting environments; a nonblaming relationship between home and school; and encouragement, praise, and involvement in the youth's life from key adults. The degree of continuity of these relationships and interactions—between adults at home and at school—influences the degree of academic achievement of the youth. It is how adults in the home, in the school, and in the community help youth to be learners.

Modeling—how adults demonstrate desired behaviors and commitment/value toward learning and working hard in their daily lives. Student success at school is enhanced when teachers establish an academically demanding classroom that has clearly defined objectives, explicit instructions, and an orderly and efficient environment, and when parent(s) or other adults read, ask questions, discuss the importance/value of education, set long-term goals, and are able to intervene and be involved with the youth's school.

Source: Christenson & Peterson, 1998.

These students tended to lack a connection with school and often displayed behavior such as disruptions, tardiness, absenteeism, lack of listening, and not completing assignments. Results revealed that both types of learners experienced each factor. However, the home and school experiences described by consistent learners were more frequent, systematic, and clearly more evident across grade levels than were those described by inconsistent learners.

Students and Their Multiple Worlds

Student perspectives of home, school, and peer worlds, specifically their personal meaning of how experiences in multiple environments combine to affect engagement in classrooms and school, have been investigated by Phelan, Davidson, and Yu (1998). Using ethnographic procedures, the researchers studied the experiences of ethnically diverse adolescents in urban high schools. They found students have extreme difficulty in making transitions when they experience borders (i.e., the values, beliefs, and actions of one group are more valued than those of another) among these worlds. Students, even those who were academically successful and described their home, peer, and school contexts as congruent, reported psychosocial pressures (e.g., pressure to succeed in terms of high grades and test scores). Students who experienced extreme discontinuity among these contexts had the most difficulty in making transitions and were most at risk for poor academic, social, and emotional outcomes. Students in this group reported a low probability of graduating from high school and perceived their personal futures as bleak.

Identification of psychosocial pressures experienced by adolescents, even those who are performing well academically, emphasizes the need to view students' schooling holistically. Fortunately, there are programs for promoting social and emotional learning in classrooms (Elias et al., 1997) that can address the psychosocial pressures identified by adolescents in this study (e.g., fear of speaking in classrooms because of classmates' prejudices, peer groups devaluing learning).

Motivational Support for Learning

Bempechat's (1998) research underscores the critical nature of motivational support for children's learning, particularly the subtle messages parents and teachers convey about children's abilities to learn and master new skills. She found that high-achieving fifth and sixth graders, regardless of ethnic background, credited success to their innate ability and effort and tended not to blame failure on lack of ability. Students who received more motivational support for learning (e.g., encouragement, messages about importance of effort and value of education, help regulating their time to complete schoolwork, focus among effort, schooling, and future goals) performed the best academically. In fact, students who received more parent-initiated academic support for learning performed less well in math, presumably because parents were involved as a reaction to low grades.

In particular, Bempechat recommends strengthening home–school partnerships by developing shared understanding of messages about the *process of learning*. Her data support the need to develop a common language about conditions that promote students' school performance and a need to encourage children's persistence and performance in the face of difficulty and challenge. Her message about learning is straightforward: It is a process that takes time, is not always interesting, and is one in which mistakes are both inevitable and invaluable. Messages from parents and teachers must stress the power of diligence, practice, persistence in the face of challenge, and ability to delay gratification, all indicators of social and emotional learning.

PROMOTING ENGAGEMENT WITH CHECK & CONNECT

Check & Connect, a model designed to promote student engagement, is a systematic monitoring procedure to address the social, emotional, and academic needs of individual students and to build capacity within families to assist their children's educational performance (Sinclair, Christenson, Evelo, & Hurley, 1998). Check & Connect is conceptualized as an SEL intervention because it places primary emphasis on student participation, belonging, and valuing educational success as prerequisites for academic performance. Mentors work to create positive relationships with youth and between family and school, promote regular school participation, and keep education a salient issue for students, parents, and teachers. Mentors work with students and families over an extended period of time, regularly checking on the educational progress of the students and intervening in a timely manner to reestablish and maintain students' connection to school and learning.

The Check component is designed to facilitate the continuous assessment of student levels of engagement according to several *alterable* indicators: attendance (skipping classes, absenteeism), social/behavior performance (suspensions, behavior referrals), and academic performance (for secondary: course failures, accrual of credits; for elementary: grades, reading/math objectives passed). The Connect component consists of two levels of student-focused interventions: basic interventions, which are the same for all students and delivered once or twice a month, and intensive interventions, which are more frequent and individualized. Existing support services for intensive interventions are used as much as possible, rather than developing a separate set of duplicative services. Check & Connect has been implemented primarily with elementary, middle, and high school students with and without disabilities who have attendance problems. Most recently, students in grades K–2 who have reading difficulties and are aggressive have been receiving the intervention. Students across the implementation sites are at risk for educational failure. Risk factors such as limited personal and financial resources (learning challenges, poverty, single-parent household, limited understanding of how schools function, physical health challenges, siblings and parents who had negative school experiences, including dropping out) confront students. These challenges commonly are compounded by mobility and, for secondary students, by the entrance into an educational system that expects the student to take full responsibility for adjusting to the rules and practices of the building.

Check & Connect Mentors

The role of the mentor is modeled after one of the commonly identified protective factors in resiliency studies—the presence of an adult who fuels the motivation and fosters the development of life skills needed to persevere in the face of obstacles. The concept of persistence-plus (persistence, continuity, and consistency) is used to build relationships with students and their families and collectively addresses student issues of autonomy, belonging, and competence.

Persistence means there is someone who is not going to give up on the student's educational attainment or allow the student to be distracted from the importance of school and learning. *Continuity* means there is someone who knows the student's educational history, is familiar with the student's family background, and is available throughout the school year, summer, and into the next year. *Consistency* means mentors reinforce the same message—caring adults who believe that school is important and the student can succeed, do the work, attend class, be on time, express frustration constructively, and stay in school. Trust and familiarity are developed over time through persistent efforts such as regularly checking on students' attendance and academic performance, providing ongoing feedback about progress, using problem solving to address students' needs, and frequently communicating with families about both "good and bad news." The mentor's role is not to replace established relationships, but to work with other adults in the process of supporting the student's school success. Specific attention is paid to critical social (building teacher–student and peer relationships) and emotional (motivation, belonging) factors for students' academic success.

Problem solving is used to teach students productive coping skills. Mentors (a) help students integrate their thoughts, feelings, and behaviors to meet the demands of the school environment; (b) provide students with opportunities for success in schoolwork (e.g., reinforcing organizational skills); (c) emphasize the relevance of education to future endeavors (e.g., setting personal goals); (d) help students contribute to a caring and supportive environment (e.g., managing anger); and (e) deal with personal concerns (e.g., family changes, soliciting parental support). We speculate that a unique feature of Check & Connect is not the specific interventions per se, but the social context for implementation. Mentors, who are trusted by students and their families and have demonstrated concern for, and a belief in, the school success of the student persistently and consistently over time, facilitate interventions.

A critical goal of parent-connect efforts is working with families as partners to increase their active participation in their children's education. Based on family-centered practices, mentors empower parents by minimizing education-related barriers identified by the family, facilitating contacts with other resources as requested by the family, encouraging parents to ask questions that demonstrate to teachers interest in education, and supporting parents in efforts to make education a priority at home.

Research Supporting the Check & Connect Intervention

Key findings across several studies suggest that Check & Connect promotes engagement among youth placed at high risk for school failure. Results from the original quasi-experimental study indicated that ninth-grade students with disabilities in the treatment group were significantly more likely to be enrolled in school, have persisted in school (never dropped out), and to be on track to graduate within 5 years than were students in the contrast group (Sinclair et al., 1998). We conclude that sustained intervention is critical and should be maintained at appropriate levels over a period of at least 2 years and through critical transitions, such as middle school to high school.

Of the high school students with emotional and behavioral disabilities, more treatment students were likely to be enrolled in school, have persisted in school, and to have fewer suspensions than students in the contrast group; however, no significant differences were found for the academic performance indicators. Preliminary data for chronically truant secondary students without disabilities in suburban schools have revealed a dramatic improvement in attendance and skipped classes.

Pre–post intervention results for elementary students with and without disabilities in suburban settings reveals that 60% of students have maintained or improved their attendance, particularly in terms of late arrivals to school. Christenson and Anderson (2001) found that the odds of being in the improving attendance group were almost six times greater for students in elementary than middle grades and that mentor and student perspectives of their relationship were significantly related to group membership (improving or declining attendance). Preliminary results from Project ELSE, a preventive intervention for kindergarten children at risk for reading disabilities, indicate that children who received the intensive intervention (Check & Connect with early literacy support) made significant gains in phonological awareness, attendance, social skills, and appropriate behavior when compared with children who received the moderate intervention (feedback to teachers and parents) (O'Shaughnessy & Christenson, 2001).

CONCLUSIONS AND RECOMMENDATIONS

To alter the culture of failure, represented by students who view school as an "interruption in their day," an emphasis must be placed on fostering student persistence in the face of challenges. Passing high-stakes assessment for graduation represents a significant challenge for far too many students, a challenge that can be addressed only by attending to the effect of social and emotional learning on academic performance. To fail to recognize the critical social and emotional factors necessary for success on these tests must be viewed as a contributing factor toward educational failure for some students.

Successful programs help students and families who feel marginalized in their relations with teachers and peers to become members of the school community. The goal in working with students who are at risk for dropout is twofold: acquisition of academic and social skills and fostering a personal investment in learning. Increasing students' engagement and enthusiasm for school is much more than simply having students stay in school—it involves supporting students to meet the defined academic standards of the school, as well as underlying social and behavioral standards. If students are engaged with school and learning over time, they should not only graduate but also complete school with academic and social competence.

To foster student motivation to stay in school and work hard at learning goals, attention must be paid to the development of quality social and emotional programs that enhance student ability to integrate their cognitions, emotions, and behavior to meet the demands of schooling *and* of social resources that foster student autonomy, belonging, and competence. Engagement with learning is fostered by relationships with teachers, parents, and peers. School policies and practices that enhance engagement create connections that help students see the relevance of their current school demands and future endeavors. These policies avoid isolating students (suspension, retention). Classroom and school environments strive to create a social climate where students are included and participate and have opportunities to make choices and experience success toward personal goals. And, families play a vital role in motivational support for learning. Most important, greater recognition of conditions among family, school, and community that foster school success is needed as a base for designing interventions.

With respect to research, unanswered questions are evident. For example, we describe variables in isolation, but have yet to learn about the potential mediating role of belonging for students' academic performance or the processes across home and school that result in engagement, persistence in the face of challenge, and enhanced academic performance. The role of peers on students' investment in learning has been identified as a critically important area for further research (Hymel et al., 1996). Longitudinal, experimental intervention research that focuses on understanding student engagement *and* academic performance within the family–school–peer relationship is warranted. Despite the need for further research, we have a promising prescription for altering the culture of failure for students.

REFERENCES

Abbott, R. D., O'Donnell, J., Hawkins, J. D., Hill, K. G., Kosterman, R., & Catalano, R. F. (1998). Changing teaching practices to promote achievement and bonding to school. *American Journal of Orthopsychiatry*, *68*(4), 542–552.

Adams, K., & Christenson, S. L. (2000). Trust and the family–school relationship: Examination of parent–teacher differences in elementary and secondary grades. *Journal of School Psychology*, *38*(5), 477–497.

Ames, C., & Archer, J. (1988). Achievement goals in the classroom: Students' learning strategies and motivation processes. *Journal of Educational Psychology*, *80*(3), 260–267.

Baker, J. A. (1998). The social context of school satisfaction among urban, low-income, African-American students. *School Psychology Quarterly*, *13*(1), 25–44.

Bempechat, J. (1998). *Against the odds: How "at-risk" children exceed expectations*. San Francisco: Jossey-Bass.

Berndt, T. J., & Keefe, K. (1995). Friends' influence on adolescents' adjustment to school. *Child Development*, *66*, 1312–1329.

Bryk, A. S., & Thum, Y. M. (1989). The effects of high school organization on dropping out: An exploratory investigation. *American Educational Research Journal*, *26*, 353–383.

Christenson, S. L., & Anderson, A. R. (2001, April). *Effectiveness of coping for students demonstrating differential success with Check & Connect*. Paper presented at the annual meeting of the American Educational Research Association, Seattle.

Christenson, S. L., & Peterson, C. J. (1998). *Family, school, and community influences on children's learning: A literature review* (Report No. 1). Parents are Teachers Project. Minneapolis: University of Minnesota Extension Service.

Clark, R. M. (1983). *Family life and school achievement*. Chicago: University of Chicago Press.

Comer, J. P., Haynes, N. M., Joyner, E. T., & Ben-Avie, M. (1996). *Rallying the whole village: The Comer process for reforming education*. New York: Teachers College Press.

Connell, J. P., Halpern-Felsher, B. L., Clifford, E., Crichlow, W., & Usinger, P. (1995). Hanging in there: Behavioral, psychological, and contextual factors affecting whether African American adolescents stay in high school. *Journal of Adolescent Research*, *10*(1), 41–63.

Deci, E. L. (1992). The relation of interest to the motivation of behavior: A self-determination theory perspective. In K. A. Renninger, S. Hidi, & A. Krapp (Eds.), *The role of interest in learning and development* (pp. 43–70). Hillsdale, NJ: Erlbaum.

Elias, M. J., Zins, J. E., Weissberg, R. P., Frey, K. S., Greenberg, M. T., Haynes, N. M., Kessler, R., Schwab-Stone, M. E., & Shriver, T. P. (1997). *Promoting social and emotional learning: Guidelines for educators*. Alexandria, VA: Association for Supervision and Curriculum Development.

Finn, J. D. (1993). *School engagement and students at risk*. National Center for Education Statistics, U.S. Department of Education, Washington, DC.

Finn, J. D., Pannozzo, G. M., & Voelkl, K. E. (1995). Disruptive and inattentive-withdrawn behavior and achievement among fourth graders. *The Elementary School Journal*, *95*(5), 421–434.

Finn, J. D., & Rock, D. A. (1997). Academic success among students at risk for school failure. *Journal of Applied Psychology*, *82*(2), 221–234.

Floyd, C. (1997). Achieving despite the odds: A study of resilience among a group of African American high school seniors. *Journal of Negro Education*, *65*(2), 181–189.

Goodenow, C. (1993a). Classroom belonging among early adolescent students: Relationship to motivation and achievement. *Journal of Early Adolescence*, *13*(1), 21–43.

Goodenow, C. (1993b). The psychological sense of school membership among adolescents: Scale development and educational correlates. *Psychology in the Schools*, *30*, 79–90.

Goodenow, C., & Grady, K. E. (1993). The relationship of school belonging and friends' values to academic motivation among urban adolescent students. *Journal of Experimental Education*, *62*(1), 60–71.

Grolnick, W. S., & Ryan, R. M. (1987). Autonomy in children's learning: An experimental and individual difference investigation. *Journal of Personality and Social Psychology*, *52*(3), 890–898.

Hansen, D. A. (1986). Family–school articulations: The effects of interaction rule mismatch. *American Educational Research Journal*, *23*(4), 643–659.

Hess, R. S., & D'Amato, R. C. (1996). High school completion among Mexican-American children: Individual and family background variables. *School Psychology Quarterly*, *11*(4), 353–368.

Hymel, S., Comfort, C., Schonert-Reichl, K., & McDougall, P. (1996). Academic failure and school dropout: The influence of peers. In J. Juvonen & K. R. Wentzel (Eds.), *Social motivation: Understanding children's school adjustment* (pp. 313–345). New York: Cambridge University Press.

Isakson, K., & Jarvis, P. (1999). The adjustment of adolescents during the transition into high school: A short-term longitudinal study. *Journal of Youth and Adolescence*, *28*(1), 1–26.

Israelashvili, M. (1997). School adjustment, school membership and adolescents' future expectations. *Journal of Adolescence*, *20*, 525–535.

Jordan, W. J., McPartland, J. M., & Lara, J. (1999). Rethinking the causes of high school dropout. *The Prevention Researcher*, *6*(3), 1–4.

Kupersmidt, J. B., & Coie, J. D. (1990). Preadolescent peer status, aggression, and school adjustment as predictors of externalizing problems in adolescence. *Child Development*, *61*, 1350–1362.

McPartland, J. M. (1994). Dropout prevention in theory and practice. In R. J. Rossi (Ed.), *Schools and students at risk: Context and framework for positive change* (pp. 255–276). New York: Teachers College Press.

National Center for Education Statistics. (1993). *Dropout rates in the United States: 1992*. Washington, DC: U.S. Department of Education, Government Printing Office.

National Center for Education Statistics. (2002). *Dropout rates in the United States: 2000* (NCES 2002-112). Washington, DC: U.S. Department of Education, Offices of Educational Research and Improvement (Institute of Education Sciences).

National Center for Education Statistics. (2003). *Overview of public elementary and secondary schools and districts: School year 2000–2001*. Washington, DC: U.S. Department of Education, Government Printing Office.

O'Shaughnessy, T. E., & Christenson, S. L. (2001). *Project ELSE—early literacy and school engagement*. San Diego: San Diego State University.

Patrikakou, E. N., & Weissberg, R. P. (1999). The seven P's of school–family partnerships. *Education Week*, *18*(21), 34, 36.

Phelan, P., Davidson, A. L., & Yu, H. C. (1998). *Adolescents' worlds: Negotiating family, peers, and school*. New York: Teachers College Press.

Resnick, M. D., Bearman, P. S., Blum, R. W., Bauman, K. E., Harris, K. M., Jones, J., Tabor, J., Beuhring, T., Sieving, R. E., Shew, M., Ireland, M., Bearinger, L. H., & Udry, J. (1997). Protecting adolescents from harm: Findings from the National Longitudinal Study on adolescent health. *Journal of the American Medical Association*, *278*(10), 823–832.

Rumberger, R. W. (1995). Dropping out of middle school: A multilevel analysis of students and schools. *American Educational Research Journal*, *32*(3), 583–625.

Ryan, R. M., Stiller, J., & Lynch, J. H. (1994). Representations of relationships to teachers, parents, and friends as predictors of academic motivation and self-esteem. *Journal of Early Adolescence*, *14*, 226–249.

Sheridan, S. M. (1997). Conceptual and empirical bases of conjoint behavioral consultation. *School Psychology Quarterly*, *12*, 119–133.

Sinclair, M. F., Christenson, S. L., Evelo, D. L., & Hurley, C. M. (1998). Dropout prevention for youth with disabilities: Efficacy of a sustained school engagement procedure. *Exceptional Children*, *65*(1), 7–21.

Steinberg, L., Dornbusch, S. M., & Brown, B. B. (1992). Ethnic differences in adolescent achievement: An ecological perspective. *American Psychologist, 47,* 723–729.

Trout, P. (2000, March 13). Low marks for top teachers: College students have a powerful say in how their teachers are graded [Letter to the editor]. *The Washington Post,* p. A17.

Voelkl, K. E. (1997). Identification with school. *American Journal of Education, 105,* 294–318.

Wentzel, K. R. (1998). Social relationships and motivation in middle school: The role of parents, teachers, and peers. *Journal of Educational Psychology, 90*(2), 202–209.

Wentzel, K. R., & Asher, S. R. (1995). Academic lives of neglected, rejected, popular, and controversial children. *Child Development, 62,* 1066–1078.

White, K. R. (1982). The relationship between socioeconomic status and academic achievement. *Psychological Bulletin, 91,* 461–481.

CHAPTER 5

Toward a Broader Education: Social, Emotional, and Practical Skills

PAULO N. LOPES AND PETER SALOVEY

How should educators choose among different programs of social and emotional learning? What skills should one really focus on? Every intervention program is inspired by different goals and assumptions. Every theory has its strengths and limitations. Studies often yield mixed findings. How are educators to make sense of it all?

In this chapter, we explore some of the theoretical and empirical underpinnings of social and emotional learning (SEL). Obviously, one chapter cannot do justice to all of the theory and research addressing children's social and emotional development. We focus on theories of intelligence—social, emotional, and practical intelligence—even though much of the research in these areas has been conducted with adults.

Overall, there is good evidence that well-designed SEL programs can promote children's social and emotional adjustment. The number of SEL programs that have been rigorously evaluated, using adequate comparison groups and following children over time, is still limited. When we synthesize the evidence for some of the best SEL programs, however, the overall picture is quite encouraging. Programs such as Promoting Alternative THinking Strategies, the Seattle Social Development Project, and Resolving Conflicts Creatively have undergone rigorous evaluations, and the results are promising (e.g., Hawkins, Catalano, Kosterman, Abbott, & Hill, 1999; Kusché & Greenberg, 2001; Weissberg & Greenberg, 1998).

Still, important questions remain to be addressed. Exactly how do these programs benefit children? How long do the benefits last? To what extent can social and emotional skills be generalized across settings and situations? The quality of curricula and teaching materials is important. But does choosing one quality program over another make much of a difference? How much should we emphasize formal instruction as compared with learning from experience? What approaches work best for different groups of students? How can we improve these programs to prepare children better for the challenges they are likely to face throughout life?

These are difficult questions, and we cannot wait for research to clarify them all. Given reasonable evidence that SEL programs are effective, we should seek to implement social and emotional learning on a wider scale. But exactly how should we go about this? Researchers associated with the Collaborative for Academic, Social, and Emotional Learning (CASEL) have outlined useful guidelines for effective SEL practice (Zins, Elias, Greenberg, & Weissberg, 2000; see also Payton et al., 2000). SEL programs should be comprehensive, multiyear programs, integrated into the school curriculum and extracurricular activities. They should be theoretically based, as well as developmentally and culturally appropriate. They should promote a caring, supportive, and challenging classroom and school climate; teach a broad range of skills; be undertaken by well-trained staff with adequate, ongoing support; promote school, family, and community partnerships; and be systematically monitored and evaluated.

Difficulties arise, however, when researchers try to identify a set of key skills to focus on. Payton and colleagues (2000) list key social and emotional competencies under four headings: awareness of self and others; positive attitudes and values; responsible decision making; and social interaction skills. In drawing up any such list of key skills for a domain as broad as social and emotional learning, we face several challenges:

1. Overall, the list is likely to represent a very broad range of skills, and it may be difficult to address all these skills through formal classroom instruction.
2. The skills listed (e.g., managing feelings) may encompass, or depend on, a wide array of other skills, which are not part of the list.
3. The skills to be taught may be partly domain- or context-specific, failing to transfer across situations.
4. There may be more common ground between educational programs stressing different key skills than usually is acknowledged, as these programs may operate through similar mechanisms (e.g., enhancing intrinsic motivation).
5. For all these reasons, the theoretical and empirical rationale for emphasizing one set of skills over another is often less than compelling.

It may be argued that lists of key skills are intended merely to give readers some idea about the breadth of SEL programs, rather than to present a theoretically and empirically based hierarchy of skills. But then the question remains: Given limited time and resources, what skills should educators focus on?

This question is likely to have no clear-cut answer. If schools are to prepare children for the challenges they will face in the future, then the skills emphasized depend to some extent at least on what we think these challenges will be. Such assessments are necessarily subjective because they depend on our goals and values—namely, how we would like to shape our children's development and influence the course of events in the world. Empirical studies may tell us what contributes to adaptation in the present, but they cannot always tell us how to prepare for the future. In other words, theory and research can guide decision making, but decisions about education also must be based on consensual goals and values and an appreciation of the challenges that children are likely to face over the course of their lives.

We argue that, in the absence of a clear rationale for focusing on one set of skills over another, our best bet may be to teach a broad set of competencies and capitalize on informal learning, that is, learning through experience, modeling, and observation. These ideas already figure among the guidelines outlined by CASEL, and we think they should be taken further.

Proponents of social and emotional learning often seek to teach to the whole child and promote students' balanced development. This involves going beyond the type of memory-based learning and logical-abstract thinking that has been emphasized in Western schools. We think the range of competencies addressed in schools should be broadened to encompass not only social and emotional skills, but also creative and practical abilities. We now know about different education or intervention programs that seem to be effective in promoting different goals, such as developing social and emotional skills, enhancing creativity and practical thinking, reinforcing an optimistic outlook, or stimulating intrinsic motivation for school. Ultimately, education would be better if we managed effectively to integrate important ideas and practices from these very different lines of research and intervention work.

We also need to capitalize on informal learning because we may not be able to teach through explicit instruction many of the skills that will help children to become healthy and productive adults. The number of skills involved is very large, and we may not have time to teach them effectively in the classroom. Moreover, many abilities, such as managing feelings, thinking creatively, or developing intrinsic motivation, cannot be learned through explicit instruction alone. They have to be developed through personal experience and practice. We can help children to develop such skills by constructing stimulating learning environments, creating opportunities for children to practice, providing constructive feedback, and having teachers model those skills and behaviors. To do this, we need good schools, good teachers, and quality teacher training.

SEL AND ACADEMIC ACHIEVEMENT

Social, emotional, and practical skills are likely to be important for academic achievement, both directly and indirectly. For example, emotional-regulation skills may facilitate control of attention and the development of intrinsic motivation for challenging pursuits, thus contributing to sustained intellectual engagement and studying. Children also need to control emotional outbursts and impulsive reactions in order to sit still through class and interact with teachers and peers. Children's social and emotional adaptation and their bonding to prosocial peers and adults may further contribute to their motivation for learning.

As far as we know, there is little empirical evidence linking the school-based promotion of social and emotional skills to qualities such as attention control, which are hard to assess. However, there is evidence that children's social and emotional adaptation is associated with bonding to school and with academic outcomes such as school dropout (Hawkins et al., 1999).

In this chapter we often discuss the benefits of SEL programs in terms of social and emotional adaptation, rather than academic achievement. We do this because there is a large body of theory and research on social and emotional adaptation, but little empirical data on the relationship between social and emotional skills and academic outcomes. We also think that social and emotional adaptation to school is likely to contribute to academic achievement. Moreover, we believe that social and emotional adaptation should be viewed as an essential goal of education.

Generally speaking, the extent to which social and emotional learning contributes to academic achievement is likely to depend on several factors: (1) how we define and assess academic achievement; (2) whether social and emotional learning is weaved into traditional subject matters so as to make school learning more interesting and enjoyable; and (3) the degree to which SEL programs enhance children's social and emotional adaptation to school, and bonding to prosocial peers and adults.

If developing social, emotional, practical, and creative competencies is important so that children can lead healthy and productive lives, this should be viewed as an essential goal of education. We need to revise the way that we define and assess achievement in school. We need to incorporate such skills into evaluations of academic achievement. Accountability is crucial, and decision makers will likely be wary of efforts to broaden the range of competencies addressed in schools unless these competencies can be evaluated and children's progress in these areas can be tracked over time. One of the reasons that rote learning and analytical skills have been overemphasized in Western schools is that such knowledge and skills can be assessed easily and objectively. In our discussion of emotional and practical intelligence, we describe recent efforts to develop ability measures of emotional and practical skills.

PREPARING CHILDREN FOR THE CHALLENGES AHEAD

Three or four generations ago, most children would spend only a few years in school. Classroom instruction focused on basic skills such as reading, writing, and arithmetic, and a few other traditional subjects. Parents might have been able to teach their children basic discipline, but often could not teach them to read and write. Although educators also had to enforce discipline in the classroom, they could not pay much attention to social and emotional competencies.

Times have changed. Young people are now more exposed to problems of depression, social isolation, and drug abuse. They need to build social and emotional resources to cope with these risks. Children also spend many more years in school. This requires that they develop concentration, impulse control, and emotional regulation.

Work settings now require teamwork, participative leadership, informal networks, and quality customer service. People's capacity to establish good relationships with others weighs heavily in hiring and promotion decisions. All this demands the development of elaborate social and emotional skills.

In a society undergoing rapid change, young people no longer learn a trade for life. They must constantly learn new skills and adapt to changing technology and market demands. The freedom they enjoy to make career and lifestyle decisions also requires that they plan ahead and actively manage their lives. All this puts a premium on initiative, motivation, adaptability, and self-management.

As the world has changed, so have schools. Young people spend more years in school, develop higher proficiency in basic disciplines, and study a greater range of subjects. Critical thinking is replacing rote learning. Yet educational reform continues to lag behind the changes required by modern society. As Sternberg (1985, 1999b) has argued, schooling still focuses excessively on analytical skills, encompassing logical, abstract, and critical thinking. We are neglecting the sort of practical and creative abilities that allow people to deal with real-life problems and unforeseen challenges.

Analytical intelligence (i.e., IQ) seems to account for about 10% to 15% of job performance ratings and other real-world outcomes (Herrnstein & Murray, 1994). What accounts for the rest? Children who outshine others in school are not necessarily the most successful in life. The relationship between educational achievement and life satisfaction is very weak indeed (Diener & Lucas, 1999). How can we make education more useful for what really matters?

ON WHAT SKILLS SHOULD WE FOCUS?

Most people probably agree that schools are not teaching some of the skills that are important for life. Yet they may also question whether these skills should be taught in schools at all, and whether we should be diverting time and effort away from traditional subject matters in order to do so.

It is possible to infuse social and emotional learning into existing curricula, so as to avoid overburdening teachers and students with more demands on their time. Some trade-offs are inevitable, however. Paying more attention to one set of skills is likely to detract from investment in others. So many skills are important for life that, given limited school time and resources, we cannot address them all through explicit instruction. How should we decide on what skills to focus?

There are at least three ways to approach this question. The first is that specific intervention goals may entail an emphasis on particular skills. For example, many SEL programs consider the prevention of violent and antisocial behavior a top priority, and therefore emphasize conflict resolution skills. However, prevention goals are not equally salient for all communities. If there are no acute problems and the general goal is to promote social and emotional adaptation, then the rationale for a particular focus is less clear.

The second approach is to emphasize skills that are likely to generalize across settings and situations. Self-management skills, for example, involving planning and deliberation, self-monitoring and self-reflection, are applicable to practically all domains of life. Some learning skills, including strategies for acquiring knowledge and learning from feedback, also are likely to generalize.

The third approach is to capitalize on implicit or informal learning. We may not be able to teach all relevant skills through formal instruction, but we can help children to learn through experience and practice, modeling and observation. We can use teamwork, collaborative learning, and small-group discussions to provide opportunities for children to learn to interact with others in a supportive environment. A healthy school atmosphere can help children to nurture positive relationships with others. We can take advantage of everyday problems and disputes as they arise in the classroom to help children develop perspective taking and conflict resolution skills. We can infuse social and emotional learning into the teaching of traditional subject matters.

Some of the best SEL programs use all three approaches. Still, it would be useful to have more guidance on how to promote positive youth development. While some SEL programs aim to prevent specific problems, many have much broader goals—namely, to help children lead more fulfilling lives. Whether or not it is stated as such, their ultimate goal is to help children to become healthy, well-adjusted, and happy individuals.

But what is the best way to educate children so that they will be happy and well adjusted? We may know a lot about parental and educational practices associated with positive and negative outcomes for children. In general, however, we know how to treat psychological problems much better than we understand how to promote psychological health. There are so many factors that can influence adjustment over the life course, that it becomes difficult to identify optimal strategies.

Moreover, what do we mean by happiness and adjustment? Happiness can mean different things to different people. We can think of a well-adjusted individual as one who experiences joy and excitement, peace and contentment, self-acceptance, satisfaction with life, fulfillment, meaningful engagement, or enjoyment of daily pursuits. There may be many ways to lead a good life. There may be many ways to be successful in any field. And there may be many ways to promote positive youth development.

Developing skill in any domain requires training and practice, and investing more in one set of abilities may detract from investment in others. We cannot excel at everything. Emphasizing one set of skills over another entails advantages and disadvantages, and these may be more or less salient in different environments and at different points in the life course. Every approach has its strengths and weaknesses. There may be no single best solution.

This suggests that different programs may be effective and beneficial for children, even if they target somewhat different goals and rely on different curricula. There is evidence that some SEL programs effectively promote children's social and emotional adjustment, but we have no strong reasons for claiming that one of these approaches is better than another. Can theory and research on social, emotional, and practical skills provide further guidance?

Social Skills

We all seem to think that some people are especially adept at interacting with others. We might say that these people have good social skills. But what does it take to establish and sustain good relationships with others? If we can identify a coherent and interrelated set of skills associated with positive social outcomes, perhaps we should incorporate these skills into SEL programs.

Think of all the skills and traits that may be useful for dealing with others: emotional understanding, perspective taking, communication skills, cheerfulness, sense of humor, emotional regulation, respect for social norms, empathy, agreeableness, assertiveness, negotiation skills, ability to engage in interesting conversation, plain intelligence, charm. We could go on. But do these skills and traits really go together?

Think of someone who has good social skills. Perhaps you will think of someone who might thrive at parties, receptions, and large gatherings. Maybe you will think of somebody who is generally cheerful and extroverted. But this person may not be equally adept at handling romantic relationships and intimate friendships, children and old people, subordinates and peers, teamwork and conflict.

For researchers, the attempt to define and measure social intelligence has been a frustrating endeavor. There have been more than a dozen studies of social intelligence, undertaken mostly with young adults. Although the evidence is mixed, it suggests that diverse social skills are weakly correlated (for reviews see Cantor & Kihlstrom, 1987; Hall & Bernieri, 2001; Kihlstrom & Cantor, 2000; Sternberg et al., 2000). Developing ability in one area may not ensure competence in another. Teaching some of these skills does not ensure that children will learn all the others. Because people draw upon many different skills for social interaction, and we cannot teach all of these competencies through formal instruction, we have to rely on informal learning.

Social skills training is used effectively in clinical and other settings for treating or preventing problem behaviors. However, various evaluation studies suggest that social skills training in the classroom may not always translate well into natural settings or have a strong impact on children's peer relations (La Greca, 1993). One set of skills that seems to generalize across domains and situations is linked to the theory of social information processing, which looks at how people interpret and respond to social events. They have to analyze what happened, consider possible responses, choose and plan a course of action, then monitor and evaluate the effectiveness of their reply. Deficits in these skills are associated with aggressive behavior and poor social adjustment (Crick & Dodge, 1994).

In particular, children prone to aggression often reveal deficits and biases in the way that they detect and interpret cues of aggression. They tend to attribute hostile intentions to others, even when there was no hostile intent. They tend to have limited response repertoires and generate few alternative strategies for dealing with interpersonal problems. They also tend to evaluate the outcomes of their actions from a biased perspective, so that they continue to believe that fighting is the only way to deal with similar situations, for example.

Many SEL programs now teach children that when faced with interpersonal problems, they should stop and think; identify the problem and their feelings about it; plan the best course of action by generating alternative solutions and evaluating the possible consequences of different strategies; and go ahead and try the best plan (Zins et al., 2000). Several studies suggest that this type of training helps to reduce problem behaviors, as rated by children and teachers (e.g., Caplan et al., 1992).

Practical and Creative Skills

Sternberg (1985) has argued that we should think of intelligence as something broader than IQ. His theory of successful intelligence (Sternberg, 1985, 1999b) posits three broad domains of ability in addition to memory: analytical, creative, and practical intelligence. Analytical intelligence, involving logical-abstract reasoning and critical thinking, is the one that our educational system tends to favor. Creative intelligence helps us find original solutions for new problems as we adapt to new situations. Practical intelligence helps us to solve everyday, real-life problems effectively and is based on the know-how and common sense that we acquire through experience.

Sternberg defines intelligence as one's ability to achieve success in life, given one's personal standards, and within one's sociocultural context. He views intelligence as a form of developing expertise (Sternberg, 1999a). According to him, what IQ tests really measure is achievement at the type of logical-abstract thinking skills that children learn in Western schools. The fact that IQ scores have risen significantly over the past decades suggests that intelligence can be developed. Cross-cultural studies further suggest that in communities where different skills are emphasized, IQ has less value (Sternberg, 1999b).

In Sternberg's overarching framework, practical intelligence encompasses social and emotional competencies. Among the lessons outlined by Sternberg and Grigorenko (2000) for promoting practical skills in schools are several units that one also might find in SEL programs: motivation, controlling impulses, persevering, managing self-pity, handling personal difficulties, and developing self-confidence. However, Sternberg's work tends to emphasize cognitive processes and pays less attention to emotions.

Sternberg's approach to practical intelligence focuses on the concept of tacit knowledge. This is the know-how that we acquire through experience, usually without thinking about it, so that we have trouble putting it into words. The problems we train children to solve at school are very different from the problems they often will face later in life. Academic problems usually are clearly spelled out, involve a limited number of variables, and allow only one solution. Students can solve these problems using abstract rules and principles in sequential order. And the problems allow only one correct solution. In contrast, practical problems often are poorly defined and can be tackled in many different ways. They often require creative reformulation. And they draw upon tacit knowledge that may be largely domain-specific (Sternberg et al., 2000).

Sternberg and his team have shown that taking into account analytical, creative, and practical skills permits understanding and predicting people's performance better than IQ alone (Sternberg, 1999b). Practical skills can be assessed through tests of tacit knowledge, which ask people to rate the effectiveness of different strategies for dealing with given school or workplace scenarios, for example. This type of tacit knowledge is associated with supervisors' ratings of job performance, over and above traditional measures of IQ (Grigorenko, Guillermo, Jarvin, & Sternberg, 2001; Sternberg et al., 2000).

Sternberg's team is now applying these ideas to education. They have adapted existing curricula and teaching materials for students, at different grade levels, to address analytical, creative, and practical skills in a balanced way. They found that teaching children in this way improves their academic achievement on reading and other skills, as compared with focusing solely on memory or critical thinking (Grigorenko, Jarvin, & Sternberg, 2002; Sternberg, Grigorenko, & Jarvin, 2001).

Instead of asking educators to teach a whole new curriculum, Sternberg's team is infusing creative and practical skills into existing curricula and teaching materials. This makes it easier for educators and policy makers to buy into their program. It also makes it easier to link their program to academic achievement. Moreover, they are trying to broaden the definition and assessment of academic achievement. They are developing tests of creative and practical ability to ensure that children's progress in these areas can be evaluated on a continuing basis.

Sternberg's team has done a lot to show that the range of competencies taught in school should be broadened. Many of their ideas about creative and practical skills also could be usefully applied to social and emotional learning. However, their work pays little attention to emotions and does not specify what subskills to focus on for different abilities. Moreover, we still do not know to what extent these abilities generalize across domains, cultures, and situations.

Emotional Skills

For a long time, emotions were seen as processes that disrupted rational thought and decision making. Only recently have investigators started to emphasize the adaptive value of emotions. For example, people whose capacity to process emotional information has been impaired due to brain injury have difficulty making everyday decisions and managing their lives (Damásio, 1994). Emotions tell us what we like and what to do. Feelings guide our everyday behavior and allow us to make choices without considering all the pros and cons of every option.

Moreover, some people seem to handle feelings and emotions better than others. People who are otherwise very intelligent sometimes make disastrous decisions because they fail to take into account their own and other people's feelings. Bright politicians can lose elections because their emotional reactions come across as inappropriate.

Salovey and Mayer (1990) posited a theory of emotional intelligence encompassing four basic abilities: perceiving and understanding emotions, using emotions in thought, and managing emotions (see also Mayer & Salovey, 1997). Inspired by this functional view of emotions, they focused on skills that allow people to process and interpret emotional information. Evidence suggests that these skills represent a coherent and interrelated set of information-processing abilities, distinct from other types of intelligence, and that they develop with age (Mayer, Caruso, & Salovey, 1999).

Mayer, Salovey, and Caruso (2002) developed a test to assess emotional abilities without relying on self-report: the Mayer, Salovey and Caruso Emotional Intelligence Test (MSCEIT). This test involves various tasks, including decoding facial expressions of emotion, understanding blends of emotions and emotional dynamics, integrating emotional information with other thinking processes, and managing emotions for purposes of self-regulation and social interaction. Answers on the MSCEIT can be scored against those of a sample of experts from an international society of emotion researchers, or a normative sample of several thousand people. The two scoring methods yield similar results, and the test has been shown to be reliable (Mayer, Salovey, Caruso, & Sitarenios, 2001, 2003; Salovey, Mayer, Caruso, & Lopes, 2003). Although this test was designed for adults, a version for elementary and middle school children is in the works.

A number of studies suggest that emotional intelligence, assessed in this way, is associated with a range of positive outcomes. Among school children, it was associated with lower peer ratings of aggressiveness and higher teacher ratings of prosocial behavior (Rubin, 1999). Among teenagers, it was linked to less tobacco and alcohol consumption (Trinidad & Johnson, 2002). Among college students, it was related to higher self-reported empathy, relationship quality, and psychological well-being (Brackett & Mayer, 2003; Ciarrochi, Chan, & Caputi, 2000). College students' scores on the MSCEIT were associated with the self-reported quality of relationships with both friends and parents, the self-perceived quality of daily social interactions, and peer nominations for positive social and emotional characteristics, even when basic personality traits and academic intelligence were statistically controlled (Lopes, Brackett, Nezlek, Schütz, Sellin, & Salovey, in press; Lopes, Salovey, & Beers, 2002; Lopes, Salovey, & Straus, 2003). Among leaders of an insurance company's customer claims teams, emotional intelligence was linked to higher manager ratings of effectiveness and higher team performance (Rice, 1999).

Emotional abilities are also likely to be important for academic achievement (see Salovey & Sluyter, 1997). For example, perceiving emotions may be important for artistic expression and writing, as well as for interpreting literature and works of art. Using emotions to facilitate thinking may help students to decide what activities to focus on, depending on how they feel. It may be easier to write a creative essay if one is feeling cheerful, because positive moods enhance divergent thinking and imagination. Negative moods may facilitate careful attention to detail and be more suitable for doing geometry proofs, for example. Understanding emotional vocabulary and emotional dynamics helps children to develop a good command of language and analyze the characters and plot of a novel. The ability to manage emotions may help students to handle anxiety-arousing situations, such as taking tests or starting creative projects. However, we do not yet have strong evidence linking emotional intelligence and academic achievement.

Solid evidence that emotional skills are associated with social adaptation comes from research with children, involving a variety of different assessment tools. In a large number of studies, children's abilities to read emotions in faces, understand emotional vocabulary, and regulate their emotions have been associated with their social competence and adaptation, as rated by peers, parents, and teachers (for reviews see Denham, 1998; Eisenberg, Fabes, Guthrie, & Reiser, 2000; Feldman, Philippot, & Custrini, 1991; Halberstadt, Denham, & Dunsmore, 2001; Saarni, 1999).

People's capacity for emotional regulation may be linked to genetically driven temperamental dispositions, which tend to be fairly stable. Over time, however, children can learn to cope with, and compensate for, their temperamental dispositions. In fact, about one-third of the infants who seem temperamentally predisposed to become inhibited and shy grow up to be relatively uninhibited (Kagan, 1998). Furthermore, evaluations of intervention programs that emphasize emotional competencies indicate that training in emotional skills contributes to social adaptation (Greenberg, Kusché, & Riggs, this volume).

Emotional intelligence gained popularity through Goleman's (1995) best-selling book. The idea captured educators' attention and contributed to the growing interest in social and emotional learning programs. In Goleman's writings, however, the concept was vastly expanded to include personality traits, social skills, and motivational and other factors. Other authors also have used the term to designate very broad conceptions of social and emotional adaptation.

To determine whether emotional intelligence is truly important, we need to distinguish it from other dimensions of psychological functioning to show that we are not rehashing old ideas with a new name (Brackett & Mayer, 2003). We therefore distinguish emotional intelligence, designating a set of skills for processing emotional information, as outlined above, from broader conceptions of social and emotional competence and adaptation (Mayer, Salovey, & Caruso, 2000). The skills subsumed by this definition of emotional intelligence are only a subset of the skills and qualities that SEL programs seek to address. Available evidence suggests that they are important, but further research is needed to determine to what extent they should be emphasized in programs of social and emotional learning.

In drawing implications from this type of research, we also need to keep in mind that although basic emotional skills may be important everywhere, the way that they are applied or expressed should vary according to culture and context. Particular coping strategies may be more appropriate in some contexts than others. Some people may control anger or anxiety quite well in some situations, but not in others.

TEACHING SOCIAL AND EMOTIONAL SKILLS

Teachers can enrich classroom instruction regardless of whether their schools adopt new curricula or endorse a given program of educational reform. However, school-wide changes may have far greater impact. Using appropriate teaching materials greatly facilitates teachers' work. Support from school administrators, parents, and colleagues makes it easier to implement changes. Nonetheless, teachers can start to address a broader range of competencies in their classrooms, even if changing educational practice on a broader scale takes a long time (e.g., Elias et al., 1997).

For example, teachers can use everyday situations that arise in the classroom, or in the schoolyard, as opportunities to promote a richer understanding of social and emotional issues. Conflicts and arguments may be particularly fruitful for modeling or practicing negotiation skills, perspective taking, and emotional regulation. Teachers can use literature or history classes, essays and art projects, or even sports, to discuss human nature, people's feelings, and emotional reactions. They can promote teamwork, group projects, and small discussion groups to help children learn to interact with others through experience. They can encourage children to express and discuss their emotions, listen to others, and respect other people's points of view. They can train children to breathe deeply, look at a problem from different angles, and think things through before taking action on a stressful situation.

This may be challenging. Teachers who are overwhelmed, with too many students or discipline problems, may be reluctant to take on new challenges. Some educators may feel less comfortable with social and emotional learning than others. Children's emotional reactions and coping habits may be deeply engraved and hard to change. It takes a lot of training and practice for children to develop new habits and skills. We should not expect quick changes.

Managing our emotions, and relating to others, are among the greatest challenges that we face in life. Helping children to face these challenges may not be easy, but it is essential that we try. There are no simple formulas to be applied to all children and circumstances. More than drilling a limited set of skills over and over again, we should strive to expand children's repertoire of skills and enhance their capacity to respond flexibly to the demands of the moment. Ideally, we would help our youth to relate to others by promoting a deeper appreciation of the complexity of human nature.

CONCLUSION

To prepare children for the challenges they are likely to face in a fast-changing society, we should broaden the range of competencies addressed in schools. There is evidence that SEL programs can promote children's social and emotional adaptation and bonding to school. There is also evidence that promoting a balanced mix of analytical, creative, and practical abilities may enhance children's interest in learning and school achievement. Integrating these two approaches may be a good way to help children become well-adjusted and productive adults.

There may be many ways of promoting positive youth development. We do not know exactly what components of different programs are most effective and for what purposes, groups, and contexts. We should avoid focusing public debate too much on issues of program content, as this may inadvertently undermine the higher goal of investing in quality education. In the end, investing in good schools, good teachers, and quality teacher training is likely to be more important than choosing between one quality program and another.

Future research will clarify the importance of specific social, emotional, and practical skills for adaptation over the life course. However, educators should not wait for research to clarify all questions and doubts. By adopting better curricula, or changing the way they teach, teachers can help improve children's lives. Given all the factors that impinge upon children's development, and the vast array of competencies that contribute to social and emotional adaptation, we should not expect to see dramatic changes from educational reform or intervention programs. In the long run, however, small changes can have tremendous impact.

NOTES

We thank the following individuals for their comments on earlier drafts of this chapter: Kathryn Estes, Cory Head, Linda Jarvin, Chinyelu Lee, Helena Lopes, David Pizarro, Robert Sternberg, Roger Weissberg, Andreas Xenachis, and Joseph Zins.

We also acknowledge support from the National Cancer Institute (R01-CA68427), the National Institute of Mental Health (P01-MH/DA56826), the National Institute of Drug Abuse (P50-DA13334), and the Donaghue Women's Health Investigator Program at Yale to Peter Salovey. Paulo N. Lopes was supported by a fellowship from the Portuguese Science and Technology Foundation.

REFERENCES

Brackett, M. A., & Mayer, J. D. (2003). Convergent, discriminant, and incremental validity of competing measures of emotional intelligence. *Personality and Social Psychology Bulletin 29*, 1147–1158.

Cantor, N., & Kihlstrom, J. F. (1987). *Personality and social intelligence.* Englewood Cliffs, NJ: Prentice-Hall.

Caplan, M., Weissberg, R. P., Grober, J. H., Sivo, P. J., Grady, K., & Jacoby, C. (1992). Social competence promotion with inner-city and suburban young adolescents: Effects on social adjustment and alcohol use. *Journal of Consulting and Clinical Psychology, 60*, 56–63.

Ciarrochi, J. V., Chan, A. Y. C., & Caputi, P. (2000). A critical evaluation of the emotional intelligence construct. *Personality and Individual Differences, 28*, 539–561.

Crick, N. R., & Dodge, K. A. (1994). A review and reformulation of social information-processing mechanisms in children's social adjustment. *Psychological Bulletin, 115*, 74–101.

Damásio, A. R. (1994). *Descartes' error: Emotion, reason, and the human brain.* New York: Putnam.

Denham, S. A. (1998). *Emotional development in young children.* New York: Guilford Press.

Diener, E., & Lucas, R. E. (1999). Personality and subjective well-being. In D. Kahneman, E. Diener, & N. Schwarz (Eds.), *Well-being: The foundations of hedonic psychology* (pp. 213–229). New York: Russell Sage.

Eisenberg, N., Fabes, R. A., Guthrie, I. K., & Reiser, M. (2000). Dispositional emotionality and regulation: Their role in predicting quality of social functioning. *Journal of Personality and Social Psychology, 78*, 136–157.

Elias, M. J., Zins, J. E., Weissberg, R. P., Frey, K. S., Greenberg, M. T., Haynes, N. M., Kessler, R., Schwab-Stone, M. E., & Shriver, T. P. (1997). *Promoting social and emotional learning: Guidelines for educators*. Alexandria, VA: Association for Supervision and Curriculum Development.

Feldman, R. S., Philippot, P., & Custrini, R. J. (1991). Social competence and nonverbal behavior. In R. S. Feldman & B. Rimé (Eds.), *Fundamentals of nonverbal behavior* (pp. 329–350). New York: Cambridge University Press.

Goleman, D. (1995). *Emotional intelligence*. New York: Bantam Books.

Grigorenko, E. L., Guillermo, G., Jarvin, L., & Sternberg, R. J. (2001). *Toward a validation of aspects of the theory of successful intelligence*. Unpublished manuscript, Yale University.

Grigorenko, E. L., Jarvin, L., & Sternberg, R. J. (2002). School-based tests of the triarchic theory of intelligence: Three settings, three samples, three syllabi. *Contemporary Educational Psychology, 27*, 167–208.

Halberstadt, A. G., Denham, S. A., & Dunsmore, J. C. (2001). Affective social competence. *Social Development, 10*, 79–119.

Hall, J. A., & Bernieri, F. J. (2001). *Interpersonal sensitivity: Theory and measurement*. Mahwah, NJ: Erlbaum.

Hawkins, J. D., Catalano, R. F., Kosterman, R., Abbott, R., & Hill, K. G. (1999). Preventing adolescent health-risk behaviors by strengthening protection during childhood. *Archives of Pediatric & Adolescent Medicine, 153*, 226–334.

Herrnstein, R. J., & Murray, C. (1994). *The bell curve*. New York: Free Press.

Kagan, J. (1998). *Galen's prophecy*. Boulder, CO: Westview Press.

Kihlstrom, J. F., & Cantor, N. (2000). Social intelligence. In R. J. Sternberg (Ed.), *Handbook of intelligence* (2nd ed.; pp. 359–379). New York: Cambridge University Press.

Kusché, C. A., & Greenberg, M. T. (2001). PATHS in your classroom: Promoting emotional literacy and alleviating emotional distress. In J. Cohen (Ed.), *Social emotional learning and the elementary school child: A guide for educators* (pp. 140–161). New York: Teachers College Press.

La Greca, A. M. (1993). Social skills training with children: Where do we go from here? *Journal of Clinical Child Psychology, 22*, 288–298.

Lopes, P. N., Brackett, M., Nezlek, J., Schütz, A., Sellin, I., & Salovey, P. (in press). Emotional intelligence and social interaction. *Personality and Social Psychology Bulletin*.

Lopes, P. N., Salovey, P., & Beers, M. (2002). *Emotional intelligence and social networks*. Unpublished data, Yale University.

Lopes, P. N., Salovey, P., & Straus, R. (2003). Emotional intelligence, personality, and the perceived quality of social relationships. *Personality and Individual Differences, 35*, 641–658.

Mayer, J. D., Caruso, D. R., & Salovey, P. (1999). Emotional intelligence meets traditional standards for an intelligence. *Intelligence, 27*, 267–298.

Mayer, J. D., & Salovey, P. (1997). What is emotional intelligence? In P. Salovey &

D. J. Sluyter (Eds.), *Emotional development and emotional intelligence: Educational implications* (pp. 3–31). New York: Basic Books.

Mayer, J. D., Salovey, P., & Caruso, D. (2000). Models of emotional intelligence. In R. J. Sternberg (Ed.), *Handbook of human intelligence* (2nd ed.; pp. 396–420). New York: Cambridge University Press.

Mayer, J. D., Salovey, P., & Caruso, D. (2002). *The Mayer-Salovey-Caruso Emotional Intelligence Test (MSCEIT)*. Toronto, ON: Multi-Health Systems.

Mayer, J. D., Salovey, P., Caruso, D., & Sitarenios, G. (2001). Emotional intelligence as a standard intelligence. *Emotion, 1*, 232–242.

Mayer, J. D., Salovey, P., Caruso, D., & Sitarenios, G. (2003). Measuring emotional intelligence with the MSCEIT V2.0. *Emotion, 3*, 97–105.

Payton, J. W., Wardlaw, D. M., Graczyk, P. A., Bloodworth, M. R., Tompsett, C. J., & Weissberg, R. P. (2000). Social and emotional learning: A framework for promoting mental health and reducing risk behavior in children and youth. *Journal of School Health, 70*, 179–185.

Rice, C. L. (1999). *A quantitative study of emotional intelligence and its impact on team performance*. Unpublished master's thesis, Pepperdine University, Malibu, CA.

Rubin, M. M. (1999). *Emotional intelligence and its role in mitigating aggression: A correlational study of the relationship between emotional intelligence and aggression in urban adolescents*. Unpublished dissertation, Immaculata College, Immaculata, PA.

Saarni, C. (1999). *Developing emotional competence*. New York: Guilford.

Salovey, P., & Mayer, J. D. (1990). Emotional intelligence. *Imagination, Cognition, and Personality, 9*, 185–211.

Salovey, P., Mayer, J. D., Caruso, D., & Lopes, P. N. (2003). Measuring emotional intelligence as a set of abilities with the Mayer-Salovey-Caruso Emotional Intelligence Test (MSCEIT). In S. J. Lopez & C. R. Snyder (Eds.), *Positive psychology assessment* (pp. 251–265). Washington, DC: American Psychological Association.

Salovey, P., & Sluyter, D. J. (Eds.). (1997). *Emotional development and emotional intelligence: Educational implications*. New York: Basic Books.

Sternberg, R. J. (1985). *The triarchic mind: A new theory of human intelligence*. New York: Penguin.

Sternberg, R. J. (1999a). Intelligence as developing expertise. *Contemporary Educational Psychology, 24*, 259–275.

Sternberg, R. J. (1999b). The theory of successful intelligence. *Review of General Psychology, 3*, 292–316.

Sternberg, R. J., Forsythe, G. B., Hedlund, J., Horvath, J. A., Wagner, R. K., Williams, W. M., Snook, S. A., & Grigorenko, E. L. (2000). *Practical intelligence in everyday life*. New York: Cambridge University Press.

Sternberg, R. J., & Grigorenko, E. L. (2000). *Teaching for successful intelligence: To increase student learning and achievement*. Arlington Heights, IL: SkyLight Professional Development.

Sternberg, R. J., Grigorenko, E. L., & Jarvin, L. (2001). Improving reading instruction: The triarchic model. *Educational Leadership, 58*, 48–52.

Trinidad, D. R., & Johnson, C. A. (2002). The association between emotional intelligence and early adolescent tobacco and alcohol use. *Personality and Individual Differences*, *32*, 95–105.

Weissberg, R. P., & Greenberg, M. T. (1998). School and community competence-enhancement and prevention programs. In W. Damen (Series Ed.) & I. E. Sigel & K. A. Renninger (Vol. Eds.), *Handbook of child psychology: Vol. 4. Child psychology in practice* (5th ed.; pp. 877–954). New York: Wiley.

Zins, J. E., Elias, M. J., Greenberg, M. T., & Weissberg, R. P. (2000). Promoting social and emotional competence in children. In K. M. Minke & G. C. Bear (Eds.), *Preventing school problems—promoting school success: Strategies and programs that work* (pp. 71–100). Bethesda, MD: National Association of School Psychologists.

CHAPTER 6

Social and Emotional Learning in Teacher Preparation Standards

JANE E. FLEMING AND MARY BAY

Teachers and teacher educators are increasingly aware of the extent to which children's social and emotional adjustment affects performance in school. The National Advisory Mental Health Council (2001) estimates that one in ten children and adolescents suffers from mental health problems; for significant proportions of these students, social and emotional problems interfere with learning in school (Adelman & Taylor, 2000; Hinshaw, 1992; Roeser & Eccles, 2000).

Fortunately, teaching practices that attend to students' social and emotional needs can have a significant impact on children's psychosocial adjustment. Engaging in positive teacher–child interactions, fostering positive relationships among students, employing proactive classroom management techniques, and engaging students in cooperative learning activities are associated with children's feelings of well-being and bonding to school (Huffman, Mehlinger, & Kerivan, 2000; O'Donnell, Hawkins, Catalano, Abbott, & Day, 1995). Moreover, these same factors are associated with a reduction in acting out among students (Cairns & Cairns, 1994), fewer teacher-reported behavior problems (Huffman et al., 2000), and increased levels of student academic achievement (Abbott et al., 1998; Zins, Bloodworth, Weissberg, & Walberg, this volume).

As a result, schools across the country are moving toward a preventive approach aimed at promoting development of healthy outcomes and preventing the onset of behavior problems (Greenberg, Domitrovich, & Bumbarger, 2001). Based on child development and prevention research, a "new generation" of social and emotional learning (SEL) programs has been developed to promote student social and emotional development (Elias et al., 1997). A comprehensive approach to addressing SEL is one that works to develop a wide range of social and emotional skills through developmentally appropriate instruction. This collection of skills can be organized within a framework that includes four major skill areas: (1) awareness of self and others; (2) positive attitudes and values; (3) responsible decision making; and (4) social interaction skills (Payton et al., 2000). In addition to fostering skill development among students, a comprehensive approach to SEL should include efforts to coordinate instruction across the curriculum and throughout the school, as well as collaboration with families and the school community (Payton et al., 2000).

SEL programs that incorporate some or all of these components continue to be more and more widely disseminated to schools across the country. Each year, the federal government spends hundreds of millions of dollars to fund adoption of these programs. In 2003, $716 million was appropriated to the Office of Safe and Drug-Free Schools to fund prevention activities (U.S. Department of Education, 2003).

In the majority of school districts, regular classroom teachers hold the bulk of responsibility for program implementation and teaching of SEL skills. Arguably, teachers are *the* critical element in creating learning environments in which children's understandings and skills in this domain are advanced. Despite this, few colleges of education have incorporated SEL training into their teacher preparation programs. Although teacher education programs typically require a strong foundation in child development, course offerings tend to be focused on the cognitive development of children and adolescents. More frequently, teacher candidates receive little to no instruction in social and emotional development or exposure to SEL programs until they are required to teach them in the schools.

Despite the fact that most practicing teachers and teacher candidates immediately acknowledge the salience of these issues in their work and recognize the benefits of addressing the social and emotional developmental needs of students in their classrooms (Pasi, 2001), compliance with the full range of requirements of the National Council for Accreditation of Teacher Education (NCATE) as well as state and local teacher preparation standards often leaves little room for additional coursework covering SEL in teacher education curricula. This argument against SEL training is reinforced by the supposition that SEL content is incompatible with the performance-based standards that teacher preparation programs are required to address.

In an effort to more carefully investigate this notion of "incompatibility," we were compelled to engage in a thorough examination of professional teaching standards for their congruence with principles of social and emotional learning. In this chapter we present comparisons made between the core Illinois Professional Teaching Standards (IPTS) and a framework of key social and emotional competencies developed by the Collaborative for

Academic, Social, and Emotional Learning (CASEL). Our comparison is based on the method employed by Norris and Kress (2000) in their pioneering case study of the relevance of social and emotional learning to the New Jersey State Core Curriculum Content Standards.

STANDARDS FOR TEACHER PREPARATION

There is a broad reform movement currently taking place in teacher education. Across the nation, states are shifting away from a highly prescribed, course-counting method of teacher preparation to a standards-based or outcomes approach. Given this opportunity for reform, teacher educators in colleges and universities across the country are redesigning courses and field experiences to provide their teacher candidates the opportunities to study the ideas and acquire the abilities set forth in these standards.

In 1992, the Interstate New Teacher Assessment and Support Consortium (INTASC) undertook the development of a set of performance-based standards for teacher preparation programs. These standards were developed by representatives of both state boards of education and professional standards boards, with significant participation by institutions of higher education, researchers, and professional associations (Council of Chief State School Officers, 2000). Having been developed by a wide range of stakeholders and aligned with the standards of the National Board for Professional Teaching Standards, these standards are thought to represent the best knowledge base for teaching we have to date. They are now recognized broadly as providing a useful framework for reforming many aspects of teacher education, licensing, and professional development. INTASC maintains the position that the complex art of teaching requires performance-based standards and assessment strategies that evaluate what teachers actually can do in authentic teaching situations (Indiana State University, 2000).

In addition to state boards of education adopting these standards for professional teaching, NCATE, which oversees and sanctions teacher preparation programs at many colleges and universities across the country, has incorporated the INTASC standards into its accreditation process (Council of Chief State School Officers, 2000). NCATE standards not only set the policy for preparing, licensing, and certifying educators, but also guide the regulation and accreditation of schools of education.

THE ILLINOIS PROFESSIONAL TEACHING STANDARDS

Illinois is among 49 states involved in reform initiatives around INTASC standards. Using the principles designed by INTASC, Illinois began the reform process by developing a set of Professional Teaching Standards, which have become the umbrella standards for all teaching areas. They include 11 standards that define the core expectations for all teachers and include core standards ranging from content knowledge and instructional planning and delivery, to creating positive learning environments and developing collaborative professional and community relationships (complete Illinois Professional Teaching Standards can be found on the Illinois State Board of Education website at http://www.isbe.state.il.us/).

Teacher education curricula must comply with the Illinois Professional Teaching Standards, and teacher preparation institutions must assess their preservice teacher candidates across these areas. Consequently, teacher educators across the state of Illinois are using these standards to guide the design of their teacher preparation programs. Any proposed changes to teacher education curricula undergo the scrutiny of their compatibility with the standards for teacher training.

COMPARING SEL COMPETENCIES WITH THE ILLINOIS PROFESSIONAL TEACHING STANDARDS

We undertook a review of teaching standards with a social and emotional learning lens, comparing the standards with social and emotional teacher competencies adapted from the key SEL competencies established by CASEL (Payton et al., 2000). These competencies include the teacher's responsibility to foster the skills, attitudes, and values identified as being essential to the social and emotional development of young people, as well as the teacher's role in ensuring school-wide coordination of instruction and connections to family and community resources that are critical for effective enhancement of children's SEL skills (see Table 6.1).

These competencies were compared with the complete set of Illinois Professional Teaching Standards (Illinois State Board of Education, 1999), including the Preamble to the standards and the subsets of knowledge and performance indicators associated with each of the 11 core standards. The Illinois Professional Teaching Standards were selected for a number of reasons: (1) they are aligned with national standards for beginning and accomplished teachers; (2) they serve as the core standards identifying what all teachers should know and be able to do; (3) they are used to focus teacher training programs on the knowledge and skills needed by teachers in the classroom; (4) they form the basis for assessing students in teacher education programs; and (5) they are typical of teacher standards across the nation (Illinois State Board of Education, 1999).

We took a rather conservative approach to mapping the SEL teacher competencies with the Illinois standards; while some inferences could have been made regarding the implied intent of the standards and their underly-

Table 6.1. Social and Emotional Learning Competencies Compared with the Illinois Professional Teaching Standards

	SEL Teacher Competencies						
Illinois Professional Teaching Standards	*Developing Student Awareness of Self and Others*	*Promoting Positive Student Attitudes and Values*	*Supporting Responsible Decision Making*	*Fostering Student Social Interaction Skills*	*Supporting School-wide Coordination*	*Developing School-Family Partnerships*	*Building School-Community Partnerships*
Content knowledge							
Human development and learning	√	√	√	√			
Diversity		√		√	√	√	√
Planning for instruction					√	√	√
Learning environment	√	√	√	√			
Instructional delivery		√	√				
Communication	√	√		√			
Assessment	√		√		√	√	
Collaborative relationships					√	√	√
Reflection and personal growth					√		
Professional conduct					√		√

ing SEL competencies, we made no such leaps. Only those standards that included explicit reference to social and emotional development, or that employed language used in CASEL definitions of key SEL competencies, were counted as having significant SEL content. Results of the comparison of SEL teacher competencies with the Illinois Professional Teaching Standards are summarized in Table 6.1.

Results of engaging in a review of the standards exceeded our expectations of the consistency and compatibility of key social and emotional competencies with the Illinois Professional Teaching Standards. SEL competencies are included in 10 out of 11 (91%) of the core teaching standards. Of these 10, nine (90%) of the standards incorporate multiple SEL competencies. Moreover, all of the SEL competencies outlined by Payton and colleagues (2000) are represented in the teaching standards (see Table 6.1). As with the Norris and Kress (2000) review of the New Jersey State Core Curriculum Content Standards, the Illinois Professional Teaching Standards can serve virtually as a "primer" in goals for developing social and emotional learning skills (p. 7). The alignment of specific SEL competencies with each standard is discussed in more detail below.

Standard 1: Content Knowledge

The first of the Illinois Professional Teaching Standards concerns the content knowledge that is central to a teacher's particular discipline. It ensures that teachers have a strong command of concepts, principles, and theories of their content area as well as the skills to convey this knowledge to students. Although Standard 1 is not directly related to social and emotional learning competencies, it does assert that teachers use a variety of methods in teaching subject matter that take into account "students' conceptual frameworks and misconceptions" (Illinois State Board of Education, 1999).

Although this does not necessarily involve the promotion of SEL skills among students, it does imply a degree of SEL competence on the part of the teacher in terms of awareness of self and others. In order to adjust one's teaching methods to account for "common misunderstandings that impede learning" (Illinois State Board of Education, 1999), one must be cognizant of student misconceptions and reflective on one's own teaching practices. Despite these connections, this standard was not scored as directly connected with the key SEL teacher competencies in accordance with our more conservative scoring criteria.

Standard 2: Human Development and Learning

The second standard, which focuses on human development and learning, has very explicit connections to social and emotional learning competencies.

This standard involves teacher understandings of human development in a variety of areas, including how social and emotional development influences learning (Illinois State Board of Education, 1999). The standard requires that teachers "design instruction that meets learners' current needs in the cognitive, *social*, *emotional*, *ethical*, and physical domains at the appropriate levels of development" (emphasis added). The standard also states directly that a teacher should "understand how students . . . acquire skills" in these various domains (Illinois State Board of Education, 1999), including social and emotional skills.

Standard 3: Diversity

Standard 3 stresses skills for teaching in diverse settings and ensures that teachers are prepared to create instructional opportunities to address the needs of culturally, socioeconomically, and academically diverse learners. This standard involves promotion of students' SEL skills, as well as school, family, and community coordination. In terms of student skills, Standard 3 addresses the promotion of positive attitudes and values by mandating that each teacher "facilitate a learning community in which individual differences are respected" (Illinois State Board of Education, 1999). In addition, this standard calls for school-wide coordination of "appropriate services or resources" to address the needs of diverse learners. It further ensures that teachers have an understanding of how "family and community values" influence learning, and that teachers access "information about students' families, cultures, and communities as a basis for connecting instruction to student experiences" (Illinois State Board of Education, 1999).

Standard 4: Planning for Instruction

The next IPTS standard focuses on instructional planning and calls for teachers to be skilled in designing instruction that draws upon knowledge of the discipline, the students, the community, and the curriculum goals. Standard 4 is most closely aligned with the SEL principles of school-wide coordination and school–family and school–community partnerships. In relation to school-wide coordination of instruction and joint planning by teachers, the standard calls on teachers to participate in curriculum development, creating "interdisciplinary" approaches to learning that "integrate multiple content areas."

In addition, while not specifically naming families and communities, the standard requires that teachers create learning experiences that "relate to students' current life experiences," are "relevant to the students," and are "based on students' prior knowledge" in order to build "an effective bridge between student experiences and career and educational goals" (Illinois State Board of Education, 1999).

Standard 5: Learning Environment

The fifth standard involves creating a learning environment that is conducive to positive social interaction and active engagement in learning. Standard 5 places a strong emphasis on SEL, explicitly calling for teachers to engage students in activities that enhance social and emotional development. The standard calls on teachers to establish a learning environment that is characterized by positive attitudes and values, including "mutual respect" and student "support for one another." Teachers also should create opportunities for students to "assume responsibility for themselves and one another."

Furthermore, Standard 5 establishes the expectation that teachers engage students in activities that promote SEL skills, including responsible decision making and development of social interaction skills. In particular, teachers should use strategies to create a smoothly functioning learning community in which "expectations and processes for communication and behavior" have been established and students "participate in decision making." Teachers also must analyze and make decisions about the classroom learning environment that will "enhance social relationships" through "cooperation," working "collaboratively," and engaging in "group learning activities" (Illinois State Board of Education, 1999).

Standard 6: Instructional Delivery

Standard 6 emphasizes the need for teachers to use a variety of instructional strategies to meet student needs. Included among these are strategies that "engage students in active learning opportunities" in order to promote the development of SEL skills related to responsible decision making, such as "critical thinking" and "problem solving" skills (Illinois State Board of Education, 1999). In addition, Standard 6 addresses teachers' obligation to employ teaching strategies that "help students assume responsibility" as learners, a key component of fostering SEL skills through promotion of positive attitudes and values.

Standard 7: Communication

The seventh standard calls for teachers to use a variety of effective communication techniques to foster active inquiry, collaboration, and supportive interaction. This standard also is directly reflective of a number of SEL competencies. Most explicitly, it calls on teachers to develop student awareness of self and others and to foster student social interaction skills by "practicing effective listening" and modeling "effective verbal and nonverbal communication" that reflects a sense of audience and purpose. In addition, Standard 7 specifically mandates that teachers model and practice "effective conflict resolution skills," which involves a variety of social and emotional competencies, including expressive communication, negotiation, refusal, and help seeking (Payton et al., 2000).

Standard 8: Assessment

Standard 8 focuses on teachers' use of a variety of assessment strategies to support the development of all students. This standard is reflective of a number of SEL teacher competencies, including developing student awareness of self and others, supporting responsible decision making, supporting school-wide coordination of instruction, and developing school–family partnerships. In particular, it requires that teachers involve students in self-assessments that will "help them become aware of their strengths and needs" and encourage them to engage in adaptive goal setting. In addition, Standard 8 emphasizes teacher communication and coordination with colleagues on issues related to student work performance, as well as responsible communication about student progress with parents and families.

Standard 9: Collaborative Relationships

In emphasizing that teachers should develop and maintain collaborative relationships with colleagues, parents and guardians, and the community, Standard 9 is very explicitly linked to the key social and emotional competencies for teachers. In terms of supporting school-wide coordination of instruction, Standard 9 states that teachers must "work with colleagues to develop an effective learning climate in the school" and must "participate in collaborative decision making with other professionals" aimed at achieving student success. Further, the professional teacher "works effectively with parents and guardians," as well as "other members of the community" to develop school–family and school–community "partnerships to promote student learning and well-being" (Illinois State Board of Education, 1999).

Standard 10: Reflection and Professional Growth

The tenth standard distinguishes the professional teacher as a reflective practitioner who continually evaluates how choices and actions affect students, families, and colleagues and who actively seeks opportunities for professional development. This standard is directly related to the SEL competency of supporting school-wide coordination of instruction. Teacher performance indicators explicitly stated in the standard include "collaborating with other professionals as resources for . . . seeking and giving feedback," "participating in professional dialogue," and "collaboratively sharing a variety of instructional resources with colleagues" (Illinois State Board of Education, 1999).

Standard 11: Professional Conduct

Similarly, Standard 11, which calls on teachers to maintain standards of professional conduct and provide leadership to improve student learning, is most directly related to the SEL principles of supporting school-wide coordination and developing school–community partnerships. In order to support school-wide coordination of instruction, Standard 11 establishes the expectation that teachers "actively participate in curriculum development and staff development" activities with colleagues. Toward building school–community partnerships, teachers are expected to "participate, as appropriate, with [local] professional and community organizations" in policy design and development of educational projects and programs (Illinois State Board of Education, 1999).

Evidence of SEL in Teacher Preparation Standards

After careful review of the Illinois Professional Teaching Standards for connections with key social and emotional competencies for teachers, the alignment of SEL competencies with the teaching standards is clear; social and emotional learning has a prominent place in these standards. This is especially significant given that these core standards identify what all teachers in Illinois should know and be able to do. In addition to the SEL connection with individual standards, the Preamble to the IPTS, which outlines the general beliefs of the Board of Education with regard to the Illinois educational system, specifically emphasizes supporting the social and emotional, as well as the intellectual, development of students (Illinois State Board of Education, 1999). In addition, the Preamble includes the belief that the Illinois educational system "must guarantee" a learning environment that nurtures "understanding" and "respect" and in which there is "collaboration, cooperation, and shared responsibility between the school and the family, and between the school and the community" (Illinois State Board of Education, 1999).

Clearly, social and emotional competencies are compatible with, if not central to, the Illinois standards for teachers. Given that the Illinois standards are typical of teacher standards across the nation, one would expect to find similar compatibility of SEL competencies with teaching standards for the majority of states. Moreover, given the commonalities among IPTS, INTASC, and NCATE standards for teacher preparation, SEL holds a prominent place in policy outlining the requisite content of teacher preparation programs.

Suggestions for Integrating SEL into Teacher Preparation Programs

Evidence of social and emotional learning as a thread throughout teacher preparation standards suggests that training teachers in SEL should help to *better* meet existing standards, rather than detract from them. In the face of new performance-based standards, many teacher education programs currently are engaged in program reviews and curricular revisions. The timing is right for teacher educators to consider addressing SEL more systematically throughout teacher education curricula. Proponents of social and emotional learning should work with teacher educators to integrate SEL into university teacher education curricula in ways that reinforce and further ensure teacher candidates' ability to meet professional teaching standards, while providing them with the instructional tools to create SEL-rich classroom environments.

One critical first step may be for teacher educators and proponents of SEL to find a more common language around social and emotional learning competencies. Part of the reason teacher educators don't always recognize immediately the inclusion of SEL in teacher preparation standards may be due to differences in the language used by SEL proponents and teachers to describe these principles. Instead, teacher educators may be under the impression that SEL is somehow a new educational movement rather than a fundamental part of child development that is integrally woven into the work teachers do. SEL competencies include "social norm analysis," "management of feelings," and developing a "constructive sense of self" (Payton et al., 2000), while teachers may speak more of "critical thinking skills," "self-monitoring of behavior," or "self-motivation and active engagement." Developing a common vocabulary may be essential for teacher educators and SEL proponents to more readily recognize their shared understandings and more effectively work to advance their common goals of promoting the social, emotional, and academic success of all children.

To be most effective, the integration of SEL into teacher preparation programs should involve the teaching of SEL in a "do-as-I-do"-type environment, where university instructors model good SEL practice in their own education courses, enabling their teacher candidates to experience how the classroom environment can be transformed and how their own motivation for success can be affected in a caring, cooperative community of learners. Furthermore, SEL content should be addressed within the reality of the school context in which teacher candidates are working. For example, in the urban context of our particular teacher preparation programs, SEL instruction must involve developing teacher candidates' understandings of the potential effects of poverty on social and emotional development and children's mental health, as well as ways to engage children in educational activities that foster a sense of community by capitalizing on the cultural and linguistic resources children bring to school.

Toward this end, there is a great deal of opportunity for proponents of SEL to share resources, coordinate curricular space, and engage in collaborative research with teacher educators with expertise in different, yet related, areas of teacher preparation. For example, given the need to prepare teachers for work with increasingly diverse student populations, long-overdue curricular attention is being focused on the subject of culturally relevant teaching, which shares a substantial degree of common ground with SEL, including prioritizing self-awareness, perspective taking, student–teacher connections, student interaction and collaborative learning, and family and community partnerships (see Elias et al., 1997; Ladson-Billings, 1995; Villegas, 1991; Zeichner, 1996). SEL has similar, natural connections for teacher educators interested in child and adolescent development, classroom management, and special education. Recognizing this common ground and joining forces with faculty across complementary disciplines can help further inform teacher education practices and serve to produce the best-qualified, most effective teaching corps (Cavanaugh, Lippitt, & Moyo, 2001).

In order to address issues of curricular space, some teacher educators may consider integrating training in SEL with existing, related teacher education curricula as a feasible alternative to adding SEL-specific required coursework. Even in the context of related course content, social and emotional development may be taught most effectively as a comprehensive, cohesive body of knowledge, as one would approach the teaching of cognitive development or reading development, rather than addressing SEL as fragmented components of other teaching skills (Elias et al., 1997; Jacobs, 2001). Raising teacher awareness through systematic teaching of SEL will deepen teacher candidates' understanding of the impact of SEL on student success and increase the likelihood that teachers will incorporate learning opportunities that foster social and emotional development in their classrooms.

Field Experience

Incorporating explicit coverage of SEL in teacher education programs in order to build preservice teachers' "knowledge *for* practice" is an important step (Cochran-Smith & Lytle, 1999). Equally important for effective teacher training in SEL is the opportunity for teacher candidates to build their "knowledge *in* practice" (Cochran-Smith & Lytle, 1999) through hands-on experience in SEL-rich classrooms. Newly certified teachers and teacher candidates often report their field experiences as the single most powerful element of their teacher preparation programs, particularly when they are provided with opportunities to engage in extensive fieldwork that is well coordinated with the university-based components of their teacher education programs (Darling-Hammond, 2000; Wilson, Floden, & Ferrini-Mundy, 2001). It may be particularly important for classroom immersion to begin from the start of the school year (fieldwork is often delayed for first few weeks of the school year) in order for teacher candidates to experience from the start how experienced teachers go about creating classroom community, as well as to be present from the beginning of the school year when teachers frequently engage in more explicit teaching of fundamental SEL skills as part of establishing classroom expectations and guidelines for appropriate behavior.

Mentors and Professional Development

This need for teacher candidates to have opportunities to practice integrating SEL through authentic classroom experiences further involves the challenge of identifying mentor teachers who are competent in content, teaching methodology, and creating community, and in developing children's social and emotional skills. Along these lines, opportunities must be made available for practicing teachers whose teacher education programs may not have included a focus on SEL to engage in professional development opportunities.

Professional development is tied to certification renewal in many states. Most practicing teachers would welcome the opportunity to engage in professional development experiences designed to enhance the quality of their classrooms, their relationships with students, and the school success that comes with those experiences (Pasi, 2001). However, this professional development must involve *ongoing, practical opportunities* for teachers to learn sophisticated teaching strategies for infusing SEL in daily instruction, contrary to typical professional development offerings, which often involve no more than "hit and run" workshops (Darling-Hammond, 1997, p. 2).

Practicing Teachers as SEL Partners

In addition, practicing teachers ought to be invited to the professional development table as valid and valued sources of the practical knowledge of their field (Cochran-Smith & Lytle, 1999). Although community psychologists and mental health professionals have been largely responsible for conceptualizing SEL as an important framework for describing the social and emotional skills that contribute to school success, it is critical for proponents of SEL to acknowledge that teachers also have long been concerned with these issues. Even though social and emotional learning may not always be made explicit or addressed as a specific body of knowledge in teacher education programs, teachers and teacher educators have considerable interest in the emotional health of their students and understand, through firsthand, day-to-day experience, how social and emotional difficulties can affect children's potential for success in school. Respecting and involving teachers as contributing partners in the effort to promote children's social and emotional development is key.

Experienced teachers are often the most perceptive about the needs of children in their classrooms and understand the best ways to deliver instruction to their students (Pasi, 2001). Just as it is important to provide teachers with training in SEL so they have a framework for better understanding children's social and emotional development, it is equally important to trust and encourage them to use their skills and experience in integrating SEL into the daily curriculum in the most effective ways, rather than relying solely on outside experts to develop and deliver program content (Pasi, 2001) or being bound to scripted curricula designed to reduce variation in program delivery among various teaching personnel. Teaching is not simply a technique or routine, but is a process of "acting and thinking wisely in the immediacy of classroom life [and] making split-second decisions" guided by knowledge of subject matter, understanding of students, and reflections on previous teaching experiences (Cochran-Smith & Lytle, 1999, p. 266).

SEL program developers should value the expertise teachers bring to bear and should work with them on understanding what constitutes an effective SEL lesson, while encouraging and challenging teachers to create lessons that promote SEL and also are tailored to the needs of the children in their particular local context (Pasi, 2001). Helping teachers come to view SEL as an approach to classroom instruction, rather than as a single-period, add-on program, may help foster a sense of ownership and investment among teachers in infusing SEL principles in everyday classroom activities and developing lessons across the curriculum that promote student self-awareness, responsible decision making, and social interaction skills (Pasi, 2001).

Some might argue that "that's just good teaching!" in the same way that Gloria Ladson-Billings (1995) describes the reaction to the "pedagogical excellence" that comprises culturally relevant pedagogy. Indeed, teaching practices that promote social and emotional development are fundamental to good teaching practices in general (Elias et al., 1997). This is the *very reason* SEL is well represented in teaching standards. Yet, this does not in any way diminish the value of explicit coverage of SEL as a unified, comprehensive body of knowledge in teacher preparation programs any more than it reduces the need for training in culturally relevant pedagogy (or reading development or cognitive development, for that matter).

Another way teacher educators and SEL proponents can work together is to continue to document examples of best practice in SEL instruction. Describing classroom practices in the form of documented case studies, or developing curricular materials and video resources like those put out by Developmental Studies Center (www.devstu.org) that show real teachers in real classrooms integrating SEL instruction in the context of rigorous, standards-based learning activities, provides invaluable tools to teacher educators for integrating SEL into teacher preparation coursework.

CONCLUSION AND FUTURE DIRECTIONS

On a final note, continuing to study the impact of SEL on school success is extremely important in order to build a solid empirical research base upon which teacher educators can draw when proposing revisions to teacher preparation curricula in their programs. Conducting research that continues to document the positive effects of SEL on student outcomes in school, including academic achievement, is essential. Still, the value of also examining the impact on *teacher outcomes* should not be overlooked. With our nation facing teacher shortages of crisis proportions, particularly in urban schools (Riley, 1999), teacher educators are increasingly concerned with improving teacher retention and reducing turnover, especially among new teachers.

Training in SEL has the potential to reduce teacher attrition by affecting factors associated with retention, such as reducing job-related stress, increasing feelings of effectiveness and job satisfaction, reducing student–teacher conflicts and discipline problems, and improving classroom management skills (Ingersoll, 2001; National Center for Education Statistics, 1999). Research that documents the impact of SEL training on teacher retention, in addition to student school success, would be of significant interest to teacher educators, school administrators, and educational policy makers, and would play a powerful role in further establishing SEL as an essential component of teacher preparation programs across the country.

REFERENCES

Abbott, R. D., O'Donnell, J., Hawkins, D. J., Hill, K. G., Kosterman, R., & Catalano, R. F. (1998). Changing teaching practices to promote achievement and bonding to school. *American Journal of Orthopsychiatry*, *68*(4), 542–552.

Adelman, H. S., & Taylor, L. (2000). Shaping the future of mental health in schools. *Psychology in the Schools*, *37*(1), 49–60.

Cairns, R. B., & Cairns, B. D. (1994). *Lifelines and risks: Pathways of youth in our time*. New York: Cambridge University Press.

Cavanaugh, D. A., Lippitt, J., & Moyo, O. (2001). *Resource guide to selected federal policies affecting children's social and emotional development and their readiness for school*. Retrieved September 28, 2001, from http://www.nimh.nih.gov/childhp/fdnconsb.htm

Cochran-Smith, M., & Lytle, S. L. (1999). Relationships of knowledge and practice: Teacher learning in communities. In A. Iran-Nejad & P. D. Pearson (Eds.), *Review of research in education* (Vol. 24, pp. 251–307). Washington, DC: American Educational Research Association.

Council of Chief State School Officers. (2000). *Interstate New Teacher Assessment and Support Consortium*. Retrieved October 3, 2000, from http://www.ccsso.org/intasc.html

Darling-Hammond, L. (1997). *Doing what matters most: Investing in quality teaching*. New York: National Commission on Teaching and America's Future. (ERIC Document Reproduction Service No. ED415183)

Darling-Hammond, L. (2000). How teacher education matters. *Journal of Teacher Education, 51*(3), 166–173.

Elias, M. J., Zins, J. E., Weissberg, R. P., Frey, K. S., Greenberg, M. T., Haynes, N. M., Kessler, R., Schwab-Stone, M. E., & Shriver, T. P. (1997). *Promoting social and emotional learning: Guidelines for educators*. Alexandria, VA: Association for Supervision and Curriculum Development.

Greenberg, M. T., Domitrovich, C., & Bumbarger, B. (2001, March 30). The prevention of mental disorders in school-aged children: Current state of the field. *Prevention & Treatment, 4*, Article 1. Retrieved August 5, 2001, from http://journals.apa.org/prevention/

Hinshaw, S. P. (1992). Externalizing behavior problems and academic underachievement in childhood and adolescence: Causal relationships and underlying mechanisms. *Psychological Bulletin, 111*(1), 127–155.

Huffman, L. C., Mehlinger, S. L., & Kerivan, A. S. (2000). *Risk factors for academic and behavioral problems at the beginning of school*. Retrieved September 28, 2001 from http://www.nimh.nih.gov/childhp/ goodstart.cfm

Illinois State Board of Education. (1999). *Illinois professional teaching standards*. Retrieved November 8, 2000, from http://www.isbe.state.il.us/profdevelopment/ipts.htm

Indiana State University. (2000). *Interstate new teacher assessment and support consortium: Model standards for beginning teachers licensing and development*. Retrieved October 3, 2000, from http://isu.indstate.edu/dickinson/ cimt200/intascin.htm

Ingersoll, R. M. (2001, January). *Teacher turnover, teacher shortages, and the organization of schools*. Retrieved August 5, 2001, from http://depts.washington.edu/ctpmail/Alpha.html

Jacobs, G. M. (2001). Providing the scaffold: A model for early childhood/primary teacher preparation. *Early Childhood Education Journal, 29*(2), 125–130.

Ladson-Billings, G. (1995). But that's just good teaching! The case for culturally relevant pedagogy. *Theory Into Practice, 34*, 159–165.

National Advisory Mental Health Council. (2001). *Blueprint for change: Research on child and adolescent mental health* (Report of the National Advisory Council's Workgroup on Child and Adolescent Mental Health Intervention Development and Deployment). Washington, DC: Author.

National Center for Education Statistics. (1999). *Teacher quality: A report on the preparation and qualifications of public school teachers.* Retrieved September, 28, 2001, from http://nces.ed.gov/pubs99/quarterlyapr/2-feature/ 2-esq11a.html

Norris, J. A., & Kress, J. S. (2000). Reframing the standards vs. social and emotional learning debate: A case study. *The Fourth R*, *91*, 7–10.

O'Donnell, J., Hawkins, J. D., Catalano, R. F., Abbott, R. D., & Day, L. E. (1995). Preventing school failure, drug use, and delinquency among low-income children: Long-term intervention in elementary schools. *American Journal of Orthopsychiatry*, *65*, 87–100.

Pasi, R. J. (2001). *Higher expectations: Promoting social and emotional learning and academic achievement in your school.* New York: Teachers College Press.

Payton, J. W., Wardlaw, D. M., Graczyk, P. A., Bloodworth, M. R., Tompsett, C. J., & Weissberg, R. P. (2000). Social and emotional learning: A framework for promoting mental health and reducing risk behavior in children and youth. *Journal of School Health*, *70*(5), 179–185.

Riley, R. W. (1999). *New challenges, a new resolve: Moving American education into the 21st century.* Sixth Annual State of American Education Speech. (ERIC Document Reproduction Service No. ED428052)

Roeser, R. W., & Eccles, J. S. (2000). Schooling and mental health. In A. J. Sameroff, M. Lewis, & S. Miller (Eds.), *Handbook of developmental psychopathology* (2nd ed.; pp. 135–156). New York: Kluwer Academic/Plenum.

U.S. Department of Education. (2003). *Department of Education fiscal year 2003 Congressional action.* Retrieved April 2, 2003, from http://www.ed.gov/offices/OUS/budnews.html

Villegas, A. M. (1991). *Culturally responsive pedagogy for the 1990's and beyond* (Trends and Issues Paper No. 6). Washington, DC: ERIC Clearinghouse on Teacher Education. (ERIC Document Reproduction Service No. ED 339 698)

Wilson, S. M., Floden, R. E., & Ferrini-Mundy, J. (2001, March). *Teacher preparation research: Current knowledge, gaps, and recommendations.* Seattle: University of Washington, Center for the Study of Teaching and Policy.

Zeichner, K. (1996). Educating teachers for cultural diversity. In K. Zeichner, S. Melnick, & M. L. Gomez (Eds.), *Currents of reform in preservice teacher education* (pp. 133–175). New York: Teachers College Press.

PART II

Effective Strategies for Enhancing Academic, Social, and Emotional Outcomes

CHAPTER 7

Strategies to Infuse Social and Emotional Learning into Academics

MAURICE J. ELIAS

Examining the impact of curricula that build students' social and emotional learning (SEL) along with their academic achievement is a complex task. This chapter explores this issue through the lens of one particular program, Social Decision Making and Social Problem Solving (SDM/SPS), which has been in operation for over 2 decades. SEL curricula are not simple instructional units but rather create caring learning contexts through their implementation. Therefore, looking at the way in which one program conceptualizes and approaches building social-emotional skills in students, and their generalization to academic domains, may provide the richness of understanding needed to help move research and practice ahead in this critical area.

Much has been written about social decision-making and problem-solving processes. As an approach to education, it has an extensive lineage, going at least back to the work of John Dewey (1933). In recent years, the work of the SDM/SPS project has been the vanguard of this approach. It began in 1979 as a collaboration among Rutgers University, the then-University of Medicine and Dentistry of New Jersey–Community Mental Health Center at Piscataway, and the schools, particularly in New Jersey. Years of collaborative field research and development with teachers, administrators, and parents led to the development of curriculum and instructional procedures and extensive implementation strategies (Elias, 1993; Elias, Bruene-Butler, Blum, & Schuyler, 2000; Elias & Clabby, 1989). Essential to the success of SDM/SPS is its strong linkage with the academic development of children; current understanding of the conceptual, pragmatic, and empirical aspects of this linkage is the focus of this chapter.

Building Academic Success on Social and Emotional Learning: What Does the Research Say? ISBN 0-8077-4439-5 (pbk), ISBN 0-8077-4440-9 (cloth).

OVERVIEW OF THE SDM/SPS CURRICULUM APPROACH

SDM/SPS curricula (Elias, 1993; Elias & Clabby, 1989; Elias, Friedlander, & Tobias, 2001; Elias & Tobias, 1996) operationalize a set of skills linked empirically with social competence and peer acceptance in the areas of self-control, social awareness and group participation, and critical thinking. The skills are organized into three domains, readiness, instructional, and application. Instructional design is as important as content. Systematic skill-building procedures are used as the framework for all curriculum units. The structure includes the following:

- Introducing the skill concept and motivation for learning; presentation of the skill in concrete behavioral components
- Modeling behavioral components and clarifying the concept by descriptions and behavioral examples of not using the skill
- Providing opportunities for practice of the skill in "kid-tested," enjoyable activities, to allow for corrective feedback and reinforcement until skill mastery is approached
- Labeling the skill with a prompt or cue, to establish a "shared language" that can be used to call for the skill in future situations
- Giving assignments for skill practice outside of the structured lesson
- Providing follow-through activities and ways to use prompts in academic content areas and everyday interpersonal situations

Readiness for Decision Making

This domain targets skill areas that give children valuable tools for effective social decision making and interpersonal behavior in the classroom, in the schoolyard, and with peers, family, and employers. The readiness domain includes two units, Self-Control and Social Awareness. The Self-Control Unit refers to internal or personal skills necessary for self-regulation and monitoring, while the Social Awareness Unit focuses on external social skills and awareness linked with successful participation in a group.

The Self-Control Unit includes skills such as listening, turn taking, remembering, and following a series of directions. The heart of the unit focuses on skills for regulating emotional reactions and impulsivity and developing the skills needed for social literacy. Children learn to recognize personal physical cues and situations that put them at risk of fight-or-flight reactivity and result in negative consequences and poor decisions. They also are taught skills for gaining control and access to clear thinking. Linked with the skill of regulating emotion is the ability to apply self-control in the context of interpersonal communication. Students are taught to self-monitor their body language, eye contact, the way they put their message into words, and their tone of voice, and to attend to similar signals from others.

The Social Awareness Unit emphasizes skills characteristic of children who are accepted by their peers. Research in peer relationships has found that children respond positively to peers that praise, compliment, and express positive emotion and appreciation for others. They also recognize and respond when peers need help; recognize when they need help and appropriately ask for it; and give criticism or negative feedback by clearly stating what they do not like, give reasons, and offer new ideas. They also accept constructive criticism appropriately and can take another's perspective. Lessons in this unit target these skills, in addition to activities for group building; practice in expressing feelings and thoughts in a group; and the characteristics of friendship, the importance of being a good friend, and choosing good friends.

Instructional Phase

This domain targets an eight-step framework for organizing clear thinking. The eight thinking skills are worded in language designed to provide children with a "self-talk" strategy they can use to think through a problem or make a decision. They are presented descriptively in Figure 7.1, using the acronym "FIG TESPN" as an organizing framework. The following version of FIG TESPN is presented to children in SDM/SPS curricula and related interventions:

- Feelings are my cue to problem solve.
- I have a problem.
- Goals guide my actions.
- Think of many possible things to do.
- Envision the outcomes of each solution.
- Select your best solution, based on your goal.
- Plan, practice, anticipate pitfalls, and pursue your best solution.
- Next time, what will you do—the same thing or something different?

FIG TESPN (and other comprehensive problem-solving and decision-making strategies) provides a centralized way for students to understand a strategy they can invoke when they confront a problem or decision (Wales, Nardi, & Stager, 1986). The unique name, FIG TESPN, is also a mnemonic that reinforces memory. In addition, it is a convenient prompt for teachers to use; for example, they can ask a student, "How can FIG TESPN help you with this problem?" (This point will be revisited later in the chapter.)

The objective of the instructional phase is student over-learning and internalization of a framework for thinking through a problem or making a

Figure 7.1. FIG TESPN framework for clear thinking.

When children or adults are using their social decision-making/social problem-solving skills, they are:

1. **F**ocusing on signs of feelings in themselves and others.
2. **I**dentifying issues or problems.
3. **G**uiding themselves with goals they have identified.
4. **T**hinking of many alternative solutions or ways to get to their goals.
5. **E**nvisioning possible consequences in strong visual detail.
6. **S**electing their best solution, the one that will get them to their goal.
7. **P**lanning, practicing, and preparing for obstacles before acting.
8. **N**oticing what happened when they acted and using the information for future problem solving.

decision. Because of this, continual review and recitation are built into the program. Students learn and practice these steps in diverse developmentally appropriate and salient contexts so that when they are under pressure and/or not under adult supervision, they will turn to their readiness skills and use FIG TESPN.

Application Phase

This domain focuses on structured opportunities to practice the application of the skills to everyday problems and decisions and within the context of academic content areas. Two areas are emphasized: structured lessons and facilitative questioning.

Application Phase Lessons (Structured Lessons). Sample lesson plans, worksheets, and concrete examples show how to integrate practice of the SDM skills into a wide variety of topic areas, such as social studies, stereotyping and prejudice, creative writing, and starting and completing projects.

Facilitative Questioning. Although the application phase provides concrete tools that teachers can use to launch their efforts to integrate social decision-making skills into everyday use, structured lessons are by no means the only way to help children practice their skills. Teachers model both readiness skills and FIG TESPN and translate FIG TESPN into questions that prompt an individual or group to think through a problem. Once students are trained in the discrete skills targeted in the curriculum, opportunities for extending the use or practice of these skills are almost endless. FIG TESPN and the readiness prompts and cues become a shared language to elicit use of skills and to promote transfer, generalization, and maintenance of skills beyond the classroom walls. Playground aides, bus drivers, school nurses, and other school staff as well as parents and other adults in the community can be trained to prompt and promote children's SDM/SPS abilities.

Evidence for Effectiveness

Relative to children who were not participants in SDM/SPS programs, children involved in the programs derived many benefits (Bruene-Butler, Hampson, Elias, Clabby, & Schuyler, 1997; Elias, Gara, Schuyler, Branden-Muller, & Sayette, 1991). These included the following:

- Greater sensitivity to others' feelings
- Better understanding of the consequences of their behavior
- Increased ability to size up interpersonal situations and plan appropriate actions
- Higher self-esteem
- More positive prosocial behavior
- More positive behavior and leadership behaviors with peers
- Better transition to middle school
- Lower than expected levels of antisocial, self-destructive, and socially disordered behavior, even when followed up into high school
- Improvement in their learning-to-learn skills in academic areas that had been infused with social decision making
- Improved use of skills in self-control, social awareness, and social decision making and problem solving in situations occurring both inside and outside the classroom

Recent replications of many of these original findings have been carried out. For example, extent of teacher acquisition of skills in "dialoguing" and "facilitative questioning" met or exceeded those of the original sample in new sites assessed. Comparing a replication site in Oregon and the original New Jersey site, use of inhibitory questioning strategies by teachers declined from pretest to posttest by 40% and 53%, respectively; use of facilitative questioning increased by 35% and 117%, respectively. With regard to the acquisition of skills in interpersonal sensitivity, problem analysis, and planning, students in all recent dissemination sites showed significant pre–post gains; the effect sizes in all cases were equal to or as much as twice as large as those in the original validation sample (cf. Bruene-Butler et al., 1997).

Most recently, the program was designated as a model for Goal #7 by the National Education Goals Panel (Safe, Drug Free Schools) and as a Promising Program by the U.S. Department of Education's Expert Panel on Safe, Disciplined, and Drug-Free Schools. Data also show that children, teachers, and other educators enjoy the program and put its principles to regular and frequent use. Taken together, the evidence gathered to date indicates that the SDM/SPS approach is effective and feasible in diverse settings.

THE SDM/SPS–ACADEMICS CONNECTION

Integrating SDM/SPS into the academic work of students builds their social-emotional learning skills and enriches their academics by linking cognitive and social and emotional processes. Readiness skills are essential for students to accomplish the following academic and learning tasks (among many others too numerous to list here):

- Understanding assignments and test instructions accurately
- Examining passages of text patiently and extracting necessary information across a wide range of academic subject areas
- Delaying gratification long enough to think about difficult choices on exams, or to prepare well for those exams
- Participating in cooperative learning groups
- Completing homework and short- and long-term projects in an organized way

Beyond the readiness skills, the critical thinking skills denoted by FIG TESPN are the cornerstone of academic understanding and sustained achievement. This is true both in terms of mastering the intricacies of a subject area and addressing the numerous everyday decisions that are part of life in school and among peers and family. Consider how well a student would function with deficiencies in any one, two, or three FIG TESPN skills. Imagine if the deficiencies occurred in only two or three school or home situations. Is there any doubt that the student would be at risk for academic difficulty, for substance abuse, and for not functioning as a healthy, productive adult citizen (Benard, Fafoglia, & Perone, 1987)?

Empirical Evidence for the SDM/SPS Link to Academics

Formalization of an application phase appears to be important for helping create a linkage between SDM/SPS and academics in which use of the skills in the social-emotional domain reinforces use of the skills in the academic domain. Children come to understand that the skills have universal applicability to all aspects of their life.

Elias and Clabby (1992) found that adding the application phase to an SDM/SPS instructional phase already focused on social-emotional contexts led to significant generalization to indices of academic progress in fourth and fifth graders in a blue-collar, suburban elementary school. Application lessons were in language arts and social studies, academic areas in which progress was anticipated to occur.

Report card grades were examined between marking periods 1 and 2, 2 and 3, and 2 and 4. A series of multivariate analyses of covariance in a 2-by-2 design (grades 4 and 5, SDM/SPS curriculum instructional phase only vs. instructional plus application phases) showed no differences between marking periods 1 and 2, the time when students received standard SDM/SPS instruction. However, between marking periods 2 and 3 and 2 and 4, significant interaction effects at the $p < .005$ level were found. Fifth graders showed the greatest gains in language arts; the only group not showing gain was the instructional phase only group; fourth graders receiving the application phase showed the greatest gains in social studies. It should be noted that math and science grades were examined also as a form of control on grade inflation, and no changes of any kind were observed.

Although these findings await replication, they do suggest that transfer of SDM/SPS and related SEL approaches to academics not only is a function of the generalized improvement of the learning context, but also is aided by fostering specific contexts of application. A series of examples follows showing how FIG TESPN is integrated into various aspects of academics, including traditional academic areas (language arts, social studies), personal and social development (health, family life education), and project and problem-based learning (group projects, inclusion, service learning) (Elias, 1993; Elias & Tobias, 1996). Following these sections, the special challenges of accomplishing this in the urban environment will be outlined.

Language Arts and Literature: Characters Making Decisions and Solving Problems

Much of what children read involves characters in stories making decisions, reacting to conflict, coping with strong feelings, and otherwise navigating the tricky waters of interpersonal situations. Therefore, is makes sense to have students apply the FIG TESPN framework when reading a story (Naftel & Elias, 1995). Formats for carrying out "book talks" in this manner can be found in Figure 7.2. Note that there is a simplified format for beginning readers.

When implementing book talks, teachers introduce early in the discussions consideration of how the characters feel about the situations they are

Figure 7.2. SDM/SPS applied to literature analysis and book talks.

1. Think of an event in the section of the book assigned. When and where did it happen? Put the event into words as a problem.
2. Who were the people that were involved in the problem? What were their different feelings and points of view about the problem? Why did they feel as they did? Try to put their goals into words.
3. For each person or group of people, what are some different decisions or solutions to the problem that he, she, or they thought of that might help in reaching their goals?
4. For each of these ideas or options, what are all of the things that might happen next? Envision and write both short- and long-term consequences.
5. What were the final decisions? How were they made? By whom? Why? Do you agree or disagree? Why?
6. How was the solution carried out? What was the plan? What obstacles were met? How well was the problem solved? What did you read that supports your point of view?
7. Notice what happened and rethink it. What would you have chosen to do? Why?
8. What questions do you have, based on what you read? What questions would you like to be able to ask one or more of the characters? The author? Why are these questions important to you?

Simplified Book Talk Format for Young Readers

I will write about this character . . .

My character's problem is . . .

How did your character get into this problem?

How does the character feel?

What does the character want to happen?

What questions would you like to be able to ask the character you picked, one of the other characters, or the author?

in. This prompts inferential thinking and allows for expansion of students' emotional vocabularies. Students then can identify the problem and goal in their own words, which also facilitates reading comprehension. Indeed, sometimes students must go back and look at the text quite carefully to resolve differences in opinion about what a character's goal might be.

Not only can students discuss and evaluate the options chosen by characters, they also can speculate about other possible options that a character might have taken. It is quite instructive to end Chapter 4 of a book and have the students consider what they might be reading in Chapter 5, based on an SDM/SPS analysis of the story thus far. Students can discuss options and potential outcomes, as well as evaluate any plans made by characters. Further, students enjoy inferring what happens after the story ends, with ideas for sequels becoming in-class written projects or homework assignments.

High school students can use book talk formats to consider the author's writing process. An author must make decisions about writing and solving the problem of how to convey certain feelings, goals, and the like through the written medium. Students gain great insight into writing by studying about authors and then reading a book from a formative point of view. Authors' styles, paraphrasing, use of language, and ways of having plans and outcomes crafted all can be analyzed. Dramatic tension, irony, and conflict can be understood as options and techniques for particular purposes. What feelings does the author want to convey in a particular chapter? What possibilities does the author have with regard to how to advance the plot? Using the SDM/SPS framework as a metacognitive guide for studying the writing process can enrich students' depth of understanding considerably.

The proliferation of highly structured approaches to reading and literacy in schools may limit the easy applicability of frameworks like this. However, school mental health practitioners and consultants can use the literature format to create such things as "book talk" clubs or literary review magazines and clubs, or apply the framework to the analysis of scripts of plays, movies, and even television programs. Such activities provide school professionals with innovative and stigma-free ways to build students' academic, interpersonal, and social problem-solving skills, among both at-risk and other youth populations.

Social Studies: Persons and Groups Engaging in Historically Based Decisions

Instruction in social studies (or civics or related topic areas) can become an engaging experience that emphasizes how decisions have been, and continue to be, made in the context of history. Both history and current events can be thought of as a series of decisions made by individuals and groups, often in response to actual or anticipated problems, accompanied by strong feelings, reflecting certain goals, options, consequences, plans, and implications for the future. Figure 7.3 provides an example of FIG TESPN adapted for use in current events instruction. Consider how often current events are discussed without any way to provide a unifying cognitive framework for students to use outside the school-based context. Current events lessons are an opportune time for school practitioners to bring SEL to students and also to

Figure 7.3. Thinking about current events.

1. What is the event that you are thinking about? When and where is it happening? Put the event into words as a problem or choice or decision.
2. What people or groups were involved in the problem? What are their different feelings? What are their points of view about the problem?
3. What do each of these people or groups want to have happen? Try to put their goals into words.
4. For each person or group, name some different options or solutions to the problem that they think might help them reach their goals. Add any ideas that you think might help them that they might not have thought of.
5. For each option or solution you listed, picture all the things that might happen next. Envision long- and short-term consequences.
6. What do you think the final decision should be? How should it be made? By whom? Why?
7. Imagine a plan to help you carry out your solution. What could you do or think of to make your solution work? What obstacles or roadblocks might keep your solution from working? Who might disagree with your ideas? Why? What else could you do?
8. Rethink it. Is there another way of looking at the problem that might be better? Are there other groups, goals, or plans that come to mind?

introduce teachers to the academic benefits of FIG TESPN and social problem solving.

The framework in Figure 7.3 is easily adapted for analyzing historical events. It is fascinating to help children understand a particular historical event from the perspective of the different participating groups involved. I recall vividly working with middle school students during the Reagan years and how these students were not able to grasp initially that the Soviet Union had its own particular sets of feelings and goals with regard to its relationship to the United States and other nations. But the very framework of FIG TESPN implied strongly to the students that different groups often do have different perspectives, and they eventually gained many insights into the nature of international relationships. It is likely that difficulties in perspective taking and empathy have helped fuel tragic events in the Middle East, Balkans, and Africa.

Certainly, there is greater flexibility in social studies instruction, and certainly in teaching current events, than there is in language arts and reading. Therefore, it is easier to infuse FIG TESPN into the mainstream of social studies. However, nonclassroom variations, such as the creation of a newspaper club for students (including those with behavioral problems), have been shown to improve students' social studies skills and also improve their ability to read and understand current events and historical material (Haboush & Elias, 1993).

Incorporating Historically Based Readings. Social problem-solving frameworks articulate well with social studies literature at all grade levels (Alexander & Crabtree, 1988). For young readers, books such as *Watch the Stars Come Out* by Riki Levinson (in the Dutton Reading Rainbow Library edition) contain stories that relate to historical periods (in this case, the immigration from Europe to the Land of Liberty). Older readers would enjoy anthologies that focus not only on history but America's diversity, such as *In the Spirit of Peace* (Defense for Children–International), *Goodbye Vietnam* (Knopf), *Growing Up Asian American* (Morrow), and *Visions of America: Personal Narratives from the Promised Land* (Persea Books). A continuing source of information in this area is the magazine *Teaching Tolerance*, published by the Southern Poverty Law Center (www.tolerance.org).

The FIG TESPN framework can be used to help students think more deeply about the issues presented in these and other sources. Consider a series of FIG TESPN-derived questions focused on the topic of emigration:

- How did they feel about leaving their countries?
- What countries were they leaving?
- What problems were going on that made them want to leave?
- What problems would leaving bring about?
- What would have been their goals in leaving or staying?
- What were their options and how did they envision the results of each possibility?
- What plans did they have to make? What kinds of things got in their way at the last minute? How did they overcome the roadblocks?
- Once they arrived, how did they feel? What problems did they encounter at the beginning? What were their first goals?

To help students find fact-based answers to questions posed and check their own views, further reading and research can be assigned. And there are obvious parallels to be drawn in the context of understanding the current diversity of one's classroom, school, or community.

FIG TESPN and 9/11. Although the evidence is only anecdotal, there is reason to believe that schools in which SDM/SPS and related SEL programs already existed were well able to address and respond to the events of

September 11, 2001, at the World Trade Center and the Pentagon in Washington, DC. Teachers were prepared to address the social-emotional needs of students, while the mental health and crisis teams were still being organized and mobilized. FIG TESPN and related problem-solving strategies were used as tools to help children sort through an incredibly complex and charged set of facts and feelings. Perhaps most important, the tools of SDM/SPS were found to be instruments not only of reflection but of action. Children were helped to think through how they would cope with the situation most immediately and then what they could do to help. And the problem-solving/decision-making approach continued to be used regularly in the days afterward to continually enhance children's understanding and channel their need for contribution.

Health and Family Life Education: Making Choices About How to Live

Health educators, to an increasing degree, are identifying sound decision making around health-related behaviors as an overarching instructional goal (Allensworth, 1997). Therefore, students can be taught that use and abuse of alcohol, tobacco, steroids, and other drugs, like all other health-related issues, reflect their SDM/SPS process. Every health behavior has effects on oneself and on others (friends, classmates, parents, siblings, other relatives) that must be carefully separated, specified, and examined. Any given substance—cigarettes, chewing tobacco, beer, wine, hard liquor, pills, steroids, cocaine, crack, heroin, amphetamines, barbiturates, and so on—can be introduced and discussed using FIG TESPN as a framework. One way to open such a discussion is, "How do you feel when (or, would you feel if) someone asks you to try ______?" Different ways of thinking through the problem can be shared with the class or written down; possible consequences and obstacles of trying different solutions and plans can be tried out through guided practice and rehearsal.

A more general way of introducing such discussions with younger children is to ask, "How do you feel about . . . (e.g., cigarettes)?" "What problems do you see for people who smoke?" Then, goals can be set, alternatives to smoking discussed, and plans made. As part of the last step in FIG TESPN, students can be asked to make public commitments about not smoking, an effective public health technique. This can even extend to creating public service ads. FIG TESPN also is useful for discussing the related, delicate problem of what to do when a friend or loved one is involved in some form of substance abuse. This is a volatile issue, especially when a parent is involved.

Across all health-related FIG TESPN applications, key skills to emphasize include guiding oneself through clear goals and envisioning in detail a variety of outcomes or consequences. Conflicts between long-term and short-term goals need exploration.

Creating worksheets that look something like this can link actions, goals, and consequences.

> If my goal is to ___________, then some things that can help me get there and not hurt me or others are:
>
> ____
>
> ____
>
> ____

For each goal, a "menu" or personal workbook can be created that students can review and have available to add to or look over for ideas throughout the year. Many times, teachers find it useful to provide a set of goals that are commonly implicit or hidden reasons that contribute to high-risk health behaviors, such as the following:

- To fit into a group
- To please one's friends
- To relieve "pressure"
- To imitate sports stars

With these goals placed in the format of the workbook, the idea of using risky health behaviors to reach these goals loses some of its plausibility and secrecy.

An SEL-Based Format for Deepening Academic Understanding Through Action-Oriented Projects and Reports

Educators desire children to learn deeply. This requires children to have a sustained focus on a particular topic. In addition, there must be an active component that allows children to construct what they are learning and bring it into their lives. The process of doing projects and reports most commonly leads to deep learning. Key elements for success are the SEL skills needed for preparation, planning, and carrying out the many tasks that are involved. Projects require coordination of cognition, affect, behavior, and motivation; sequences of goal-directed action; and, often, teamwork, persistence, flexibility, and creativity. In the face of such task demands, students often invoke rote procedures geared toward getting finished.

The worksheet in Figure 7.4, Taming Tough Topics (cf. Elias & Clabby, 1989, pp. 157–158), recognizes that while topics usually are determined by the teacher, at times there should be some latitude concerning what aspects of the topics students explore. Further, students usually are channeled toward a standard written report format that many find unengaging. An excursion to an encyclopedia or CD-ROM for some copying can become an appealing way to get an assignment finished fast.

Figure 7.4. Taming Tough Topics outline.

First: Define your problem and goal.

1. What is the topic?
2. What are some questions you would like to answer about the topic, or some things about the topic you would like to learn?

Second: List alternative places to look for information.

1. Write at least five possible places where you can look for information.
   a.____________________
   b.____________________
   c.____________________
   d.____________________
   e.____________________
2. Plan which ones you will try first.
3. If these ideas do not work, whom else can you ask for ideas? Where else can you look for information?

Third: List alternative ways to present the topic.

1. Write at least three ways in which to present the topic. If it is a written report, write three different ways it can be put together.
2. Consider the consequences for each way, choose your best solution, and plan how you will do it.

Fourth: Make a final check, and fix what needs fixing.

1. Does your presentation answer the topic and the questions you asked? Is it clear and neat? Is the spelling correct? Will others enjoy what you have done?

Note: Reprinted with permission from Elias & Clabby, 1989, pp. 157–158.

Typically, teachers review the Taming Tough Topics worksheet with a group or an entire class, brainstorming answers to each question and writing them on the board. This engages students in a shared SDM/SPS process, which continues as they select their own preferences and then carefully plan and check their work before deciding whether their final product is complete.

When given choices and structure, students become more motivated to expend effort. One special education class in Middlesex Borough, New Jersey, used Taming Tough Topics as a framework for studying the topic, Indians of New Jersey. When asked, students indicated they wanted to learn more about what happened to the Indians, the sports they played, even the radio stations they listened to. The teacher accepted the students' questions, as they reflected genuine concerns that would serve to motivate the ensuing learning process. (Of course, this format also provides interesting diagnostic/assessment information to teachers about their students' state of thinking about a particular topic.) They generated places to look for information, including museums, sound filmstrips, and finding people of Indian ancestry. Their presentation formats ranged from a written interview with a Native American to a series of dioramas to a "period play"; older students also have created videos for other topics.

Creating Student Action Groups. The idea of organizing students as problem-solving teams using Taming Tough Topics is complementary to ongoing curricular initiatives, such as terrorism, world peace, school violence, cultural/ethnic stereotyping, prejudice, vandalism, poverty, education, toxic waste, social justice, race relations, future jobs, and the elderly (Crabbe, 1989; Kniep, 1986). It also links well with initiatives in service learning, such as Lions-Quest International's Skills for Action Program (cf. *www.Quest.edu* for the most updated information about this curriculum). The latter is based on a process of organizing service learning experiences around the following activities: preparation (acquire background related to the recipients of the service), action (provide meaningful service with real consequences, based on appropriate social-emotional and academic skills), reflection (keep records of the experience, discuss thoughts and feelings, look at broader perspective), and demonstration (show others what one has done, learned, accomplished through service, perhaps including carrying out projects in the community). This sequence has clear parallels to both Taming Tough Topics and FIG TESPN.

One example of such an application took place in Berkeley Heights, NJ. Sixth-grade students addressed local environmental problems with recycling. Plans they generated led the students to receive community-wide attention and recognition by the state legislature, culminating in a Presidential Environmental Award, complete with a White House ceremony (Johnsen & Bruene-Butler, 1993).

Preparation for Inclusive Education. For students in classes in which children with handicapping conditions will be included, a valuable project is to learn about the conditions of these children. In one situation, when a child diagnosed with autism was going to join a third-grade class, the class used Taming Tough Topics as a way to learn about autism. By the time the student was ready to enter the class, the class was ready for him. They had an understanding of autism and of how best to include their new classmate in activities and respond to him during difficult times (Epstein & Elias, 1996). Relatedly, some special education classes actually turn projects on their own disabilities into presentations to educate other members of the school community.

Exploring How Role Models Attained Their Status. Role models play a substantial part in students' learning. This can be capitalized on by having them write biographies. Taming Tough Topics can be an excellent vehicle for teaching students about the role of hard work, determination, commitment, and other character attributes and skills in the successes of the people they find admirable. Individuals can be selected from a wide range of backgrounds, including political figures, explorers, inventors, scientists, sports and entertainment figures, musical performers—the list is endless. Then, students use Taming Tough Topics to learn more about the person in areas of their interest. Such assignments bring to life the realities of success, as well as issues relating to certain historical periods and to diversity, depending on how a teacher chooses to construct the assignment. The main instructional goal is always kept in focus: building students' thinking abilities and SDM/SPS skills—essential for students to function effectively in a sophisticated, twenty-first century society.

MOVING TOWARD PRE-K TO GRADE 12 SEL IN URBAN SCHOOLS: INITIAL LESSONS LEARNED FROM THE PLAINFIELD PROJECT

Perry London, writing in *Phi Delta Kappan*, articulated the need to integrate social-emotional and academic concerns:

> For the common good, a sane society needs to educate its citizens in both civic virtue and personal adjustment. . . . The schools must become more important agents of character development, whose responsibility goes beyond such matters as dress, grooming, and manners. Their new role must include training for civility and civic virtue, as well as a measure of damage control for personal maladjustment. (London, 1987, p. 667)

As educators look toward the future, the challenge of bringing SDM/SPS and related approaches into urban schools looms large. In New Jersey, the focus is the 30 "Abbott" school districts, the locations where youth are at highest risk for problem behaviors and poor academic outcomes. Of particular concern is children's literacy, as students in urban Abbott districts have poor reading scores. In response, districts place a huge emphasis on improving reading, at times to the exclusion of much else. As the link of SEL and academics has grown stronger, there is a greater imperative for bringing SEL approaches into urban schools as an integral part of larger education reform and improvement of literacy skills. However, while SDM/SPS and related SEL programs have been widely implemented with effectiveness in suburban and rural settings, this has not been true in urban contexts. What follows are some learnings from a project designed to help fill some of our knowledge and practice gaps in this area.

As of this writing, I am in the latter stages of working directly with the Plainfield, NJ, school district as it embarks on a 7-year effort to bring SEL from pre-K to grade 12. These years have focused on bringing an SDM/SPS-based SEL curriculum to the elementary level and piloting infusion of SEL into character and health education at the middle and high school levels. In all cases, it has been necessary to simultaneously align SEL with the district's adoption of whole school reform models, especially (but not exclusively) America's Choice and its highly prescriptive approaches to literacy. This has created difficult conditions in which to engage in bringing in a systematic approach to SEL instruction. Yet, students cannot wait to begin focusing systematically on their SEL until academically oriented school reforms have been successfully implemented. Thus, two significant innovations must occur in tandem, something that will be the rule and not the exception in urban settings.

Reading and Emotion

Reading standards for grade 3 promulgated by the U.S. Department of Education show considerable overlap in the skills required for reading and the skills of SEL/emotional intelligence. This is particularly true in the area of reading comprehension, where impulse control, attention to sequence, focusing, and making careful, informed choices are part of both reading and assessment. Not emphasized, although it should be, is the issue of expanding children's feelings vocabulary, another area in which life and literacy skills converge.

Literacy performance also is related to the boundaries between home and school. Strong emotions in the home context have a profound impact on how and what children learn. Stories that contain common referents—mother, father, sister, brother, home—can evoke surprisingly powerful emotional reactions in young readers. Once this charge is activated, many children lack the skills to put aside their feelings and continue with the task at hand. Observing reading instruction in urban schools, I have seen this happen repeatedly. I have even observed children taking assessments associated with our interventions who were so put off by a question about doing things with their fathers, when they had no contact with their fathers, that they were not able to complete the assessments in a reliable manner.

On the other hand, I also have seen techniques that provide emotional buffers between home and school, serving as mediators and allowing children to differentiate conditions at "home" and conditions at "school." The active ingredients in the Responsive Classroom program, with its Morning Meetings and Greetings (Kriete, 1999), as well as the SDM/SPS Sharing Circle (Elias & Clabby, 1989), serve to create an emotional bridge that allows students to ease their way into the school environment as members of a safe community of learners.

Instruction That Leads to Social-Emotional Skills and Their Application

For SEL skills to become salient to children, their acquisition and use must be clear, visible, and fully integrated into the school day. Instructional processes must be used that ensure that children will access and use SEL skills in reading, in other areas of academic instruction, and in everyday life decisions and contexts, particularly when under stress.

Much is known about how to teach skills and create environments in which those skills will become reinforced and generalized. It matches the instructional design used in the vast majority of empirically supported curriculum-based approaches to SEL. The core is "formal" or "structured" lessons that include these features: (1) identify a skill and create/discuss a rationale for its use in children's lives, (2) model/teach components of the skill and their integration, (3) provide students with kid-tested activities for practice with feedback opportunities, (4) establish *prompts and cues* that refer to the behavioral components rehearsed in the lesson, and (5) ensure recognition/reinforcement for real-world skills application.

In Plainfield, an adaptation of the SDM/SPS curriculum was made around a fictional multiethnic set of characters working in a radio station. These characters, led by "TJ the DJ"—a wheelchair-bound African American teenager who handles the calls—help kids who call in to figure out how to solve their problems, prompting them to build their skills in the process. Vignettes presented in video and story-based formats (to build various types of literacy skills) are followed by a series of SEL lessons designed to explicate, build, and reinforce the skills presented in the stories. Lessons have been developed through grade 5 (Rutgers Social and Emotional Learning Laboratory, 2002) and research studies have confirmed both positive outcomes of the program (Dilworth, Mokrue, & Elias, 2002) and the linkage of social competence skills to academic outcomes in our urban sample (Mitchell, 2003).

However, gains cannot be attributed to the formal lesson structure alone. Built into the instructional plan are external prompts, such as posters, cue cards, visual cues, and signals that are established between a teacher and students or groups of students to serve as reminders to use the skills presented in formal lessons. For example, in Plainfield's program, TJ-related posters remain on the walls of the classroom throughout the school year as prompts for students to use the teamwork and conflict resolution skills that were introduced and practiced in formal lessons. In Martin Luther King School in Piscataway, NJ, a Keep Calm Force of students volunteer their services for a marking period and wear big, bright T-shirts on the playground (over their jackets in winter) with "Keep Calm Force" written in black letters. The goal is to interrupt potentially disruptive situations by showing up at recess quarrels as in vivo posters, thereby prompting emotional regulation and problem-solving thinking among the disputants. (Should this not be sufficient, the force members are trained in ways to get an adult quickly, which also serves many valuable functions.) The experience in Plainfield has illustrated clearly that curriculum-based approaches may be necessary but clearly are not sufficient for SEL skill acquisition with the strength needed to also affect academic functioning. For learning in academic subject areas to proceed effectively in the face of the powerful distractions found so commonly in low socioeconomic urban environments, children need structures and skills that will help them channel their energies and emotions into learning. Unless students are given strategies to regulate their emotions and direct their energies toward learning, it is unlikely that added instructional hours or days will eventuate in corresponding amounts of academic learning. Students need tools to self-monitor and regulate their emotions. Questions such as, "How do you know when you are upset?" and "What will you do in this class when you are distracted by your strong feelings, or when your feelings are about to 'burst,' or when you don't understand what is being taught to you?" must become part of commonplace classroom conversation and climate. Prompts to use skills taught in formal lessons, advisories, or group guidance periods are essential stops along the road to internalization of skills, a road that is traveled over the course of years, not weeks or months.

CONCLUDING THOUGHTS

Curriculum-based lessons provide structured opportunities for skill instruction and practice that then can combine with students' self-monitoring of their own skill development, and ongoing external prompts by adults to promote skill use. These skills also must be integrated into everyday academic instruction if generalization is to be maximized. Clearly, our understanding of what a curriculum or program does and how it works to build "individual" skills has become much more sophisticated. The broader classroom and school context—including parents, bus drivers, community sports coaches, for example—must reinforce the use of skills. The combination of these elements yields positive student outcomes and significant behavior change.

The SDM/SPS approach, like many related approaches identified as exemplary SEL curricula by the Collaborative for Academic, Social, and Emotional Learning (2003; Cohen, 1999; Elias et al., 1997; Payton et al., 2000), builds competence and confidence. A basic set of skills is taught explicitly, but for generalization, it is essential to regularly make applications to social and academic aspects of school learning and life. SDM/SPS skills foster clarity amid many competing influences on a student's heart and mind. They help form the basis of coping skills and strategies that students must possess because one cannot prepare children for every problem they will face and all the ways in which problems might occur.

In that sense, SDM/SPS and related approaches serve as beacons in a fog or as lifelines when one is overboard at sea. This has been amply demonstrated in schools' use of SDM/SPS in response to the tragic events of September 11, 2001, and their aftermath. But like a beacon, the light must shine continuously. And lifelines, once proffered, should not be pulled in. There is never a time when SEL instruction stops and the assumption is made that children have seen enough light or grabbed enough rope so they can navigate themselves to safety. They must be explicitly guided all the way, until high school graduation.

Social Decision Making and Social Problem Solving, and the many related approaches discussed here and elsewhere, provide tools for all educators to decisively confront the task of how, not whether, to enhance children's social-emotional competencies and life skills and how to do so in a way that simultaneously lifts all students' academic potential.

REFERENCES

Alexander, F., & Crabtree, C. (1988). California's new history–social science curriculum promises richness and depth. *Educational Leadership*, *46*, 10–13.

Allensworth, D. (1997). *Schools and health: Our national investment*. Washington, DC: IOM/National Academy Press.

Benard, B., Fafoglia, G., & Perone, J. (1987, February). Knowing what to do—and not to do—reinvigorates drug education. *Association for Supervision and Curriculum Development Curriculum Update*, pp. 1–12.

Bruene-Butler, L., Hampson, J., Elias, M. J., Clabby, J., & Schuyler, T. (1997). The Improving Social Awareness–Social Problem Solving Project. In G. Albee & T. Gullotta (Eds.), *Primary prevention works* (pp. 239–267). Newbury Park, CA: Sage.

Cohen, J. (Ed.). (1999). *Educating minds and hearts: Social emotional learning and the passage into adolescence*. New York: Teachers College Press & Alexandria, VA: Association for Supervision and Curriculum Development.

Collaborative for Academic, Social, and Emotional Learning. (2003). *Safe and sound: An educational leader's guide to evidence-based social and emotional learning programs*. Chicago: Author.

Crabbe, A. (1989). The future problem solving program. *Educational Leadership*, *46*, 27–29.

Dewey, J. (1933). *How we think*. Boston: Heath.

Dilworth, J. E., Mokrue, K., & Elias, M. J. (2002). The efficacy of a video-based teamwork-building series with urban elementary school students: A pilot investigation. *Journal of School Psychology*, *40*(4), 329–346.

Elias, M. J. (Ed.). (1993). *Social decision making and life skills development: Guidelines for middle school educators*. New Brunswick, NJ: Rutgers University Center for Applied Psychology.

Elias, M. J., Bruene-Butler, L., Blum, L, & Schuyler, T. (2000). Voices from the field: Identifying and overcoming roadblocks to carrying out programs in social and emotional learning/emotional intelligence. *Journal of Educational and Psychological Consultation*, *11*(2), 253–272.

Elias, M. J., & Clabby, J. F. (1989). *Social decision making skills: A curriculum guide for the elementary grades*. New Brunswick, NJ: Rutgers University Center for Applied Psychology.

Elias, M. J., & Clabby, J. F. (1992). *Building social problem solving skills: Guidelines from a school-based program*. San Francisco: Jossey-Bass.

Elias, M. J., Friedlander, B. S., & Tobias, S. E. (2001). *Engaging the resistant child through computers: A manual for social and emotional learning*. Portchester, NY: National Professional Resources. (www.nprinc.com)

Elias, M. J., Gara, M. A, Schuyler, T. F, Branden-Muller, L. R., & Sayette, M. A. (1991). The promotion of social competence: Longitudinal study of a preventive school-based program. *American Journal of Orthopsychiatry*, *61*, 409–417.

Elias, M. J., & Tobias, S. E. (1996). *Social problem solving interventions in the schools*. New York: Guilford Press.

Elias, M. J., Zins, J. E., Weissberg, R. P., Frey, K. S., Greenberg, M. T., Haynes, N. M., Kessler, R., Schwab-Stone, M. E., & Shriver, T. P. (1997). *Promoting social and emotional learning: Guidelines for educators*. Alexandria, VA: Association for Supervision and Curriculum Development.

Epstein, T., & Elias, M. J. (1996). To "reach for the stars": How social/affective education can foster truly inclusive environments. *Phi Delta Kappan*, *78*(2), 157–162.

Haboush, K., & Elias, M. J. (1993). The social decision making approach to social studies, citizenship, and critical thinking. In M. J. Elias (Ed.), *Social decision making and life skills development: Guidelines for middle school educators* (pp. 79–104). New Brunswick, NJ: Rutgers University Center for Applied Psychology.

Johnsen, R., & Bruene-Butler, L. (1993). Promoting social decision making skills of middle school students: A school/community/environmental service project. In M. J. Elias (Ed.), *Social decision making and life skills development: Guidelines for middle school educators* (pp. 241–250). New Brunswick, NJ: Rutgers University Center for Applied Psychology.

Kniep, W. (1986). Defining a global education by its content. *Social Education*, *50*, 437–445.

Kriete, R. (1999). *The morning meeting book*. Greenfield, MA: Northeast Foundation for Children.

London, P. (1987). Character education and clinical intervention: A paradigm shift for U.S. schools. *Phi Delta Kappan*, *68*, 667–673.

Mitchell, K. (2003). *Social competence and social support in third grade, minority, low-income, urban school children*. Unpublished dissertation, Rutgers University, New Brunswick, NJ.

Naftel, M., & Elias, M. J. (1995). Building problem solving and decision making skills through literature analysis. *The Middle School Journal*, 26(4), 7–11.

Payton, J. W., Wardlaw, D. M., Graczyk, P. A., Bloodworth, M. R., Tompsett, C. J., & Weissberg, R. P. (2000). Social and emotional learning: A framework for promoting mental health and reducing risk behavior in children and youth. *Journal of School Health*, *70*(5), 179–185.

Rutgers Social and Emotional Learning Laboratory. (2002). *Talking with TJ social-emotional learning curriculum for urban youth*. Piscataway, NJ: Center for Applied Psychology.

Wales, C., Nardi, A., & Stager, R. (1986). Decision making: A new paradigm for education. *Educational Leadership*, *43*, 37–42.

CHAPTER 8

Social Development and Social and Emotional Learning

J. DAVID HAWKINS, BRIAN H. SMITH, AND RICHARD F. CATALANO

This chapter explores the contribution of a social developmental perspective to the understanding and design of social and emotional learning programs, and illustrates this approach through the Seattle Social Development Project (SSDP), a universal preventive intervention delivered in elementary schools.

A social developmental perspective focuses on the importance of creating the conditions that lead youths to develop strong bonds to family, school, and community. The social development model (SDM) suggests that these bonds are created through providing children with opportunities for involvement with prosocial peers and adults, ensuring they have the skills to participate effectively, and recognizing and rewarding them for this involvement. A social developmental perspective suggests that social and emotional learning (SEL) interventions should include elements designed to increase opportunities for children to be involved in prosocial activities and to be effectively rewarded for that participation, in addition to teaching social and emotional competence.

We begin with an overview of social developmental theory and the social development model. Next we discuss why the goals behind social and emotional learning are likely to be more fully realized when skills-training interventions are provided in the context of opportunities and rewards for prosocial involvement. This is followed by examples of effective program components and interventions from elementary through high school that illustrate the implications of the social development model for SEL interventions. We then examine the SSDP, a school-based intervention grounded in the social development model that has durable effects on a wide range of

 ISBN 0-8077-4439-5 (pbk), ISBN 0-8077-4440-9 (cloth).

behaviors. We conclude with a discussion of the implications of these findings for efforts to improve social and emotional competencies in creating positive outcomes for children.

A THEORY OF SOCIAL DEVELOPMENT

A social developmental perspective seeks to integrate social and emotional competencies into theory that explains how children develop along prosocial or antisocial pathways. Our theory of social development, the SDM, integrates propositions from three theories of human behavior and development: social learning (Bandura, 1977; Burgess & Akers, 1966; Krohn, Lanza-Kaduce, Radosevich, & Akers, 1980), social control (Hindelang, 1973; Hirschi, 1969; Kornhouser, 1978), and differential association theories (Cressey, 1953; Matsueda, 1988; Sutherland, 1973).

Both social learning and differential association theories contribute to an understanding of how children learn patterns of behavior. Modeling, reinforcement, and rewards are seen to shape children's skills and choices. The social environment forms the context within which children develop and the nature of that environment guides children either toward or away from prosocial behavior and beliefs. In addition to the direct effects of social learning processes involving the learning of skills through differential reinforcement (Akers, 2000), the model borrows from control theory to assert the importance of social bonds in shaping behavior. The social development model asserts that children develop bonds of attachment to the extent that they consistently experience rewards and recognition for their involvement with individuals, families, and institutions. Bonds of attachment are built through social interaction and involvement that is reinforced.

The degree of social and emotional competence manifested by the child in these interactions and involvements is important to producing reinforcement that leads to bonding. These bonds create an investment in the norms, values, and beliefs held by these groups that has the power to influence behavior. To the extent that an individual is bonded to prosocial others, that person is less likely to violate their expectations by engaging in antisocial behavior. Conversely, bonds to people engaged in antisocial behavior can lead to increased antisocial behavior.

SOCIAL DEVELOPMENT AND SOCIAL-EMOTIONAL LEARNING

Programs to enhance SEL in school settings seek to achieve higher levels of student success while protecting students from barriers to learning such as substance abuse, school failure, delinquency, teen pregnancy, and violence (Adelman & Taylor, 1998). As the social and emotional learning field has developed, it has moved away from short-term, sporadic efforts focused on specific problems and toward comprehensive, multiyear interventions designed to affect a wide range of behavioral and academic outcomes (Elias, 1995; Payton et al., 2000). Fueling this development is a growing recognition that the teaching of social and emotional competence is most effective when it is supported by the larger environment surrounding the child (Elias, 1995; Elias et al., 1997; Payton et al., 2000; William T. Grant Consortium on the School-Based Promotion of Social Competence, 1992; Zins, Elias, Greenberg, & Weissberg, 2000).

According to the social development model, if social and emotional competencies are to lead to social bonding, children must be provided with developmentally appropriate opportunities to use these skills and must be rewarded for exercising them successfully. The creation of opportunities for prosocial interaction and involvement throughout school, community, and family life allows children to use their social and emotional competencies while developing powerful protective attachments to positive social influences. Social and emotional learning confined to a period of classroom skills instruction is stripped of much of its power to shape behavior and create academic and social success. Students' motivation to acquire social and emotional competence is enhanced by an environment that offers opportunities for prosocial involvement and reinforces skillful participation.

The conditions required for developing prosocial attachments specified by the social development model are consistent with the best practice recommendations of SEL researchers. Zins and colleagues (2000) emphasize the importance of integrating classroom-acquired social and emotional competencies into the daily routines of the classroom, school, and extracurricular activities, as well as assisting parents to support SEL at home. According to Elias and colleagues (1997), one of the foundational goals of SEL is to help students develop a sense of belonging or attachment to their school. In the framework developed by the Collaborative to Advance Social and Emotional Learning (Payton et al., 2000), effective social competence promotion includes reinforcement for successful use of these skills throughout a range of social contexts.

Involvement alone is not enough to create attachment to prosocial groups and individuals. A child's participation must be accomplished with sufficient competence to produce reinforcement for making a contribution. Social and emotional competence can have a dramatic effect on the rewards and reinforcements available to students through their involvement in prosocial activities. Providing opportunities for students to take part in classroom, family, or after-school activities will be effective only if students possess the skills required for successful performance. Successful participation, combined with consistent recognition or reinforcement, creates strong prosocial bonds.

That reinforcement is what motivates students to become repeatedly involved in the classroom or other prosocial environments, building a behavioral and attitudinal chain that ultimately predisposes them to prosocial behavior. The social development model posits that it is the combination of opportunities for prosocial involvement, skills for successful participation, and rewards and recognition that works together to create a bond that then can increase positive choices even in the face of negative influences and opportunities.

IMPLICATIONS FOR SCHOOL-BASED INTERVENTIONS

The Elementary Years

During the elementary school years, the classroom setting provides a major opportunity for developing prosocial bonds that lead to a commitment to schooling and academic success. The social development model implies that interventions that improve children's academic success in their early school years can lead to increased bonding to school staff and positive peers.

There are a variety of proven strategies for increasing academic success in elementary school. Effective classroom management increases the amount of time spent on academic tasks, which in turn has been associated with improved achievement and better grades (Brophy & Good, 1986). One effective classroom strategy is proactive classroom management (Evertson, 1985; Kellam & Rebok, 1992). By minimizing disruptions and decreasing negative behavior, this approach increases focused work time while creating more opportunities for positive interactions with peers and teachers, creating the preconditions for increased bonding.

Another classroom strategy to increase student learning consistent with the tenets of the social development model is cooperative learning, which consistently has been found to effectively increase academic success, including with students at risk of failure (Slavin, Karweit, & Wasik, 1994; Johnson & Johnson, this volume). Social competence gives students the tools to succeed in cooperative learning settings. In cooperative learning, students are able to increase their opportunities for building prosocial bonds by gaining rewards for academic achievement created through prosocial interactions. Cooperative learning has been a component in the Child Development Project (Battistich, Schaps, Watson & Solomon, 1996; Schaps, Battistich, & Solomon, this volume) and Success for All (Slavin et al., 1996), which have shown positive effects in improving students' behavior and academic competencies.

Tutoring by adults or by older or same-age peers is an individually focused intervention that provides opportunities for children to develop rewarding prosocial relationships. The academic, social, and emotional benefits children accrue when they receive tutoring have been well documented (Coie & Krehbiel, 1984; Greenwood, Terry, Utley, Montagna, & Walker, 1993; Wasik & Slavin, 1994). In addition, student tutors themselves make academic and attitudinal gains when involved in peer tutoring (Cohen, Kulik, & Kulik, 1982). This strategy provides opportunities for students to build prosocial relationships with their peers, while gaining recognition for social competence and rewards for academic progress. Effective programs that utilize tutoring with elementary students include the Woodrock Youth Development Project (LoSciuto, Freeman, Harrington, Altman, & Lanphear, 1997), the Fast Track Prevention Project (Greenberg, 1998), and Success for All (Slavin et al., 1996).

Late Elementary to Middle School Years

As children move into late elementary and middle school, they are exposed to increased negative behavior modeling from peers, combined with the decrease in prolonged interaction with an adult that accompanies the expanded geographies of middle and high school. Children whose bonding to prosocial peers and adults is weak at the time they leave elementary school are more vulnerable during these transitions. The School Transitional Environment Program (STEP) (Felner & Adan, 1988) is an effective intervention that aptly illustrates several implications of social developmental theory. The STEP intervention was designed explicitly to provide conditions for vulnerable students to establish bonds with peers and school staff as they moved from elementary to middle school and middle to high school. Students were kept together in homerooms and core classes throughout their first year in the larger school, and teachers received training to enhance their academic and social-emotional counseling skills. In these ways, STEP increased students' opportunities for consistent involvement with prosocial adults, while improving their ability to gain recognition for academic success, and limited their exposure to social pressures from older students who may have developed norms more favorable to antisocial behavior. In the study by Felner and Adan (1988), students who received the STEP intervention at the transition from middle to high school were only half as likely to drop out and had significantly higher grades and fewer absences than the control group.

The High School Years

The extent of youths' belief in the moral order and the types of behavioral choices they make during high school are strongly influenced by the bonds they develop to pro- or antisocial adults and peers in elementary and middle school. Nevertheless, it is still possible to have an impact on the type of influences youth experience during this developmental period by providing them with prosocial opportunities and rewards. Programs that utilize youths as leaders and role models are consistent with the social developmental goal of providing opportunities for prosocial involvement and have been shown to provide an effective means of social competence promotion (William T. Grant Consortium on the School-Based Promotion of Social Competence, 1992). Peer tutoring remains a developmentally appropriate strategy at this age and was used successfully in the effective Teen Outreach Program (Allen, Philliber, Herrling, & Kuperminc, 1997).

Another program that provides key social developmental components to high school students is the Quantum Opportunities Program (Hahn, Leavitt, & Aaron, 1994). This intervention specifically sought to create long-term relationships between disadvantaged students and prosocial adults working in the program. Staff worked intensively with the youth in small groups from ninth through twelfth grade, seeking to build bonds through intensive involvement focused on students' academic success, personal and cultural development, and community service. Students remained in the same small group throughout their 4 years in the program, a strategy designed specifically to enhance group cohesion and bonding among students. Fully one-third of the time in the program was spent in activities designed to help youths build a positive connection to their community. Students applied their social and emotional skills to challenges in the real world by participating in community service projects, assisting at public events, and working as volunteers in various community agencies. This program is illustrative of how intervention components can work together to promote the development of prosocial bonds to adults and peers. Students interacted with caring adults over time in prosocial activities focused on their academic skills, social interactions, and community contributions. Graduates of the program were more likely to graduate from high school, more likely to go on to postsecondary education, less likely to drop out of school, more likely to receive an honor or award, and less likely to become teen parents.

SEATTLE SOCIAL DEVELOPMENT PROJECT

The Seattle Social Development Project was a school-based test of a set of interventions based explicitly on the principles of the social development model. The SSDP intervention package was tested in elementary schools whose students overrepresented high-crime neighborhoods. The intervention sought to directly affect the processes hypothesized by the SDM to strengthen children's bonds to school and family. It was hypothesized that training teachers to teach and manage their classrooms in ways that promote greater opportunities for active student involvement and recognition for positive participation in the classroom, training parents to manage their families in ways that increase opportunities and recognition for positive involvement in the family and school, and providing children with training in skills for social interaction, would strengthen children's bonds of commitment to education and attachment to family and school. In turn, stronger bonding to school and family was expected to improve children's academic achievement and to decrease the likelihood that they would engage in behaviors disapproved of by school personnel and family members, including school misbehavior, aggressive and violent behavior, alcohol and other drug abuse, and risky sexual behavior. In short, it was thought that increasing opportunities, skills, and recognition for positive involvement in school and family during the elementary grades would set children on a positive developmental trajectory observable in more positive academic outcomes and fewer health-risk behaviors later in adolescence. The components of the SSDP are shown in Figure 8.1.

Classroom Components of SSDP

The classroom-based aspects of the intervention included two components: (1) a classroom element focused on teacher training, and (2) a child-focused social competence promotion component. To increase students' opportunities for successful involvement, teachers were trained in proactive classroom management in order to minimize disruptions, while discouraging negative and rewarding positive classroom behavior. Prior to the beginning of each year, intervention teachers were taught to give clear expectations and explicit instructions about attendance, classroom procedures, and student behavior, and to maintain control of the classroom while minimizing disruption of classroom activities.

Based on the premise that virtually all students can develop the skills necessary to succeed in the classroom under appropriate instructional conditions, teachers also received training in interactive teaching techniques, with the twofold goal of improving academic success and increasing the amount of rewarding student–teacher involvement. The components of interactive teaching used in this project were assessment, mental set, objectives, input, modeling, checking for understanding, and remediation (Barber, 1981). Finally, to increase students' opportunities for productive involvement, academic achievement, and prosocial interactions with peers, teachers also were trained to use cooperative learning methods.

Students of different abilities were provided the opportunity to work together in small groups as learning partners to master curriculum materials

Figure 8.1. Seattle Social Development Project interventions.

TEACHER TRAINING IN CLASSROOM INSTRUCTION AND MANAGEMENT

Proactive classroom management

Establish consistent classroom expectations and routines at the beginning of the year

Give clear, explicit instructions for behavior

Recognize and reward desirable student behavior and efforts to comply

Use methods that keep minor classroom disruptions from interrupting instruction

Interactive teaching

Assess and activate foundation knowledge before teaching

Teach to explicit learning objectives

Model skills to be learned

Frequently monitor student comprehension as material is presented

Re-teach material when necessary

Cooperative learning

Involve small teams of students of different ability levels and backgrounds as learning partners

Provide recognition to teams for academic improvement of individual members over past performance

CHILD SOCIAL AND EMOTIONAL SKILL DEVELOPMENT

Interpersonal problem-solving skills

Communication

Decision making

Negotiation

Conflict resolution

Refusal skills

Recognize social influences to engage in problem behaviors

Identify consequences of problem behaviors

Generate and suggest alternatives

Invite peer(s) to join in alternatives

(continued)

Figure 8.1 (*cont.*)

PARENT TRAINING

Behavior management skills

Observe and pinpoint desirable and undesirable child behaviors

Teach expectations for behaviors

Provide consistent positive reinforcement for desired behavior

Provide consistent and moderate consequences for undesired behaviors

Academic support skills

Initiate conversation with teachers about children's learning

Help children develop reading and math skills

Create a home environment supportive of learning

Skills to reduce risks for drug use

Establish a family policy on drug use

Practice refusal skills with children

Use self-control skills to reduce family conflict

Create new opportunities in the family for children to contribute and learn

and receive recognition as a team for their group's performance. The cooperative learning techniques used in this intervention were student teams achievement divisions and teams–games–tournaments. These were developed by Slavin (1980).

All of the above approaches were supported by providing training to children in basic social competencies in grade 1. Students in the intervention condition were provided training in interpersonal cognitive problem solving (Shure & Spivack, 1988), a cognitive-based social competence training focused on building communication, decision-making, negotiation, and conflict resolution skills. This program component sought to help students develop the skills needed for successful engagement in the expanded opportunities for classroom involvement being created by their teachers, such as cooperative learning groups. In sixth grade, students received training in refusal skills to help them recognize and resist social influences to engage in problem behaviors and to generate and suggest positive alternatives to stay out of trouble while keeping friends.

Parent Training

The SSDP sought to support students' social development by enhancing the family environment as well. In first and second grades, parents were offered training in child behavior management skills through a seven-session curriculum, "catch 'em being good" (McCarthy & Brown, 1983). This curriculum helps parents improve their ability to monitor their children's behavior, communicate clear expectations to their children, and provide both positive reinforcement for good behavior and moderate negative consequences for undesirable behavior in a consistent and contingent fashion.

In the spring of second grade and again in third grade, parents also were offered a four-session curriculum, "preparing for school success" (Hawkins & Catalano, 1999). This program was designed to improve parent–child involvement and enhance children's school success by improving parents' abilities to provide a positive learning environment at home, help their children develop reading and math skills, communicate effectively with their children's teachers, and support their children's school success. These intervention components were designed to strengthen bonding to family and school by providing children with clear guidelines for behavior consistent with school success, additional skills for successful school participation, and consistent rewards from parents for prosocial involvement in both arenas.

When children in the intervention reached fifth and sixth grades, their parents were offered a five-session curriculum, "preparing for the drug-free years" (Hawkins & Catalano, 2002), to strengthen their skills to reduce their children's risks for drug use. Preparing for the Drug Free Years (PDFY) is found to be effective in helping parents of children aged 9–14 protect their children from substance abuse (Kosterman, Hawkins, Spoth, Haggerty, & Zhu, 1997; Spoth et al., 1998). PDFY seeks to reduce drug abuse and related barriers to learning and increase prosocial bonding by helping parents create opportunities for children to be involved in meaningful ways with their families, set and reinforce clear expectations for their children's behaviors, teach their children to resist negative peer influences, reduce family conflict and control emotions, and practice consistent family management.

SSDP Study Outcomes

Studies of the SSDP intervention show that it created the preconditions for bonding laid out in the SDM, improved bonding to school, and improved academic and behavioral outcomes. A study by Abbott and colleagues (1998) examined data from students in fifth and sixth grades and showed that greater teacher implementation of SSDP-targeted teaching practices increased students' reports of classroom opportunities for involvement, their actual involvement in classroom activities, their perception that their classroom participation was recognized, and their degree of actual bonding to school. Thus, teachers' use of the intervention teaching practices led to changes in students' perceptions of the opportunity and reward structure of the classroom and resulted in stronger bonding to school, as hypothesized.

Low-Income Children

A study of the intervention's effects on low-income children at the end of grade 6 found effects on both preconditions for bonding and bonding itself. Low-income girls in the intervention group reported significantly more classroom and team learning opportunities, more classroom participation, and more bonding and commitment to school than their low-income comparison counterparts.

Low-income boys in the intervention group were significantly more likely to report improved social skills, schoolwork, and commitment to school, and to have better achievement test scores and grades; and were less likely to have antisocial peers than were low-income comparison boys (O'Donnell, Hawkins, Catalano, Abbott, & Day, 1995).

School Bonding

Given the central role of bonding to school in the SDM, it is important to examine the SSDP's long-term impact on school bonding. Hawkins and colleagues (2001) used hierarchical linear modeling to analyze the changes in school bonding from age 13 to age 18. Although overall school bonding declined with age, bonding trajectories appeared to diverge increasingly with age across the intervention groups. The full intervention group had a significantly higher level of bonding to school than the control group at ages 16 and 18, 6 years after the SSDP intervention.

Problem Behaviors

These effects on school bonding were accompanied by both short- and long-term effects of the SSDP intervention on problem behaviors. In a study of early intervention effects, teachers reported that boys involved in the intervention were significantly less aggressive and demonstrated significantly less externalizing behavior than boys in the control group, and that girls in the intervention condition were less self-destructive than were controls (Hawkins, Catalano, Kosterman, Abbott, & Hill, 1999).

Direct effects of the intervention were found on alcohol initiation and on delinquency initiation by fifth grade, with intervention students reporting significantly less initiation for both behaviors than control students. When low-income students were compared in sixth grade, low-income girls in the intervention group reported significantly less cigarette use initiation than their control counterparts as well as fewer opportunities to get marijuana, and low-income boys were reported by their teachers to be less likely to have antisocial peers (O'Donnell et al., 1995).

Positive effects of the SSDP intervention on behavioral outcomes extended through adolescence. Hawkins and colleagues (1999) found a range of significant impacts of this elementary intervention on students at age 18. Participants in the intervention condition showed less school misbehavior and were significantly less likely to report lifetime violence, heavy alcohol use in the past year, lifetime sexual activity, and lifetime multiple sex partners by age 18, compared with controls. The intervention was found to be particularly effective for youth from working- and middle-class families with regard to pregnancy and parenthood. Interactions with gender showed that the intervention had significantly greater effects in preventing boys from engaging in sexual activity.

Academic Performance

A common critique of social and emotional curricula is that they focus time and energy on social and behavioral goals at the expense of academic learning. The assumption behind this view is that academic achievement and social and emotional learning compete in a zero sum game, and schools must choose between the two. The social development model suggests that improved social competence, in an environment rich with opportunities for successful involvement, can enhance bonding and commitment to school and prosocial adults, which can contribute to both improved behavioral outcomes and greater academic success. Long-term results of the SSDP show this to be true.

This program was able to increase school bonding and improve behavioral and health outcomes while simultaneously having a positive impact on academic performance. Abbott and colleagues (1998) used hierarchical linear modeling to show that by fifth and sixth grades students assigned to intervention classrooms had a significant improvement in achievement test scores compared with control classrooms. Low-income intervention boys in sixth grade also were found in another analysis significantly more likely to have better achievement test scores and grades (O'Donnell et al., 1995).

When outcomes were examined for students at age 18, intervention students showed a significant improvement in self-reported achievement ($p = .01$); a near-significant improvement in school-reported grade point average (2.18 for controls vs. 2.42 for intervention participants; $p = .09$); a decreased proportion who had repeated a grade (22.8% of controls vs. 14.1% of intervention participants; $p = .05$); and a nonsignificant reduction in the proportion who had dropped out of school (26.2% vs. 18.9%; $p = .14$). This study also showed that the intervention had particularly strong effects for working- and middle-class students on reduced grade repetition (Hawkins et al., 1999).

CONCLUSION

Social and emotional learning programs in schools can increase academic achievement while reducing antisocial behavior. Social developmental theory has important implications for the design of programs to increase school success through enhancing social and emotional learning. Social and emotional skills training will have limited effectiveness in environments that do not support social development by rewarding the skillful application of social competencies in ways that promote prosocial bonding. Students who perceive opportunities for involvement in prosocial activities, possess the skills for success, and are appropriately rewarded are more likely to develop strong bonds to schooling and to develop values and beliefs that create greater academic achievement and less antisocial behavior.

The Seattle Social Development Project illustrates the central message of this chapter: Social and emotional learning programs do not improve students' behavior at the expense of academics. Rather, when children's social and emotional competence is enhanced in the context of opportunities and recognition for prosocial involvement, both better behavior and academic achievement follow.

NOTES

Work on this chapter was supported by research grants No. 1R24MH56587 and No. 1R24MH56599 from the National Institute of Mental Health, and No. R01DA09679 from the National Institute on Drug Abuse.

For more information on the programs used in the Seattle Social Development Project, contact Channing Bete Company, Inc., One Community Place, South Deerfield, MA 01373, 1-800-477-4776, www.channing-bete.com

REFERENCES

Abbott, R. D., O'Donnell, J., Hawkins, J. D., Hill, K. G., Kosterman, R., & Catalano, R. F. (1998). Changing teaching practices to promote achievement and bonding to school. *American Journal of Orthopsychiatry*, *68*(4), 542–552.

Adelman, H. S., & Taylor, L. T. (1998, July). *How school reform is failing to address barriers to learning*. Center for Mental Health in Schools, UCLA.

Akers, R. L. (2000). *Criminological theories: Introduction, evaluation, and application.* Los Angeles: Roxbury.

Allen, J. P., Philliber, S., Herrling, S., & Kuperminc, G. (1997). Preventing teen pregnancy and academic failure: Experimental evaluation of a developmentally-based approach. *Child Development, 68*, 729–742.

Bandura, A. (1977). *Social learning theory.* Englewood Cliffs, NJ: Prentice-Hall.

Barber, C. (1981). *Methods of instruction: Interactive teaching component III. Trainer's manual.* Columbia, MD: Westinghouse National Issue Center.

Battistich, V., Schaps, E., Watson, M., & Solomon, D. (1996). Prevention effects of the Child Development Project: Early findings from an ongoing multisite demonstration trial. *Journal of Adolescent Research, 11*, 12–35.

Brophy, J., & Good, T. L. (1986). Teacher behavior and student achievement. In M. C. Wittrock (Ed.), *Handbook of research on training* (3rd ed.; pp. 328–375). New York: Macmillan.

Burgess, R., & Akers, R. (1966). A differential association-reinforcement theory of criminal behavior. *Social Problems, 4*, 128–147.

Cohen, P. A., Kulik, J. A., & Kulik, C. C. (1982). Educational outcomes of teaching. *American Educational Research Journal, 19*, 237–248.

Coie, J. D., & Krehbiel, G. (1984). Effects of academic tutoring on the social status of low-achieving, socially rejected children. *Child Development, 55*, 1465–1478.

Cressey, D. (1953). *Other people's money.* New York: Free Press.

Elias, M. (1995). Primary prevention as health and social competence promotion. *The Journal of Primary Prevention, 16*, 5–24.

Elias, M. J., Zins, J. E., Weissberg, R. P., Frey, K. S., Greenberg, M. T., Haynes, N. M., Kessler, R., Schwab-Stone, M. E., & Shriver, T. P. (1997). *Promoting social and emotional learning: Guidelines for educators.* Alexandria, VA: Association for Supervision and Curriculum Development.

Evertson, C. M. (1985). Training teachers in classroom management: An experimental study in secondary school classrooms. *Journal of Educational Research, 79*, 51–58.

Felner, R. D., & Adan, A. M. (1988). The School Transitional Environment Project: An ecological intervention and evaluation. In R. H. Price, E. L. Cowan, R. P. Lorion, & J. Ramos-McKay (Eds.), *Fourteen ounces of prevention: A casebook for practitioners* (pp. 111–122). Washington, DC: American Psychological Association.

Greenberg, M. T. (1998, August). *Testing developmental theory of antisocial behavior with outcomes from the Fast Track Prevention Project.* Paper presented at the annual meeting of the American Psychological Association, Chicago.

Greenwood, C. R., Terry, B., Utley, C. A., Montagna, D., & Walker, D. (1993). Achievement, placement, and services: Middle school benefits of classwide peer tutoring used at the elementary school. *School Psychology Review, 22*, 497–516.

Hahn, A., Leavitt, T., & Aaron, P. (1994). *Evaluation of the Quantum Opportunities Program (QOP). Did the program work? A report on the post secondary outcomes and cost effectiveness of the QOP Program (1989–1993).* Waltham, MA: Brandeis University, Heller Graduate School Center for Human Resources.

Hawkins, J. D., Catalano, R. F. (1999). *Preparing for school success: A parent teaching tool.* South Deerfield, MA: Channing Bete Company, Inc.

Hawkins, J. D., Catalano, R. F. (2002). *Guiding good choices: A program for parents of children ages 9–14.* South Deerfield, MA: Channing Bete Company.

Hawkins, J. D., Catalano, R. F., Kosterman, R., Abbott, R., & Hill, K. G. (1999). Preventing adolescent health-risk behaviors by strengthening protection during childhood. *Archives of Pediatrics and Adolescent Medicine, 153*, 226–234.

Hawkins, J. D., Guo, J., Hill, K. G., Battin-Pearson, S., & Abbott, R. D. (2001). Long term effects of the Seattle Social Development intervention on school bonding trajectories. In Prevention as altering the course of development [Special issue]. *Applied Developmental Science, 5*, 225–236.

Hindelang, M. (1973). Causes of delinquency: A partial replication and extension. *Social Problems, 20*, 471–487.

Hirschi, T. (1969). *Causes of delinquency.* Berkeley: University of California Press.

Kellam, S. G., & Rebok, G. W. (1992). Building developmental and etiological theory through epidemiologically based preventive intervention trials. In J. McCord & R. E. Tremblay (Eds.), *Preventing antisocial behavior* (pp. 162–195). New York: Guilford.

Kornhouser, R. (1978). *Social sources of delinquency: An appraisal of analytic models.* Chicago: University of Chicago Press.

Kosterman, R., Hawkins, J. D., Spoth, R., Haggerty, K. P., & Zhu, K. (1997). Effects of a preventive parent training intervention on observed family interactions: Proximal outcomes from preparing for the drug free Years. *Journal of Community Psychology, 25*, 277–292.

Krohn, M., Lanza-Kaduce, L., Radosevich, M., & Akers, R. (1980, August). *Cessation of alcohol and drug use among adolescents: A social learning model.* Paper presented at the annual meeting of the Society of Social Problems, New York.

LoSciuto, L., Freeman, M. A., Harrington, E., Altman, B., & Lanphear, A. (1997). An outcome evaluation of the Woodrock Youth Development Project. *Journal of Early Adolescence, 17*, 51–66.

Matsueda, R. (1988). The current state of differential association theory. *Crime and Delinquency, 34*, 277–306.

McCarthy, S., & Brown, E. O. (1983). *Catch 'em being good.* Seattle: Center for Law and Justice.

O'Donnell, J., Hawkins, J. D., Catalano, R. F., Abbott, R. D., & Day, L. E. (1995). Preventing school failure, drug use, and delinquency among low-income children: Long-term intervention in elementary schools. *American Journal of Orthopsychiatry, 65*, 87–100.

Payton, J. W., Wardlaw, D. M., Graczyk, P. A., Bloodworth, M. R., Tompsett, C. J., & Weissberg, R. P. (2000). Social and emotional learning: A framework for promoting mental health and reducing risk behavior in children and youth. *Journal of School Health, 70*, 179–185.

Shure, M. B., & Spivack, G. (1988). Interpersonal cognitive problem solving. In R. H. Price, E. L. Cowan, R. P. Lorion, & J. Ramos-McKay (Eds.), *Fourteen ounces of prevention: A casebook for practitioners* (pp. 69–82). Washington, DC: American Psychological Association.

Slavin, R. E. (1980). *Using student team learning*. Baltimore: Johns Hopkins University.

Slavin, R. E., Karweit, N. L., & Wasik, B. A. (Eds.). (1994). *Preventing early school failure: Research, policy, and practice*. Boston: Allyn & Bacon.

Slavin, R. E., Madden, N. A., Dolan, L. J., Wasik, B. A., Ross, S., Smith, L., & Dianda, M. (1996). Success for All: A summary of the research. *Journal of Education for Students Placed at Risk*, *1*, 41–76.

Spoth, R., Redmond, C., Shin, C., Lepper, H., Haggerty, K., & Wall, M. (1998). Risk moderation of proximal parent and child outcomes of a universal family-focused preventive intervention: A test and replication. *American Journal of Orthopsychiatry*, *68*, 565–579.

Sutherland, E. H. (1973). Development of the theory [private paper published posthumously]. In K. Shuessler (Ed.), *Edwin Sutherland on analyzing crime* (pp. 13–29). Chicago: University of Chicago Press.

Wasik, B. A., & Slavin, R. E. (1994). Preventing early reading failure with one-to-one tutoring: A review of five programs. In R. E. Slavin, N. L. Karweit, & B. A. Wasik (Eds.), *Preventing early school failure: Research, policy, and practice* (pp. 143–174). Boston: Allyn & Bacon.

William T. Grant Consortium on the School-Based Promotion of Social Competence. (1992). Drug and alcohol prevention curricula. In J. D. Hawkins & R. F. Catalano (Eds.), *Communities that care: Action for drug abuse prevention* (pp. 129–148). San Francisco: Jossey-Bass.

Zins, J. E., Elias, M. J., Greenberg, M. T., & Weissberg, R. P. (2000). Promoting social and emotional competence in children. In K. M. Minke & G. C. Bear (Eds.), *Preventing school problems—promoting school success: Strategies and programs that work* (pp. 71–99). Bethesda, MD: National Association of School Psychologists.

CHAPTER 9

The Resolving Conflict Creatively Program: A School-Based Social and Emotional Learning Program

JOSHUA L. BROWN, TOM RODERICK, LINDA LANTIERI, AND J. LAWRENCE ABER

The Resolving Conflict Creatively Program (RCCP) is one of the oldest and largest school-based conflict resolution programs in the United States. Beginning in 1994, we planned and implemented a rigorous scientific evaluation of the RCCP, involving over 350 teachers and 11,000 children from 15 public elementary schools in New York City. In this chapter, we describe the RCCP, explain the rationale for and design of the study, summarize the major results related to the program's impact on children's trajectories of social and emotional learning (SEL) and academic achievement, and discuss the implications of these findings for research, practice, and policy.

THE RESOLVING CONFLICT CREATIVELY PROGRAM

At the Patrick Daly School in Brooklyn, teacher Sarah Button is telling her fifth graders a story about a girl named Maria who experiences one put-down after another as she goes through her day. After each put-down, Button tears off a piece of a red paper heart taped to her chest. By the end of the story, the heart lies in pieces on the floor. The students describe the feelings Maria is having and make connections to their own lives. Then Button says, "I'm going to tell the story again, and this time you're going to help Maria by suggesting put-ups instead of put-downs." The children oblige, and Maria has a better day. The lesson concludes with a discussion of how to make the classroom a "put-down-free zone."

Identifying feelings and developing empathy are aspects of a comprehensive effort at the Patrick Daly School to teach young people critical life skills in conflict resolution and intercultural understanding through the Resolving Conflict Creatively Program. The school is one of 400 schools in the country that have implemented the RCCP since its founding in 1985 as a collaboration of Educators for Social Responsibility Metropolitan Area (ESR Metro) and the New York City Board of Education.

The founders of the RCCP are Linda Lantieri, then a curriculum specialist for the Board of Education, and Tom Roderick, executive director of ESR Metro. Since 1985, the RCCP has trained and coached approximately 6,000 teachers in providing instruction in the RCCP curriculum to more than 200,000 children in schools throughout New York City. The RCCP also is being replicated in 12 other diverse school systems around the country. These include: the Anchorage School District in Alaska; the Roosevelt School District in Phoenix; the Vista Unified School District, the West Contra Costa School District, and the Modesto City Schools in California; the Atlanta Public Schools; the New Orleans Public Schools; the Boston Public Schools; the West Orange, South Orange–Maplewood School District, the Kinnelon and Newark School Districts in New Jersey; the Lawrence Public Schools in Long Island, New York; and the Lincoln County School District in Oregon.

The RCCP started with what is still its core component: professional development of teachers to support them in providing regular classroom instruction based on the RCCP curriculum. The professional development includes: (1) a 25-hour course to introduce teachers to the concepts and skills in social and emotional learning, with a focus on conflict resolution and diversity education, and to the RCCP's interactive approach to teaching these skills to children; and (2) regular classroom coaching by staff developers (generally 10 classroom visits for each teacher during the course of the school year).

Regular instruction is designed to mean at least one lesson from the RCCP curriculum each week. The length of the lessons varies from 20 minutes to 1 hour depending on the age of the students. RCCP staff developers also help teachers integrate the ideas and skills of social and emotional learning, into other areas of the curriculum (such as language arts and social studies) and throughout the school day. Over the years, the RCCP has added other components, including peer mediation, training for parents, training for administrators, and training of trainers to build local capacity.

The RCCP teaching guides provide age-appropriate interactive activities designed to develop students' understandings and skills in a wide range of topics related to social and emotional learning, including active listening, assertiveness, handling feelings, negotiation, mediation, celebrating differences, and countering bias.

The RCCP expanded rapidly between 1988 and 1993, fueled by concern about the surge in violence among young people. After several highly publicized juvenile homicides in New York City, violence prevention became a top-priority political issue, and the RCCP became an item in the New York City Board of Education's budget. By 1993 the RCCP was serving approximately 110 schools in New York City. While Roderick and ESR Metro continued to implement the program in New York City in collaboration with the Board of Education, Lantieri left the Board of Education to start the RCCP National Center (under the auspices of ESR National, based in Cambridge, MA) to spread the RCCP to other sites around the country and to advocate for social and emotional learning as an educational "basic."

Two independent evaluations by Metis Associates in 1988 and 1989—both based on teachers' reports—indicated the program was reducing violence and violence-related behavior, and promoting caring and cooperative behavior in classrooms. But ESR Metro felt the need for a more scientifically rigorous evaluation of the RCCP that would be based on a larger sample and on data gathered directly from children, and that would include a comparison of children who were participating in the program with those who were not.

Working together, Dr. J. Lawrence Aber of the National Center for Children in Poverty (NCCP) at Columbia University and ESR Metro secured funding from the federal Centers for Disease Control and the William T. Grant Foundation to plan and launch a major study of the RCCP. (Later, the Kellogg Foundation, the Pinkerton Foundation, the Ford Foundation, and the Surdna Foundation provided additional funding.) The evaluation has included three components: a large-scale child outcome study carried out by NCCP; a teacher perception study based on in-depth interviews with a subset of participating teachers, conducted by the Education Development Center; and a management information system to document levels of and variation in program implementation.

EVALUATION OF THE RCCP

Rationale

This brief history of the RCCP is critical to understanding the rationale and design for the evaluation of the program. The RCCP originally was not a program designed on the basis of scientific theory and research findings. Rather, it was based on an implicit theory of change derived from educational practice. Unlike some interventions, it was not rigorously evaluated for its efficacy in a small number of sites and then broadly replicated, but rather it spread because of the practitioners' convictions and the schools' perceptions of need. The practitioners only later sought the opportunity to systematically examine and evaluate their practice and its impact on children. Thus, the RCCP began as a practice-driven school reform effort rather than a science-driven program intervention. Also, the diversity of students, schools, and communities served by the RCCP led the planning team to select a research design capable of examining the possible differential effects of the RCCP by student, school, and community characteristics.

For all these reasons, RCCP's leaders, in consultation with a small group of scientific advisors convened by the William T. Grant Foundation, decided to mount a large-scale, short-term longitudinal, quasi-experimental evaluation of the RCCP. The design needed to be large-scale to effectively include and study Black, White, and Hispanic students in grades 1 through 6; short-term longitudinal to examine changes over time in children based on varying levels of participation in the RCCP; and quasi-experimental to evaluate the RCCP as it actually was being implemented in the New York City public school system.

Design

Participating in the study were more than 11,000 children, grades 1 through 6, in over 350 classrooms in 15 elementary schools across four school districts in New York City (see Figure 9.1 for sample characteristics). Since the schools in New York City involved with the RCCP at the time of school selection varied in their degree of program implementation, the study was designed to capture this natural variation by initially dividing schools into four groups in varying stages of intervention: beginning stage, integration of some program components, and integration of all program components, as well as nonintervention. To reduce possible confounds, schools in each group were drawn equally from four major school districts within the city. Groups of schools were chosen whose student race/ethnicity, poverty status, and school size were comparable both across district and stage of RCCP evolution, and that were representative of the public elementary school population in New York City.

Over the course of a year of intensive planning, RCCP program leaders and evaluation researchers decided on the most effective way to (1) capture the variation in teacher implementation of and child exposure to the RCCP, and (2) identify and measure the key processes and outcomes that both program theory and developmental theory suggest might be affected by children's participation in the RCCP.

Variation in RCCP Implementation. In order to assess variation in teacher implementation and child exposure to the RCCP, the practitioners and re-

Figure 9.1. Demographic characteristics of sample.

Total *N*, children	11,160
Total *N*, teachers	
Year 1	375
Year 2	371
Mean age (in years)	
Wave 1	8.81
Wave 2	9.13
Wave 3	8.62
Wave 4	8.99
Grade (%)	
Year 1	
Grades 1, 2, and 3	57.30
Grades 4, 5, and 6	42.70
Year 2	
Grades 1, 2, and 3	58.50
Grades 4, 5, and 6	41.50
Gender (%)	
Boys	51.90
Girls	48.10
Race/ethnicity (%)	
Hispanic	41.10
Black	39.60
White	14.50
Other	4.80
School lunch eligibility status (%)	
Free	85.90
Full and reduced price	14.10

Note: Reprinted from "Developmental Trajectories Toward Violence in Middle Childhood: Course, Demographic Differences, and Response to School-Based Intervention," by J. L. Aber, J. L. Brown, and S. M. Jones, 2003, *Developmental Psychology, 39,* p. 327.

search team members developed a management information system (MIS) by which staff developers collected and recorded data in each year of the evaluation on the two core components of RCCP, namely (1) the amount of *staff development* (both initial training and ongoing coaching) a teacher received from an RCCP staff developer, and (2) the number of *lessons* in RCCP a teacher taught to the children in his/her classroom. Based on these MIS data, individual children were assigned scores reflecting the total amount of *lessons* they received from their Year 1 and Year 2 classroom teachers and the total amount of *staff development* received by their Year 1 and Year 2 teachers.

Assessing Impact on Social and Emotional Learning. Data on children's social and emotional learning were collected via child- and teacher-report assessment in both the fall and spring of 2 consecutive school years (1994–1996). Three domains of social and emotional development were assessed that (1) are consistent with the RCCP's intervention goals, and (2) represent aspects of children's thinking, feeling, and behavior associated with the development of aggressive and violent behavior (Coie & Dodge, 1998; Selman, Beardslee, Schultz, Krupa, & Podoresky, 1986; Zelli, Dodge, Lochman, Laird, & Conduct Problems Prevention Research Group, 1999). For a complete description of all child- and teacher-report measures, see Aber, Brown, Chaudry, Jones, and Samples (1996).

The first domain, children's *social-cognitive processes*, includes children's tendency to attribute hostile intent to perceived threats in ambiguous social situations (hostile attribution bias) (Dodge, 1986), and the extent to which aggressive responses are both mentally accessible and perceived as leading to desirable consequences (aggressive and competent interpersonal negotiation strategies) (Dodge, 1986; Lochman & Dodge, 1994). These mental processes have been identified as risk factors for aggressive behavior in young children and adolescents (Dodge, 1986; Dodge, Pettit, McClaskey, & Brown, 1986; Dodge, Price, Bachorowski, & Newman, 1990; Zelli et al., 1999).

The second domain, children's reports of their own *behavioral symptomatology*, focuses on feelings and behaviors—such as conduct problems (e.g., get into a lot of fights) (Greenberg, 1994), depressive symptoms (e.g., feel unhappy a lot) (Greenberg, 1994), and aggressive fantasies (i.e., frequency of aggressive or violent content in daydreams) (Huesmann & Eron, 1986; Rosenfeld, Huesmann, Eron, & Torney-Purta, 1982)—each associated with developmental maladjustment (Huesmann & Eron, 1986; Loeber, 1991; White, Moffitt, Earls, Robins, & Silva, 1990).

The third domain, *teachers' perceptions of children's behavior*, includes teacher-reported aggressive behavior (e.g., threatens or bullies others) (Dodge & Coie, 1987) and prosocial behavior (e.g., is helpful to others) (Conduct

Problems Prevention Research Group, 1991). Given the central role of teachers in school-based interventions, teacher assessments of child behavior serve as face-valid indicators of program impact (Greenberg, Kusché, Cook, & Quamma, 1995; Kellam, Ling, Merisca, Brown, & Ialongo, 1998).

Assessing Impact on Academic Achievement. In addition to assessing the impact of the RCCP on a broad range of key SEL competencies (Payton et al., 2000), we also conducted preliminary analyses examining the direct effects of the RCCP on a fourth domain, children's academic achievement as measured by standardized test performance. Data on children's achievement in mathematics during the Spring 1994, 1995, and 1996 testing periods were obtained from the New York City Board of Education (CTB Macmillan/McGraw-Hill, 1992). The Spring 1994 test was administered to children in grades 2 through 6, while the Spring 1995 and 1996 tests were administered to children in grades 3 through 6.

Taken together, the outcomes assessed within each of the four domains described above (1) target specific SEL competencies identified within the CASEL framework as key indicators of successful program practice (Elias et al., 1997; Payton et al., 2000, Zins, Elias, Greenberg, & Weissberg, 2000), and (2) provide insight into the RCCP's impact on school success defined broadly as a combination of both primary indicators (e.g., test achievement) and secondary indicators (e.g., problem-solving strategies, teacher-reported aggressive behavior) found to be associated with overall academic functioning (Dryfoos, 1990, 1997; Wang, Haertel, & Walberg, 1997; Wentzel, 1991, 1993; Zins, Bloodworth, Weissberg, & Walberg, this volume).

Analytical Framework

Taking advantage of the research study's design (referred to as an accelerated longitudinal design) and a relatively new statistical procedure (hierarchical linear modeling), we first estimated children's unconditional developmental trajectories (rates of growth) from ages 6 to 12.5 (grades 1 to 6) in the domains of social-cognitive processes, behavioral symptomatology, and teachers' perceptions of children's behavior, and from ages 7 to 12.5 (grades 2 to 6) in academic achievement, not controlling for their demographic characteristics or their exposure to the RCCP. Next, we examined how variation in children's exposure to each of the two main RCCP components—RCCP lessons and staff development—affected their rates of growth in each of the four domains, controlling for demographic characteristics.

Earlier results of tests of change in child outcomes during Year 1 identified three key patterns of RCCP implementation, characterized primarily by differences in the relative amount of lessons teachers taught and the amount of staff development they received (see Aber, Jones, Brown, Chaudry, & Samples, 1998). Building on this work, our hypothesis was that children whose teachers implemented more lessons in the RCCP, while receiving only a moderate amount of staff development, would exhibit slower growth in negative outcomes (e.g., hostile attributional bias, aggressive interpersonal negotiation strategies, teacher-reported aggressive behavior) and faster growth in positive outcomes (e.g., competent interpersonal negotiation strategies, prosocial behavior and school achievement) (Aber et al., 1998; Aber, Brown, & Jones, 2003).

While RCCP lessons and staff development were tested formally both as main and interaction effects (for technical explanation, see Aber et al., 2003), findings are presented in this chapter for three combinations of the intervention components selected on the basis of earlier results that identified significant associations between profiles of RCCP intervention and changes in child outcomes from the fall to the spring of the first year of the study: (1) high lessons (children who received greater than the average number of lessons but whose teachers received only average amounts of staff development), (2) low lessons (children who received only a few RCCP lessons and whose teachers received greater than the average amount of staff development, and (3) no RCCP intervention (children who received no lessons and whose teachers received no staff development).

Results

The following is a brief summary of a few of the key results in each of the four domains that are especially relevant to educators.

Social and Emotional Learning. First, not controlling for children's demographic characteristics or their exposure to RCCP intervention, we found three patterns of growth in children's social and emotional competencies from ages 6 to 12.5: (a) increasing rates of growth, or acceleration, for outcomes such as hostile attributional bias, aggressive interpersonal negotiation strategies, and teacher-reported prosocial behavior; (b) steady rates of growth, or linear increases, for outcomes such as conduct problems; and (c) decreasing rates of growth, or deceleration, for outcomes such as competent interpersonal negotiation strategies, depressive symptoms, aggressive fantasies, and teacher-reported aggressive behavior (Aber et al., 2003; see Figure 9.2 for representative examples).

Second, we hypothesized that children whose teachers taught above-average amounts of lessons while receiving only average amounts of staff development across 2 years would exhibit slower growth in negative outcomes such as hostile attributional bias, aggressive interpersonal negotiation

Figure 9.2. Three patterns of unconditional growth in children's social and emotional competencies.

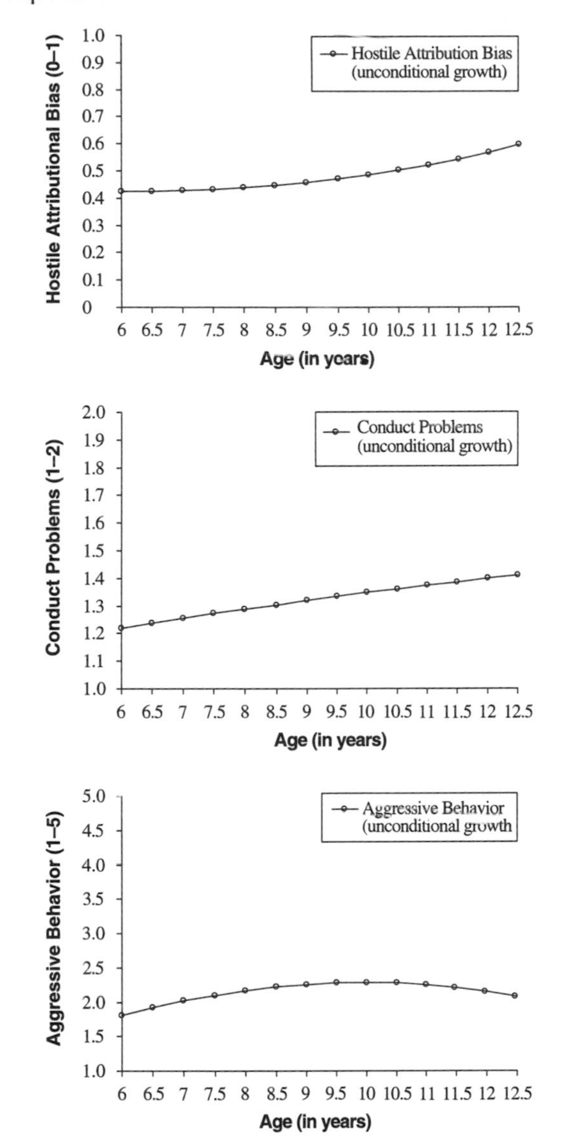

Note: Adapted from "Developmental Trajectories Toward Violence in Middle Childhood: Course, Demographic Differences, and Response to School-Based Intervention," by J. L. Aber, J. L. Brown, and S. M. Jones, 2003, *Developmental Psychology, 39,* p. 333. Copyright © 2003 by the American Psychological Association. Adapted with permission.

strategies, and teacher-reported aggressive behavior, and faster growth in positive outcomes such as teacher-reported prosocial behavior. Results reported by Aber and colleagues (2003) confirmed each of these predictions. Figure 9.3 illustrates the differences in rates of growth in hostile attribution bias for the three key patterns of program exposure described earlier (high lessons, low lessons, no RCCP exposure).

One puzzling finding, but one that is consistent with previous results (Aber et al., 1998), concerns the negative impact of RCCP on children receiving the "low lessons" combination of program exposure (i.e., teachers who received above-average amounts of staff development but taught only a few lessons). Why would children of teachers who taught some lessons and received above-average staff development do worse than children with no RCCP exposure? One set of hypotheses is that "low lessons" teachers were more likely to be experiencing "burnout" in their work, to be having difficulty effectively managing discipline problems in their classrooms, and/or to be manifesting negative attitudes toward their students, and therefore possibly absorbing more of the staff developer's time. Each of these factors, either individually or in combination, could lead principals to perceive a teacher as "needing" the RCCP and to coerce or "recommend" his/her participation. Although RCCP staff developers made efforts to assist these teachers, they ultimately could not mitigate the overall negative impact these teachers were having on children.

Figure 9.3. Hostile attributional bias: Effects of Year 1 and Year 2 lessons and staff development.

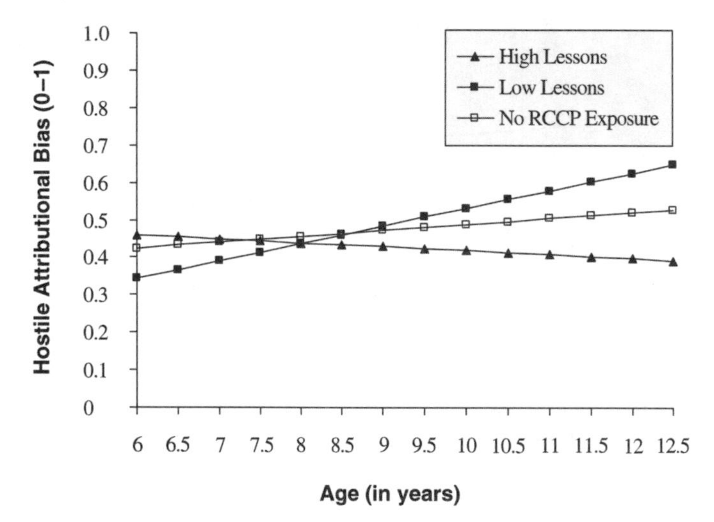

School Achievement. Preliminary analyses suggest that the pattern of children's development in math achievement, not controlling for their demographic characteristics or exposure to RCCP intervention, reflected a steady rate of growth, or linear increase, from a normal curve equivalency score of approximately 43 at age 7 to a score of 56 at age 12.5. Consistent with the stated hypothesis about program impact, children whose teachers taught above-average numbers of lessons but received only average amounts of staff development had the greatest increases in math test performance from age 7 to 12.5 (Brown & Aber, 2003). Figure 9.4 illustrates the differences in linear growth in math achievement for the three patterns of program exposure.

Evaluation Summary

High rates of instruction in the RCCP curriculum across 2 years were significantly related to positive changes in children's academic achievement and social and emotional developmental trajectories, reducing their risk of future school failure, aggression, and violence. Because children were not assigned to teachers based on teacher participation in RCCP (for explanation, see Aber et al., 1998), we can be sure these are unbiased estimates of the effects of exposure to teachers who taught a high number of lessons across the 2 years on children's developmental trajectories. But because the study is quasi-experimental in design (specifically, because teachers decided whether

Figure 9.4. Mathematics achievement: Effects of Year 1 and Year 2 lessons and staff development.

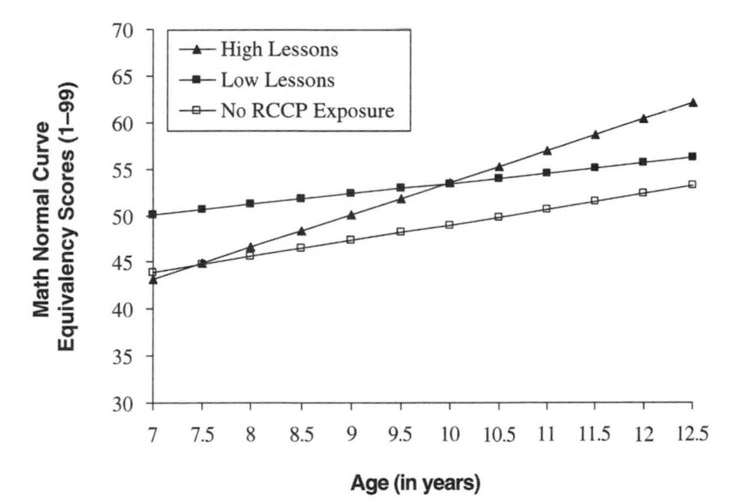

and how much to participate in the RCCP), we cannot be sure whether the observed effects are due to the lessons per se, to unobserved characteristics of teachers who teach a high number of lessons, or to some combination of teacher characteristics and lessons.

IMPLICATIONS AND RECOMMENDATIONS FOR RESEARCH, PRACTICE, AND POLICY

From the outset of our collaboration, we hoped to make contributions through this study to research, practice, and policy. In the following sections we discuss the implications of our work in each of these areas.

Research

Our collaborative work has produced several important advances. We have demonstrated it is possible for practitioners and researchers to identify and operationalize program goals and draw on the tools of the developmental and prevention sciences to design an evaluation of those goals. We have demonstrated that the effects of a large complex program serving a diverse range of students, schools, and communities can be studied using innovative field methods that permit the inclusion of *all* children in a participating school (Aber et al., 1996). Finally, we have shown that the use of an accelerated longitudinal design, coupled with the administration of measures sensitive to developmental change, allows for an examination of the effects of program participation on children's developmental trajectories (Aber et al., 1998, 2003).

With these advances, we have been able to demonstrate that children receiving higher levels of RCCP lessons from their classroom teachers across 2 years benefit most. More specifically, children of "high lessons teachers" exhibit trajectories in the domains of social-cognitive processes, behavioral symptomatology, teachers' perceptions of behavior, and school achievement that reduce the risk of future school failure and aggressive and violent behavior.

Despite these promising findings, there are several important limits to this study. The most important of these derives from the use of a quasi-experimental design. As described earlier, because teachers volunteer for the RCCP and decide how many lessons to teach, this design does not permit us to be certain whether the observed effects on children are due to unmeasured characteristics of the teachers, to RCCP lessons, or to a combination of the two. In this section we refer to children of "high lessons teachers" to emphasize this point.

Consequently, with funding from the Federal Institute of Education Sciences at the U.S. Department of Education and the Centers for Disease Control and Prevention, our researcher-practitioner team now is collaborating in conducting a classic experimental study in which schools are randomly assigned to a control condition or to an intervention condition in which teachers will teach at least 25 lessons per year and in which key teacher characteristics are measured. This experimental design will significantly improve the ability to attribute the *cause* of changes in children's developmental trajectories to the RCCP lessons per se.

But the current design has its advantages too. Having evaluated the program as implemented at scale, we have increased our confidence that the findings from this study can be generalized to how children are affected by other RCCP schools and classrooms. In addition, we evaluated the impact of the program on a broad age range of children from diverse race/ethnic backgrounds in quite different elementary schools and communities, and found the developmental effects of "high lessons teachers" to be robust across child demographic subgroups.

The implications of these findings for practice and policy are great, regardless of whether future research indicates the causal factor to be teacher characteristics, the RCCP lessons, or a combination of the two. If it is the RCCP lessons per se, then the task is to train and support teachers to teach more lessons. If teacher characteristics are the causal factor, the implications for teacher selection and retention are profound. In any case, it is clear that being the student of a "high lessons teacher" promotes social and emotional learning as well as academic development.

In addition to the paramount question of causation, future research should address a number of other unanswered questions: Why do some teachers teach more lessons than others? Can modifications in the program lead to larger effects on children's developmental trajectories? How replicable are these findings in other school systems (especially suburban and rural schools) and in other age groups (junior and senior high school)? How can we examine the role of parents in supporting or detracting from the efforts of school-based SEL programs? Finally, do the short-term changes we have documented in this study have longer-term positive effects on development, especially in the high school years when aggression/violence and school disengagement peak? This last question is the topic of a 6-year, follow-up study of the RCCP mounted in 2002 with funding from the Centers for Disease Control and the National Institute of Mental Health.

Practice and Policy

We base the following discussion of implications for practice and policy on what we consider the most plausible interpretation of our findings: that the positive impact of "high lessons teachers" resulted from a *combination* of teacher characteristics and children's exposure to the RCCP curriculum. This fits with the RCCP's experience in the schools and with the findings of the teacher perception study conducted by the Education Development Center. Participating teachers consistently attributed the positive changes they saw in student behavior to their teaching of the RCCP curriculum, which they reported to be an extremely useful tool. RCCP staff, however, have observed that teachers' attitudes toward students, toward themselves, and toward their profession have a large impact on the effectiveness of the lessons. Teachers who model the skills they are trying to teach are much more effective than those who do not (Mize & Ladd, 1990).

In the interviews, teachers also reflected very favorably on the RCCP's approach to professional development. They enjoyed the introductory training course and found the ideas and skills useful in their personal and professional lives. Many reported that coaching by the staff developer was instrumental in helping them launch the program effectively in their classrooms.

Thus, this study documents that the RCCP reached some teachers and supported them in providing effective instruction in conflict resolution for their students. Further, it suggests that the RCCP's success with those teachers and students was due to the quality of the curriculum, the amount and quality of the training and classroom coaching, and the talent and dedication of the teachers themselves who were able to use these tools to benefit the children in their classrooms.

The key issue was implementation, which varied widely from school to school and classroom to classroom. For example, in one school during 1994–95, teachers taught a total of 136 RCCP lessons. In another school, which received comparable service from RCCP staff, teachers taught a total of 305 lessons. And in schools that were fully implementing the program during 1994–95, 24% of the teachers taught 84% of the lessons. Over the years it has become evident that some schools embrace the RCCP and integrate it into their school culture, while in others it never takes root. Likewise, some teachers enthusiastically teach dozens of lessons, while others who receive comparable service never teach more than one or two.

RCCP practitioners have identified a number of factors that affect the extent and quality of RCCP implementation at a school. They include support from the principal, the quality of the principal's leadership, staff morale, the quality and experience of the faculty, teacher enthusiasm and aptitude for the RCCP, other demands on staff time, the overall priorities of the school system, and the quality of service provided by RCCP trainers and staff developers.

As a large-scale evaluation of a program being implemented widely in the New York City public schools, this study addresses a major challenge facing practitioners of school-based social and emotional learning programs:

how to take programs to scale in the face of competing demands for teachers' time and the financial and organizational constraints of urban public schools. Below are suggestions for practitioners, based on what we have learned through the RCCP.

- *Monitor classroom implementation closely.* One of the great discoveries made in carrying out this study was the usefulness of a management information system. Since the study found that the positive impact on children came from "high lessons teachers," a MIS is a relatively inexpensive way to assess whether the program is thriving in a school. The system needs to track teacher participation in training, school visits by the staff developer, and especially the number and content of the lessons each teacher conducts. Effective monitoring enables program managers to identify weaknesses or inconsistencies in implementation and address them in a timely fashion.
- *Assess a school's organizational readiness before investing resources.* The principal's active support for a program is critical. Other factors include strong support from teachers and the willingness and ability of school staff to make the program a priority. To improve the likelihood that a school is truly ready to embrace the program, the NYC Department of Education office of RCCP is making a 70% yea vote by the faculty a requirement for participation.
- *Provide orientation and training for principals.* Even principals highly committed to the program need guidance in providing effective support. Training for principals includes discussion and clarification of the principal's role in effective implementation of the program, time for sharing experiences and concerns, skills relevant to the principal's role as school leader, and problem solving on issues that arise in implementing the program.
- *Develop implementation strategies that account for differences in teachers' interests and strengths at promoting social and emotional learning.* Although many teachers embrace the RCCP, others are uncomfortable with the curriculum for a variety of reasons: fear of giving up some of their control (Elias & Tobias, 1996); concern that a Pandora's box will open if children are allowed to share feelings and experiences (Elias et al., 1997); and disappointment that the RCCP is not a magic formula for solving discipline problems. Differences in teachers' receptiveness to and skill at using the program warrant attention to both the quantity and quality of program implementation in the classroom. Accepting that not all teachers will respond to the program favorably, the challenge becomes pursuing the most effective ways to include SEL as an integral part of every child's education.

  In the past, the RCCP's strategy has been to train approximately five teachers in a school in Year 1, five more in Year 2, and so on until staff-wide implementation of the curriculum is reached. Unfortunately, the MIS data reveal that of 20–25 teachers who become involved in the RCCP in a school over a period of several years, four or five typically teach the curriculum regularly, while the rest drop away. As a result, some classes receive a lot of RCCP instruction, and others none. RCCP practitioners are working with schools to find creative ways to make RCCP instruction more systematic. One approach being implemented in several schools is to create a position for an RCCP cluster teacher. This experienced RCCP cluster teacher travels from classroom to classroom each day, teaching RCCP lessons to children throughout the school and giving classroom teachers ideas for follow-up.

- *Reform methods of teacher selection and preparation.* Teachers must become able and willing to view the fostering of children's social and emotional development as an integral part of their calling. During the next decade, the United States will hire over 2 million new teachers. This represents an opportunity to train a new generation of educators in the importance of social and emotional learning for reducing violence, promoting social competence, and bolstering academic achievement.
- *Argue that programs to promote social and emotional learning can improve academic achievement.* As a result of the standards movement, schools currently are placing almost exclusive emphasis on improving academic achievement, leaving little time for programs that promote SEL. The RCCP has been addressing this challenge in several ways. One is to share the findings of this research: that children in classes of "high lessons teachers" demonstrate greater academic improvement than children in other classes. Another is to integrate conflict resolution into a core academic subject, which ESR Metro has done recently with its new Reading, Writing, Respect, and Resolution (4Rs) program for grades K–5. It is this evolution of the program that is the current focus of the federally funded experimental study on which the researcher-practitioner team is now collaborating.

  Teachers and schools do not need to choose between academic achievement and social-emotional learning. The two can go hand in hand. The findings from this study are consistent with research on brain functioning suggesting a powerful link between learning and the social, emotional, and behavioral contexts in which it takes place (Blair, 2002; Nummela & Rosengren, 1986; Sylwester, 1995).
- *Establish social and emotional learning as a national priority.* The RCCP has been working at the grassroots level for many years. But without consistent support from education policy makers and political leaders, the broad replication of effective SEL programs will remain limited. Motivating the interest, attention, and support of school board members, superin-

tendents, chancellors, mayors, governors, and presidents is critical for generating the financial resources and political will to have SEL integrated into every child's education.

CONCLUSION

In initiating this major research study of the RCCP, practitioners had one primary goal in mind: to gain insights into the impact of their program as implemented in the New York City public school system on the lives of children and to use those insights to improve practice. Accordingly, the strength of the study is the information it provides about how variation in the implementation of school-based programs influences children's social, emotional, and academic development.

The findings clearly show the potential of the RCCP for improving children's lives. Children whose teachers provided substantial instruction in the RCCP curriculum developed more positively than peers who received less or no instruction. And this was true for children across the board—boys and girls, children of different races/ethnicities, and children of different economic strata.

The study also highlights the challenges of running effective school-based programs. The extent of classroom implementation varied greatly from school to school and from classroom to classroom. Some teachers embraced the program; others resisted it. Factors that appear to affect implementation included the effectiveness of the principal's leadership and the characteristics of individual teachers.

The RCCP's practitioners are modifying their implementation strategies to take into account what has been learned from this study. The RCCP evaluation provides a good example of how researchers and practitioners can work together to gain knowledge and improve practice.

REFERENCES

Aber, J. L., Brown, J. L., Chaudry, N., Jones, S. M., & Samples, F. (1996). The evaluation of the Resolving Conflict Creatively Program: An overview. *American Journal of Preventive Medicine*, *12*(Suppl. 5), 82–90.

Aber, J. L., Brown, J. L., & Jones, S. M. (2003). Developmental trajectories toward violence in middle childhood: Course, demographic differences, and response to school-based intervention. *Developmental Psychology*, *39*(2), 324–348.

Aber, J. L., Jones, S. M., Brown, J. L., Chaudry, N., & Samples, F. (1998). Resolving conflict creatively: Evaluating the developmental effects of a school-based violence prevention program in neighborhood and classroom context. *Developmental Psychopathology*, *10*, 187–213.

Blair, C. (2002). School readiness: Integrating cognition and emotion in a neurobiological conceptualization of children's functioning at school entry. *American Psychologist*, *57*(2), 111–127.

Brown, J. L., & Aber, J. L. (2003). The impact of the Resolving Conflict Creatively Program on elementary school students' math achievement. Unpublished manuscript, Teachers College, Columbia University, New York.

Coie, J. D., & Dodge, K. A. (1998). Aggression and antisocial behavior. In N. Eisenberg (Ed.), *Handbook of child psychology: Vol. 3. Social, emotional, and personality development* (5th ed.; pp. 779–862). New York: Wiley.

Conduct Problems Prevention Research Group. (1991). *Technical report for the Social Competence Scale*. Unpublished manuscript.

CTB Macmillan/McGraw-Hill. (1992). *The California Achievement Tests* (5th Ed.). Monterey, CA: Author.

Dodge, K. A. (1986). A social information processing model of social competence in children. In M. Perlmutter (Ed.), *Minnesota symposium on child psychology* (Vol. 18, pp. 77–125). Hillsdale, NJ: Erlbaum.

Dodge, K. A., & Coie, J. D. (1987). Social information-processing factors in reactive and proactive aggression in children's peer groups. *Journal of Personality and Social Psychology*, *53*, 1146–1158.

Dodge, K. A., Pettit, G. S., McClaskey, C. L., & Brown, M. (1986). Social competence in children. *Monographs of the Society for Research in Child Development*, *51*(2, Serial No. 213).

Dodge, K. A., Price, J. M., Bachorowski, J. A., & Newman, J. P. (1990). Hostile attribution biases in severely aggressive adolescents. *Journal of Abnormal Psychology*, *99*, 385–392.

Dryfoos, J. G. (1990). *Adolescents at risk: Prevalence and prevention*. New York: Oxford University Press.

Dryfoos, J. G. (1997). The prevalence of problem behaviors: Implications for programs. In R. P. Weissberg, T. P. Gullota, R. L. Hampton, B. A. Ryan, & G. R. Adams (Eds.), *Healthy children 2010: Enhancing children's wellness* (pp. 17–46). Thousand Oaks, CA: Sage.

Elias, M. J., & Tobias, S. E. (1996). *Social problem solving interventions in the schools*. New York: Guilford Press.

Elias, M. J., Zins, J. E., Weissberg, R. P., Frey, K. S., Greenberg, M. T., Haynes, N. M., Kessler, R., Schwab-Stone, M. E., & Shriver, T. P. (1997). *Promoting social and emotional learning: Guidelines for educators*. Alexandria, VA: Association for Supervision and Curriculum Development.

Greenberg, M. T. (1994). *Draft manual for the Seattle Personality Inventory–Revised: A self-report measure of child symptomatology*. Unpublished manuscript, University of Washington, Seattle.

Greenberg, M. T., Kusché, C. A., Cook, E. T., & Quamma, J. P. (1995). Promoting emotional competence in school-aged deaf children: The effects of the PATHS curriculum. *Development and Psychopathology*, *7*, 117–136.

Huesmann, L. R., & Eron, L. D. (1986). *Television and the aggressive child: A cross-national comparison*. Hillsdale, NJ: Erlbaum.

Kellam, S. G., Ling, X., Merisca, R., Brown, C. H., & Ialongo, N. (1998). The effect of the level of aggression in the first grade classroom on the course and malleability of aggressive behavior into middle school. *Development and Psychopathology, 10*(2), 165–186.

Lochman, J. E., & Dodge, K. A. (1994). Social-cognitive processes of severely violent, moderately aggressive, and nonaggressive boys. *Journal of Consulting and Clinical Psychology, 62*, 366–374.

Loeber, R. (1991). Antisocial behavior: More enduring than changeable? *Journal of the American Academy of Child and Adolescent Psychiatry, 30*, 393–397.

Mize, J., & Ladd, G. W. (1990). A cognitive-social learning approach to social skill training with low-status preschool children. *Developmental Psychology, 26*(3), 388–397.

Nummela, R., & Rosengren, T. (1986). What's happening in students' brains may redefine teaching. *Educational Leadership, 43*(8), 49–53.

Payton, J. W., Wardlaw, D. M., Graczyk, P. A., Bloodworth, M. R., Tompsett, C. J., & Weissberg, R. P. (2000). Social and emotional learning: A framework for promoting mental health and reducing risk behavior in children and youth. *Journal of School Health, 70*(5), 179–185.

Rosenfeld, E., Huesmann, L. R., Eron, L. D., & Torney-Purta, J. V. (1982). Measuring patterns of fantasy behavior in children. *Journal of Personality and Social Psychology, 42*(2), 347–366.

Selman, R. L., Beardslee, W., Schultz, L. H., Krupa, M., & Podoresky, D. (1986). Assessing adolescent interpersonal negotiation strategies: Toward the integration of structural and functional models. *Developmental Psychology, 22*, 450–459.

Sylwester, R. (1995). *A celebration of neurons: An educator's guide to the human brain.* Alexandria, VA: Association for Supervision and Curriculum Development.

Wang, M. C., Haertel, G. D., & Walberg, H. J. (1997). Learning influences. In H. J. Walberg & G. D. Haertel (Eds.), *Psychology and educational practice* (pp. 199–211). Berkeley: McCutchan.

Wentzel, K. R. (1991). Relations between social competence and academic achievement in early adolescence. *Child Development, 62*, 1066–1078.

Wentzel, K. R. (1993). Does being good make the grade? Social behavior and academic competence in middle school. *Journal of Educational Psychology, 85*, 357–364.

White, J. L., Moffitt, T. E., Earls, F., Robins, L., & Silva, P. A. (1990). How early can we tell? Predictors of childhood conduct disorder and adolescent delinquency. *Criminology, 28*(4), 507–533.

Zelli, A., Dodge, K. A., Lochman, J. E., Laird, R. D., & Conduct Problems Prevention Research Group. (1999). The distinction between beliefs legitimizing aggression and deviant processing of social cues: Testing measurement validity and the hypothesis that biased processing mediates the effects of beliefs on aggression. *Journal of Personality & Social Psychology, 77*(1), 150–166.

Zins, J. E., Elias, M. J., Greenberg, M. T., & Weissberg, R. P. (2000). Promoting social and emotional competence in children. In K. M. Minke & G. C. Bear (Eds.), *Preventing school problems—promoting school success: Strategies and programs that work* (pp. 71–100). Bethesda, MD: National Association of School Psychologists.

CHAPTER 10

The PATHS Curriculum: Theory and Research on Neurocognitive Development and School Success

MARK T. GREENBERG, CAROL A. KUSCHÉ, AND NATHANIEL RIGGS

This chapter examines both a theoretical model as well as empirical findings regarding the relationship between cognitive-academic development and social-emotional development. The model is contextualized in a series of research projects involving the PATHS curriculum. The PATHS (Promoting Alternative THinking Strategies) curriculum is a comprehensive prevention program for elementary school-aged children that is intended primarily to improve both social-emotional functioning and specific neurocognitive functioning, as well as to secondarily affect academic functioning.

We utilize our work over the past 20 years with the PATHS curriculum to illustrate several points. First, educational interventions, including those focused on the promotion of social-emotional learning (SEL), should be grounded in broader, interdisciplinary models of the developing child (Elias et al., 1997). Second, it is optimal for these broader theories to specify the manner in which the development of skills in the child affects the neurocognitive development of the maturing child. Third, in developing and testing the effectiveness of SEL curricula or models, researchers should be examining not only influences on behavioral adaptation and mental health, but also influences on neurocognitive development, personality maturation, and indices of school success. Finally, we call for the development of integrative models and research regarding social-emotional development, developmental neuroscience, behavioral adaptation, and academic success.

Surprisingly, there has been little interest, in the behavioral sciences or in educational research, in the relationship between social-emotional functioning and academic success. The study of child development has long had three streams of research, with only occasional interface: cognitive development, language development, and social-emotional development. The field of social cognition (the child's knowledge, attitudes, and thoughts about oneself, others, and one's behavioral options and their likely consequences) has been one of the few bridges that have attempted to bring cognition to bear on interpersonal behavior (Dodge, 1986). However, the field of social cognition has been accurately critiqued for not placing emotion and emotion regulation as core features of its models (Greenberg & Kusché, 1993; Lemerise & Arsenio, 2000).

In spite of the absence of empirical integration, a number of theoretical models have clearly linked affect, cognition, and behavior, including those of psychoanalytic theory (Freud, 1981; Freud, 1957; Pine, 1985), educational theory (Dewey, 1933), social-cognitive theory (Bandura, 1986), and neurocognitive theories (Luria, 1980; Vygotsky, 1978). At a general level, these theories all support the notion that one's ability to regulate strong emotions (anger, anxiety, sadness) and to have self-awareness will have direct impacts on one's performance, whether social or academic. Further, teaching children how to have better self-control (especially under conditions of strong emotions or high stress), and to more effectively utilize their cognitive and communicative skills, should lead to better interpersonal functioning as well academic performance (Greenberg & Kusché, 1993).

At a general level, these integrative theories are supported by research indicating that individual differences in social-emotional functioning significantly predict later academic achievement and cognitive functioning. These findings suggest not only that positive prosocial skills are valued outcomes, but that these SEL skills can be instrumental in the acquisition of knowledge and in the development of cognitive abilities. Caprara and colleagues (Caprara Barbaranelli, Pastorelli, Bandura, & Zimbardo, 2000) provide robust findings demonstrating that prosocial peer relations in elementary school years have a strong and positive impact on later academic achievement and social preferences during middle school. Similarly, Wentzel (1993) found a positive relationship between sixth- and seventh-grade students' prosocial behavior and grade point average. However, Wentzel also found a significant negative relationship between antisocial behavior and grade point average, whereas Caprara and colleagues found no such relationship. Finally, Feshbach and Feshbach (1987) found that empathy (in girls) was a significant predictor of later reading and spelling achievement. Although these studies indicate that there are causal associations between social-emotional functioning and cognitive and academic achievement, there has been a dearth of research to investigate whether improving children's social-emotional skills also can improve their cognitive functioning.

THE PATHS CURRICULUM

The PATHS curriculum (Kusché & Greenberg, 1994) was developed to fill the need for a comprehensive, developmentally based curriculum intended to promote social and emotional competence and prevent or reduce behavior and emotional problems. From its inception, the goal of PATHS was focused on prevention through the development of essential developmental skills in emotional literacy, positive peer relations, and problem solving. PATHS is designed to be taught by elementary school teachers from grade K through grade 5. Two decades of prior research indicated an increasing emphasis on the need for universal, school-based curricula for the purposes of both promoting emotional competence and decreasing risk factors related to later maladjustment (Zins, Elias, Greenberg, & Weissberg, 2000).

In addition, we believe that the rapid and complex cultural changes of the past few decades, as well as those predicted for the foreseeable future, make emotional and social competence crucial requirements for adaptive and successful functioning of children and for their continuing adaptation as adolescents and adults (Kusché & Greenberg, 2001). Although social and emotional competence had never been considered to be a necessary component of education in the past, we feel that it has become as critical for the basic knowledge repertoire of all children as are reading, writing, and arithmetic (Kusché, Riggs, & Greenberg, 1999). Many teachers acknowledge that they have little background or established strategies to deal with emotional and social competency, so we believe that it is necessary to provide detailed lessons, as well as materials and instruction.

As with many of the more recent school-based preventive interventions, PATHS is designed to be taught by regular classroom teachers (initially with support from project staff) as an integrated component of the regular yearlong curriculum. However, it is important to ensure that children generalize (i.e., apply the skills to new contexts) the use of PATHS skills to the remainder of the day as well as to other contexts. Thus, generalization activities and strategies are incorporated to be used in (and outside) the classroom throughout each school day and materials are included for use with parents.

More recent literature reviews indicate that successful programs have the following characteristics: (1) are of longer duration, (2) synthesize a number of successful approaches, (3) incorporate a developmental model, (4) provide greater focus on the role of emotions and emotional development, (5) provide increased emphasis on generalization techniques, (6) provide ongoing training and support for implementation, and (7) utilize multiple measures and follow-ups for assessing program effectiveness (Payton et al., 2000; Zins, Elias, Greenberg, & Kline Pruett, 2000; Zins, Elias, Greenberg, & Weissberg, 2000).

All seven of these underemphasized, critical factors are incorporated into the PATHS curriculum and research. Furthermore, as PATHS has been utilized with different cohorts and populations over the past 15 years, multiple field tests, with extensive feedback from teachers, have led to expansion and improvement in PATHS over time.

THEORETICAL RATIONALE AND CONCEPTUAL FRAMEWORK

The PATHS program is based on four conceptual models. Aspects of all of these models are integrated into the paradigm that is known popularly as "emotional intelligence."

The ABCD Model

The ABCD (Affective-Behavioral-Cognitive-Dynamic) model incorporates aspects of diverse theories of human development and places primary importance on the *developmental* integration of affect (i.e., emotion, feeling, mood) and emotion language, behavior, and cognitive understanding to promote social and emotional competency. A basic premise is that a child's coping, as reflected in his or her behavior and internal regulation, is a function of emotional awareness, affective-cognitive control, and social-cognitive understanding. Implicit in the ABCD model is the idea that during the maturational process, emotional development precedes most forms of cognition. That is, young children experience and react on an emotional level long before they can verbalize their experiences. As a result, in early life, affective development is an important precursor of other ways of thinking and later needs to be integrated with cognitive and linguistic abilities, which are slower to develop (see Greenberg & Kusché, 1993; Kusché et al., 1999, for elaboration of this model).

The Eco-Behavioral Systems Model

The second conceptual model incorporates an eco-behavioral systems orientation and examines learning primarily at the level of systems change (Weissberg, Caplan, & Sivo, 1989). School-based programs that focus independently on the child or the environment are not as effective as those that simultaneously educate the child and instill positive changes in the ecology of the school. Ecologically oriented programs emphasize not only the teaching of skills, but also the creation of meaningful real-life opportunities to use skills and the establishment of structures to provide reinforcement for effective skill application.

From this perspective, the success of SEL programs clearly depends on their attention to encouraging school environments that are supportive and nurturing. Thus, PATHS promotes both skill building as well as adaptive relationships that aim to improve the child's behavior, the teacher's manner of interacting, the relationship between the teacher and child, and classroom and school-level resources and procedures.

Neurobiology and Brain Organization

When designing PATHS, we paid special attention to developmental models of brain organization. Two of the most relevant concepts we incorporated involve "vertical" control and "horizontal" communication (Kusché & Greenberg, in press).

"Vertical" control refers to higher-order processing and regulation of emotion and actions by the frontal lobes over the limbic system and sensory-motor areas. When we first experience emotional information, it is rapidly perceived and processed in the limbic system in the middle part of the brain. This initial information then is transmitted to the frontal lobes in the neocortex for further interpretation, and subsequently the frontal lobes can transmit messages back to the limbic system to modify our emotion signals and to the sensory-motor cortex to influence potential actions.

For example, if you saw a car coming toward you and you startled and jumped to the side of the road, all of this rapid processing would have occurred primarily in the limbic system without any real conscious awareness on your part. Afterward, however, you would take in and process further information at a cortical level (e.g., the thought, "That car almost hit me!"; the color of the car; the license plate number, etc.). In addition to the initial fear, you probably would start to feel angry, as well as relieved, and you might decide to report the incident to the police. Rapid primary processing is sometimes crucial for survival, but secondary processing in the frontal cortex allows us to integrate information and assists with making appropriate plans for further action.

Early in development (i.e., by the time of toddlerhood), there are few interconnections between the limbic system and the frontal lobes; thus, during the "terrible twos," children frequently hit, bite, or kick "automatically" when they feel angry. As children mature, however, increasing neuronal interconnections evolve between the frontal lobes and the limbic system. This is especially important with regard to the development of self-control, because the frontal cortex becomes increasingly able to regulate impulses from the limbic areas and to modify potential actions. Between the ages of 5 and 7, a major shift occurs in which networks in the frontal areas achieve significant dominance with regard to exerting emotional self-regulation and behavioral self-control.

The "executive" functions of the left and right frontal lobes (including such domains as attention, concentration, frustration tolerance, social problem-solving skills, and self-control) are crucial for both higher-level learning and mature behavior (Kusché & Greenberg, in press). Moreover, these abilities do not develop automatically, but rather must be learned and are heavily influenced by environmental input throughout early childhood.

Thus, in order to promote the development of executive or vertical control with PATHS, we teach children to practice conscious strategies for self-control, including self-talk (i.e., verbal mediation and the Control Signals Poster). For younger children and those with either delayed language or difficulties in behavioral and emotional control, we utilize the "Turtle Technique," which includes a motor-inhibiting response in addition to self-talk.

"Horizontal" communication refers to a phenomenon that results from the asymmetry of information processing in the two halves of the neocortex. The left hemisphere is responsible for processing receptive and expressive language as well as the expression of positive affect. The right hemisphere is specialized for processing both comfortable and uncomfortable receptive affect and uncomfortable expressive affect (Bryden & Ley, 1983).

Nonlinguistic information (such as emotional signals) often is processed without awareness unless we verbally "think" about it. To verbally label our emotional experiences, and thus become consciously aware of them, this information must be transmitted to the left hemisphere. However, the left and right hemispheres can communicate with one another only via the corpus callosum, a "bridge" that horizontally connects the two sides of the brain. Thus, in order to be truly aware of our emotional experiences, we must utilize both the right and left hemispheres.

Based on this theory of *horizontal* communication and control, we hypothesized that verbal identification and labeling of feelings would assist powerfully with managing these feelings and controlling behavior. Thus, PATHS uses Feeling Face cards that include both the facial drawing of each affect (recognition of which is mediated by the right hemisphere) and its printed label (which is mediated by the left). In addition, encouraging children to talk about emotional experiences further strengthens neural integration.

Psychoanalytic Theory

Psychoanalytic theory was central to the development of PATHS, and its incorporation distinguishes PATHS from the vast majority of other social-learning curricula. PATHS has been conceptualized as applied psychoanalytic prevention, which, among other things, includes teaching children the process of joyful discovery, as well as learning how to learn (Kusché, 2002). In our American zeal to promote precocity and acceleration in academic achievement, we sometimes seem to forget that education should be fun, which paradoxically has the effect of turning children off to learning. Thus, special emphasis is placed on respect for the integrity of each child, as well as on the encouragement of active student participation and interaction in the learning process. In other words, this model is not one of teaching *to* children or of shaping children to conform to external adult expectations, but rather one of providing conditions that will result in optimal internalization, integration, personality maturation, and cognitive growth. Children are encouraged to be aware of and to express their emotions, rather than to repress or stifle them, so as to promote developmental integration; and teachers are encouraged to utilize actual classroom experiences as well as children's creative, imaginal processes.

In summary, both psychoanalytic theory and recent findings in neuroscience strongly influenced the development of PATHS. Research strongly suggests that learning experiences in the context of meaningful relationships during childhood influence the development of neural networks between different areas of the brain, which in turn affect self-control and emotional awareness. Thus, we incorporated strategies in PATHS to optimize the nature and quality of teacher–child and peer–peer interactions that are likely to have an impact on brain development as well as learning (Greenberg & Snell, 1997).

Becoming Emotionally Intelligent

As children develop more complex and accurate plans and strategies regarding emotions, these plans have a major influence on their social behavior. For example, the ability to think through problem situations and to anticipate their occurrence is critical for socially competent behavior. However, these "cold" cognitive processes are unlikely to be effectively utilized in real-world conditions (e.g., when one is being teased) unless children can identify what they are feeling and effectively regulate their emotional arousal so that they can think through the problem. Similarly, if children misidentify their own feelings or those of others, they are likely to generate maladaptive solutions to a problem, regardless of their intellectual capacities.

Recently, emotional competency has been subsumed under a new, more popular term, *emotional intelligence* (Goleman, 1995; Mayer & Salovey, 1997), defined as the ability to recognize emotional responses in oneself, other people, and situations, and to use this knowledge in effective ways (e.g., in managing one's own emotional responses, to motivate oneself, and to handle relationships effectively). "Self-awareness—recognizing a feeling *as it happens*—is the keystone of emotional intelligence. . . . The ability to monitor feelings from moment to moment is [also] crucial to psychological insight and self-understanding. An inability to notice our true feelings leaves us at their mercy. People with greater certainty about their feelings are better pilots of their lives" (Goleman, 1995, p. 43; emphasis in original). As such, a central focus of PATHS is to encourage children to discuss feelings and experiences that are personally meaningful in the context of a supportive classroom environment.

Basic Principles of the PATHS Curriculum

The PATHS prevention model contains a number of basic principles that are drawn from the theories previously discussed. First, the school environment is a fundamental ecology and can be a central locus of change. Second, to effect significant changes in children's social and emotional competency, it is necessary to take a holistic approach that includes a focus on affect, behavior, and cognitions. Third, children's ability to understand and discuss emotions is related to their ability to inhibit behavior and utilize effective problem solving in social interactions. Fourth, building protective factors (e.g., promoting reflective thinking, problem solving, and the ability to accurately anticipate and evaluate situations) that decrease maladjustment is important. Promoting these protective factors also contributes to the amelioration of significant underachievement and promotes skills and the prevention of adolescent problem behaviors (e.g., aggression, substance abuse, dangerous risk taking).

BRIEF DESCRIPTION OF THE PATHS INTERVENTION

The PATHS curriculum consists of an Instructional Manual, six volumes of lessons, pictures, photographs, posters, Feeling Faces, and additional materials (see Greenberg & Kusché, 1998a, for more detailed information). PATHS is divided into three major units: (1) the readiness and self-control unit, 12 lessons that focus on readiness skills and development of basic self-control; (2) the feelings and relationships unit, 56 lessons that focus on teaching emotional and interpersonal understanding (i.e., emotional intelligence); and (3) the interpersonal cognitive problem-solving unit, 33 lessons that cover 11 steps for formal interpersonal problem solving. Two further areas of focus in PATHS involve building positive self-esteem and improving peer communications/relations. Rather than having separate units on these topics, relevant lessons are interspersed throughout the three units. There is also a supplementary unit containing 30 lessons, which review and extend PATHS concepts that are covered in the three major units. The PATHS units cover five conceptual domains: self-control, emotional understanding, positive self-esteem, relationships, and interpersonal problem-solving skills. Each of these domains has a variety of subgoals, depending on the particular developmental level and needs of the children receiving instruction.

PATHS is an expansive and flexible program that allows implementation of the 131 lessons over a 5-year period, but it should be noted that any particular lesson can run from one to five or more PATHS sessions, depending on the needs of any specific classroom. Most of the materials that are needed are included in the PATHS curriculum kit, but supplementary materials certainly can be added as desired. A separate volume also is included with PATHS to serve as an instructional manual for teachers. To encourage generalization to the home environment, parent letters and information are provided periodically in the curricular lessons and can be sent home by teachers as desired. "Home activity assignments" also are included for children to do at home to further involve parents (see Greenberg & Kusché, 1998a, for a more extensive discussion of PATHS and issues in implementation).

EVIDENCE OF PROGRAM EFFECTIVENESS: COGNITIVE-ACADEMIC AND BEHAVIORAL FINDINGS

The effects of the PATHS curriculum were investigated in four settings: regular education classrooms, special education classrooms, and intervention project, and a program for deaf children. The regular education and special education studies consisted of two randomized trials, with extensive data collection. The first involved children in grades 2 and 3 in regular education classrooms. The second involved children in grades 1–3 who were classified as special needs due to learning and/or behavioral problems. Schools were randomly assigned to intervention versus control status, and there were no significant differences between the groups on outcome measures at the beginning of the intervention. In both trials, data were collected to assess behavioral, cognitive, and academic domains. Children were initially tested in either the spring or fall prior to the intervention year; they were then assessed again each spring. In order to assess efficiency of problem solving, the Wechsler Intelligence Scale for Children (WISC-R) subtests of Coding and Block Design were utilized. Nonverbal cognitive flexibility was assessed using the Analogies subtest of the Test of Cognitive Skills (TCS). To assess school achievement, the California Achievement Test subtest of

Mathematics Calculation and Reading achievement subtest of Comprehension were used. Additional measures included a child interview of social problem solving, and teacher, parent, and child ratings of behavioral difficulties and emotional distress. We hypothesized that skill generalization from learning PATHS would lead to improvements in neurocognitive skills related to planning and problem solving as well as to improvements in behavior. Samples and methodology for the other two studies are described in the sections "PATHS Curriculum in the Fast Track Project" and "PATHS Curriculum in the Study of Deaf Children."

Study of Regular Education Students

This study examined the effects of the PATHS curriculum in a sample of 200 children in regular education at posttest, 1-year, and 2-year follow-up (87 intervention and 113 comparison students). Students received the intervention in either second or third grade. The sample included 65% Caucasian, 21% African American, and 14% children from other ethnic minority populations (Greenberg & Kusché, 1996, 2003).

Cognitive and Academic Findings. The intervention group showed significant improvements in two areas of problem solving: nonverbal reasoning on the TCS ($p < .01$) and on the Block Design subscale of the WISC-R ($p = .03$). Contrary to our hypothesis, no effects were found for mathematics achievement on the CAT.

At 1-year follow-up, cognitive processing was again assessed and a measure was added to assess cognitive planning skills. Intervention children showed significantly higher scores on the quality of planning ($p < .05$) as well as on Coding and Block Design subtests of the WISC-R ($p < .05$). No differences were found on reading or mathematics achievement.

Social-Cognition and Behavioral Outcomes. At posttest and follow-up, students who received PATHS also showed improvements in social problem-solving skills and emotional understanding compared with the matched controls. Intervention children were significantly less likely to provide aggressive solutions and more likely to endorse prosocial solutions to interpersonal conflicts and dilemmas. At the second (but not the first) period of follow-up, significant differences were found in teacher ratings on subscales of externalizing behavior problems and of total adaptive functioning, with intervention children showing lower externalizing scores and higher social/school functioning. In addition, intervention students self-reported a significantly lower rate of conduct problems and a trend toward lower symptoms of somatization, anxiety, and depression.

Study of Behaviorally At-Risk Children

This study examined the effects of the PATHS curriculum in a sample of 108 behaviorally at-risk students at posttest, 1-year, and 2-year follow-up. These children had been assigned by their schools to special education classes (grades 1–3) prior to their inclusion in this study. Forty-nine children received the intervention and 59 children were comparisons. The sample included 52% Caucasian, 40% African American, and 8% children from other ethnic minority populations (Kam, Greenberg, & Kusché, in press).

Cognitive and Academic Findings. A strong trend for mathematics achievement on the CAT was found that favored the intervention special needs students ($p = .07$). The intervention group also showed trends for higher scores on both the Block Design ($p = .07$) and Coding subscales ($p < .10$) of the WISC-R. No significant effects were hypothesized or found for reading achievement. At follow-up, significant differences were found on the quality of planning skills ($p < .05$) as well as on the Coding subtest of the WISC-R ($p < .05$). No differences at follow-ups one or two were found on reading or mathematics achievement.

Social-Cognitive and Behavioral Findings. At posttest and follow-up, students who received PATHS also showed improvements in social problem-solving skills and emotional understanding compared with the matched controls. As with the regular education sample, special education intervention children were significantly less likely to provide aggressive solutions and more likely to endorse prosocial solutions to interpersonal conflicts and dilemmas. Although no differences were found on teacher ratings of externalizing behavior, significant differences were found for internalizing symptoms. In addition, teachers rated the intervention participants as showing better functioning with regard to frustration tolerance, assertiveness, task orientation, and peer social skills. Teachers also reported significantly more change in the intervention group on the following identified areas of concern: ability to stop and calm down, ability to resolve peer conflicts, ability to identify feelings, ability to identify problems, and empathy for others. There were no significant changes on either activity level or quality of schoolwork. Finally, intervention students reported significantly fewer symptoms of depression.

At follow-up one, intervention students reported a significantly lower rate of conduct problems, depressive symptoms, and somatic complaints. At follow-up two (but not follow-up one), significant differences were found in teacher ratings on subscales of internalizing behavior problems and externalizing behavior problems. This finding was due primarily to worsening of symptomology among the comparison group over time. In addition, intervention students self-reported a significantly lower rate of conduct problems and depression.

PATHS Curriculum in the Fast Track Project

Fast Track was a large, randomized trial of an intervention to reduce serious aggression and conduct problems (Conduct Problems Prevention Research Group, 1992). It was conducted in four American locations (Seattle, WA; Nashville, TN; Durham, NC; rural Pennsylvania), and in each location approximately 14 schools were randomized equally to intervention versus comparison conditions. The central goal of Fast Track was to create both an integrated set of prevention programs that served the entire school population (universal) as well as selective programs targeted to children who were already showing signs of early behavioral and academic difficulties at entrance to first grade (Conduct Problems Prevention Research Group, 2000).

PATHS served as the universal intervention and it was integrated with five other targeted interventions that were designed to be used only with children with early, significant behavior problems. The intervention was conducted in 3 successive years with three cohorts of first graders. There were 198 intervention classrooms and 180 matched comparisons across the three cohorts. These classrooms included approximately 9,000 children.

Although there were substantial differences between school locations in the degree of risk shown, there was considerable risk in the average school. The percentage of children receiving free or reduced price lunch was 55%, and the mean percentage of ethnic minority children attending the schools was 49%. There were no demographic differences between intervention and control schools. Three types of measures were utilized to assess the effects of the PATHS curriculum: (1) peer-sociometric interviews with each child regarding the behavior of each child in the class, (2) teacher ratings of each child's behavior, and (3) ratings of the classroom atmosphere (10-item rating scale on an average of 2 hours per classroom). Analyses were conducted with the classroom as the unit of analysis.

Findings at the end of first grade indicated that in schools in which PATHS was operating, there was improved social adaptation as indexed by more positive reports of the following dimensions as compared with matched comparison schools: lower peer-sociometric ratings of aggression and disruptive behavior, lower teacher ratings of disruptive behavior, and improved classroom atmosphere as assessed by observers (Conduct Problems Prevention Research Group, 1999). No cognitive or academic data were collected in this study.

PATHS Curriculum in the Study of Deaf Children

A trial was conducted with deaf children using the first version of the PATHS curriculum (Greenberg & Kusché, 1993, 1998b). The study employed a waiting-list control design with randomization at the level of the classroom. This trial involved 79 children, all of whom were being educated utilizing Total Communication (e.g., some variant of sign language along with speech).

Cognitive and Academic Findings. Findings on two tests of neurocognitive functioning that have some specificity to the prefrontal area were utilized to assess intervention effects. First, compared with the control children, intervention children showed improved scores on the Mazes subtest of the WISC-R test ($p < .01$) at posttest. Second, a trend ($p = .07$) indicated that intervention children showed fewer errors at posttest on the Matching Familiar Figures Test, which was intended to examine impulsive responding on academic analogue materials. In addition, the Reading section of the Stanford Achievement Test was utilized to measure changes in academic achievement. Compared with the control group, the intervention children showed significantly greater reading improvement on both measures of grade level ($p = .05$) and scale scores ($p < .05$). These findings were replicated in the succeeding year when the waiting-list control group received the PATHS intervention.

Social-Cognitive and Behavioral Findings. Results indicated that the intervention led to significant improvement in students' social problem-solving skills, emotional recognition skills, and teacher- and parent-rated social competence. Teacher ratings of behavior indicated that there were significant improvements in social competence and in frustration tolerance (Greenberg & Kusché, 1998b).

It is interesting to note that the deaf intervention children showed significant improvement in reading comprehension as compared with their matched controls. Although we do not know the process of transfer between these domains, there are at least four possibilities: (1) with less behavioral disruption, children spent more time on-task; (2) improved comprehension was due to the generalization of problem-solving skills to reading; (3) the children actually learned new strategies, developed improved neuronal networks for language, and/or developed new capacities for encoding written information; or (4) the children responded more carefully to the achievement test due to decreased impulsivity. As we do not have sufficient information to test these four hypotheses, it is not clear how the curricular innovation affected these outcomes and it may be that different pathways may account for reading improvements for different children.

Thus, the PATHS curriculum led to improvements in cognitive functioning in deaf children. Moreover, successful completion of the tests of cognitive functioning utilized in the studies of both deaf and hearing children requires at least two underlying core skills: verbal self-direction and planning. Thus, the linkage between language, self-regulation, and cognition appears critical for task performance. These findings fit well with recent research in neuroscience indicating that the areas of cognitive and emotion regulation in the frontal areas are very close together, with central cognitive regulation occurring in the dorsal area of the anterior cyngulate and emotional regulation occurring in the ventral area of the anterior cyngulate (Berger & Posner, 2000). Further, it appears that these two areas are mutually inhibitory; when activity in the emotional area is activated, activity in the cognitive area is reduced, and vice versa (Drevets & Raichle, 1998).

Summary of PATHS Findings Across Studies

There were four clinical trials of PATHS. Two involved special needs students and two involved regular education students. Across these trials, PATHS was shown to improve protective factors (social cognitions, social and emotional competencies) and to reduce behavioral risk (aggression and depression) across a wide variety of elementary school-aged children. These findings clearly indicate that a social-emotional learning model can improve not only social-emotional functioning, but also cognitive abilities that are clearly linked to school success. In addition, these findings show cross-rater validity, as they have been reflected in teacher ratings, self-reports, and child testing/interviewing.

The findings of the first two studies in particular indicate that an intervention that is focused primarily on social and emotional development can have clear and significant effects on cognitive processing abilities that are important for school success and that are maintained after the intervention has been completed. Significant effects were found on cognitive skills that involve cortical integration and flexibility in thinking. In addition, in a very high-risk sample, differences in math achievement favoring the intervention sample were very close to conventional significance. Furthermore, the intervention also led to persistent improvements in classroom behavior as rated by both teachers and students.

Thus, PATHS had a reasonably enduring impact on important cognitive and social aspects of children's development that affect both classroom behavior and long-term school success. Further, it is quite clear that time spent on PATHS in no way reduced "standardized measures" of academic achievement. In both intervention groups, PATHS appeared to improve the efficiency of problem solving on cognitive tasks. This may reflect an improvement in the ability to focus attention, in decreased impulsivity, or, more generally, in the ability to regulate affect during cognitive tasks. The use of more specific neuropsychological measures to assess underlying dimensions of frontal lobe functioning and attentional capacities would be helpful in clarifying the pathways of these gains.

IMPLICATIONS AND DISCUSSION

The Integration of Affect, Cognition, and Performance

The four studies conducted over the past 2 decades indicate that PATHS shows efficacy in improving the social competence and adaptation of a wide variety of children. We believe that a central reason for these findings is that PATHS is well grounded in a broader, interdisciplinary model of the developing child. Our theoretical paradigm regarding the integration of affective, cognitive, and linguistic development; our utilization of theoretical models from modern neuroscience and psychoanalytic thinking; and our conceptualization of the eco-behavioral interactions within the school, all drive the actual activities utilized in the PATHS curriculum model. Further, both our data and recent findings in neuroscience point to the importance of considering social-emotional development as best understood within broader theories that take into account how children's experience affects their neurocognitive development (Luria, 1980).

It should be noted that the measures of neurocognitive development utilized in our studies were relatively primitive. This was due primarily to the fact that there were few validated measures of specific-site, neurocognitive functioning for young school-aged children when we began our research. Thus, in some cases, we utilized measures known to assess prefrontal abilities in adults, but these may not necessarily do so in children. With the advent of improvements in more direct measurement of brain localization and organization, however, it is now possible to better examine how preventive interventions may directly affect brain activity (both structural and functional dimensions), for example, through the use of positron emission tests (PET scans), magnetic resonance imaging (MRI), or evoked response potential (ERP) testing.

The Importance of Effective Implementation

All of the results presented in this chapter focus on "intent to treat" models where intervention children are compared with comparison children, irrespective of the quality and dosage of PATHS they have received or other factors that may have influenced the quality of implementation (Domitrovich & Greenberg, 2000; Zins, Elias, Greenberg, & Kline, 2000). However, we previously have shown that the quality of the teacher's implementation of PATHS *does* significantly affect both students' reduction in aggressive behavior and their improvements in competency (Conduct Problems Prevention Research Group, 1999). Recently, we also have shown that in addition to the quality of the teacher's implementation, the quality of the principal's instructional leadership plays a significant role in the degree of behavior change shown by students (Kam, Greenberg, & Wells, 2003). There is clearly a need for much greater emphasis on what factors in training and school climate most influence the quality of implementation in social-emotional learning programs (Greenberg, Domitrovich, Graczyk, & Zins, 2001).

CONCLUSION

In summary, in developing and testing the effectiveness of social-emotional curricula or models, researchers should examine not only influences on behavioral adaptation, but also effects on neurocognitive development, personality maturation, emotional health, environmental domains (e.g., the classroom and the school), and other indices of school success. We emphasize the need for the development of integrative models, as well as multidimensional research, to incorporate all of the important factors that contribute to healthy development and adaptive functioning, during childhood as well as in adulthood. There is little doubt that well-developed SEL programs in schools can provide beneficial results for many individuals, if they are implemented in a thoughtful, caring, and integrated manner.

REFERENCES

Bandura, A. (1986). *Social foundations of thought and action.* Englewood Cliffs, NJ: Prentice-Hall.

Berger, A., & Posner, M. I. (2000). Pathologies of brain attentional networks. *Neuroscience & Biobehavioral Reviews, 24,* 3–5.

Bryden, M. P., & Ley, R. G. (1983). Right-hemispheric involvement in the perception and expression of emotion in normal humans. In K. M. Heilman & P. Satz (Eds.), *Neuropsychology of human emotion* (pp. 6–44). New York: Guilford Press.

Caprara, G. V., Barbaranelli, C., Pastorelli, C., Bandura, A,. & Zimbardo, P. G. (2000). Prosocial foundations of children's academic achievement. *Psychological Science, 11,* 302–306.

Conduct Problems Prevention Research Group. (1992). A developmental and clinical model for the prevention of conduct disorders: The FAST Track Program. *Development and Psychopathology*, *4*, 509–527.

Conduct Problems Prevention Research Group. (2000). Merging universal and indicated prevention programs: The Fast Track Model. *Addictive Behaviors*, *25*, 913–928.

Dewey, J. (1933). *How we think*. Boston: Heath.

Dodge, K. A. (1986). A social information processing model of social competence in children. In M. Perlmutter (Ed.), Cognitive perspectives on children's social behavior and behavioral development. *The Minnesota Symposium on Child Psychology*, (Vol. 18, pp. 77–125). Hillsdale, NJ: Erlbaum.

Domitrovich, C., & Greenberg, M. T. (2000). The study of implementation: Current findings from effective programs for school-aged children. *Journal of Educational and Psychological Consultation*, *11*, 193–221.

Drevets, W. C., & Raichle, M. E. (1998). Reciprocal suppression of regional cerebral blood flow during emotional versus higher cognitive processes: Implications for interactions between emotion and cognition. *Cognition & Emotion*, *12*, 353–385

Elias, M. J., Zins, J. E., Weissberg, R. P., Frey, K. S., Greenberg, M. T., Haynes, N. M., Kessler, R., Schwab-Stone, M. E., & Shriver, T. P. (1997). *Promoting social and emotional learning; Guidelines for educators*. Alexandria, VA: Association for Supervision and Curriculum Development.

Feshbach, N. D., & Feshbach, S. (1987). Affective processes and academic achievement. *Child Development*, *58*, 1335–1347.

Freud, A. (1981). *The writings of Anna Freud: Vol. 8. Psychoanalytic psychology of normal development*. New York: International Universities Press.

Freud, S. (1957). The unconscious. In J. Strachey (Ed. and Trans.), *The standard edition of the complete psychological works of Sigmund Freud* (Vol. 14, pp. 159–215). London: Hogarth Press. (Original work published 1915)

Goleman, D. (1995). *Emotional intelligence*. New York: Bantam Books.

Greenberg, M. T., Domitrovich, C., Graczyk, P. A., & Zins, J. E. (2001). *The study of implementation in school-based prevention research: Theory, research and practice*. Report to the Center for Mental Health Services (SAMHSA), Washington, DC.

Greenberg, M. T., & Kusché, C. A. (1993). *Promoting social and emotional development in deaf children: The PATHS Project*. Seattle: University of Washington Press.

Greenberg, M. T., & Kusché, C. A. (1996). *The PATHS Project: Preventive intervention for children*. Final Report to the National Institute of Mental Health, Grant No. R01MH42131.

Greenberg, M. T., & Kusché, C. A. (1998a). *Blueprints for violence prevention: The PATHS Project* (Vol. 10). Boulder: Institute of Behavioral Science, Regents of the University of Colorado.

Greenberg, M. T., & Kusché, C. A. (1998b). Preventive intervention for school-aged deaf children: The PATHS curriculum. *Journal of Deaf Studies and Deaf Education*, *3*, 49–63.

Greenberg, M. T., & Kusché, C. A. (2003). *Promoting social competence and preventing maladjustment in school-aged children: The direct and mediated effects of the PATHS curriculum.* Manuscript submitted for publication.

Greenberg, M. T., & Snell, J. (1997). The neurological basis of emotional development. In P. Salovey & D. J. Sluyter (Eds.), *Emotional development and emotional intelligence: Educational implications* (pp. 93–119). New York: Basic Books.

Kam, C.-M., Greenberg, M. T., & Kusché, C. A. (in press). *Promoting social competence and preventing maladjustment in special needs children: The effects of the PATHS curriculum. Journal of Emotional and Behavioral Disorders.*

Kam, C.-M., Greenberg, M. T., & Wells, C. T. (2003). Examining the role of implementation quality in school-based prevention using the PATHS curriculum. *Prevention Science*, 4, 55–63.

Kusché, C. A. (2002). Psychoanalysis as prevention: Using PATHS to enhance ego development, object relationships, and cortical integration in children. *Journal of Applied Psychoanalytic Studies*, 4, 283–301.

Kusché, C. A., & Greenberg, M. T. (1994). *The PATHS curriculum.* Seattle: Developmental Research and Programs.

Kusché, C. A., & Greenberg, M. T. (2001). PATHS in your classroom: Promoting emotional literacy and alleviating emotional distress. In J. Cohen (Ed.), *Social emotional learning and the elementary school child: A guide for educators* (pp. 140–161). New York: Teachers College Press.

Kusché, C. A., & Greenberg, M. T. (in press). Brain development and social-emotional learning: An introduction for educators. In M. Elias, H. Arnold, & C. Steiger (Eds.), *Educating students for academic success, high EQ, and sound character: A best practices casebook.* New York: Corwin Press.

Kusché, C. A., Riggs, R. S., & Greenberg, M. T. (1999). Using analytic knowledge to teach emotional literacy. *The American Psychoanalyst*, *33*, 20–21.

Lemerise, E. A., & Arsenio, W. F. (2000). An integrated model of emotion processes and cognition in social information processing. *Child Development*, *71*, 107–118.

Luria, A. R. (1980). *Higher cortical functions in man.* New York: Basic Books.

Mayer, J. D., & Salovey, P. (1997). What is emotional intelligence?. In P. Salovey & D. J. Sluyter (Eds.), *Emotional development and emotional Intelligence: Educational implications* (pp. 3–31). New York: Basic Books.

Payton, J. W., Wardlaw, D. M., Gracyzk, P. A., Bloodworth, M. R., Tompsett, C. J., & Weissberg, R. P. (2000). Social and emotional learning: A framework for promoting mental health and reducing risk behavior in children and youth. *Journal of School Health*, *70*(5), 179–185.

Pine, F. (1985). *Developmental theory and clinical process.* New Haven: Yale University Press.

Vygotsky, L. S. (1978). *Mind in society.* Cambridge, MA: Harvard University Press.

Weissberg, R. P., Caplan, M. Z., & Sivo, P. J. (1989). A new conceptual framework for establishing school-based social competence promotion programs. In L. A. Bond & B. E. Compas (Eds.), *Primary prevention and promotion in the schools* (pp. 255–296). Newbury Park, CA: Sage.

Wentzel, K. R. (1993). Does being good make the grade? Social behavior and academic competence in middle school. *Journal of Educational Psychology, 85,* 357–364.

Zins, J. E., Elias, M. J., Greenberg, M. T., & Kline Pruett, M. (2000). Issues in the implementation of prevention programs [Special issue]. *Journal of Educational and Psychological Consultation, 11*(1), 1–2.

Zins, J. E., Elias, M. J., Greenberg, M. T., & Weissberg, R. P. (2000). Promoting social and emotional competence in children. In K. M. Minke & G. C. Bear (Eds.), *Preventing school problems—promoting school success: Strategies and programs that work* (pp. 71–100). Bethesda, MD: National Association of School Psychologists.

CHAPTER 11

Community in School as Key to Student Growth: Findings from the Child Development Project

ERIC SCHAPS, VICTOR BATTISTICH, AND DANIEL SOLOMON

Nearly 20 years ago, we at the Developmental Studies Center (DSC) began working intensively on a comprehensive elementary school improvement program aimed at enhancing students' academic, ethical, emotional, and social learning. This program is called the Child Development Project (CDP). In the course of this work, we found that helping schools to become a "caring community of learners" proved pivotal for enabling the full range of students to progress along these several dimensions of development (Schaps, Battistich, & Solomon, 1997). Along with other researchers (e.g., Bryk & Driscoll, 1988; Elias et al., 1997; Hallinger & Murphy, 1986; Hawkins & Weiss, 1985; Higgins, Power, & Kohlberg, 1984; Osterman, 2000), we now believe that this priority on community building in school provides a powerful focus for improving educational practice, and especially for practice aimed at helping children to become caring, principled, and intrapersonally and interpersonally effective. But we also have come to believe, based on evaluation data gathered over time and described here, that a singular focus on community building may *not* be sufficient for promoting academic achievement, and that it must be combined and integrated with two other school improvement priorities—high expectations and challenging, engaging opportunities to learn—in order to promote achievement, especially among low-income students.

In this chapter we first focus on the importance of strengthening students' sense of community in school and on how this has been accomplished in the CDP program. Then we report the findings from a series of evaluation studies of CDP. We conclude with a discussion of the relationship of community building to academic achievement.

 ISBN 0-8077-4439-5 (pbk), ISBN 0-8077-4440-9 (cloth).

A CARING COMMUNITY OF LEARNERS

Our phrase "caring community of learners" is only one of several terms used in the literature to refer to the prevalence of positive relationships, norms, and values within a school. Other researchers and theoreticians use such terms as "connectedness" (Resnick et al., 1997), "social bonding" (Hawkins & Weiss, 1985), and "social climate" (Comer & Haynes, 1999). Just as the terms themselves vary, so do their definitions and emphases. Perhaps the most critical dimension on which these conceptualizations vary, is the degree to which they refer to observable characteristics of the school's social environment or, alternatively, refer to students' subjective sense of positive connections and roles in the school. Despite these differences in conceptualization, researchers consistently have found that building students' sense of connection to and engagement in school has important benefits for a range of socioemotional outcomes, including, for example, avoidance of problem behaviors such as drug use (Hawkins, Smith, & Catalano this volume), student misconduct and rebellious behavior in school (Gottfredson, Gottfredson, & Hybl, 1993), social skills and assertive and cooperative behavior (Elliot, 1995), and violence and sexual activity in later life (Hawkins, Catalano, Kosterman, Abbot, & Hill, 1999).

For us, a "caring community of learners" exists when the full range of students experience themselves as valued, contributing, influential members of a classroom or school that they perceive as dedicated to the welfare and growth of all its members. We regard the key components of a caring community of learners as the following:

- *Respectful, supportive relationships among students, teachers, and parents.* Stable, supportive relationships with peers and adults affirm students, inspire their effort and initiative, and enable them to ask questions, venture opinions, make mistakes, reflect on experience, tackle new subjects, and otherwise do all the risk taking that true learning entails. Supportive, mutually respectful relationships between parents and school enable communication and coordination on behalf of each student's interests, and make it easier for parents to take active roles in the school and in their children's education.
- *Frequent opportunities to help and collaborate with others.* We all learn by doing. We learn to do things well by doing them often; things done often can become second nature. So it follows that students should have regular opportunities to collaborate with or help others (whether in academic groupwork, community service, tutoring, or any other realm)—and they should be encouraged to reflect on the ins and outs and ups and downs of these interactions. They need to learn how to work well with others, and for the welfare *of* others, and why it feels good to do so.

- *Frequent opportunities for autonomy and influence.* People are invested in the choices they make for themselves; they feel little personal responsibility for the choices made for them. When students have a genuine say in the life of the classroom—class norms, study topics, conflict resolution, field trip logistics, and so on—then they are committed to the decisions they have been trusted to make and feel responsible for the community they have helped shape.
- *Emphasis on common purposes and ideals.* Part of being a community is having a sense of common purpose; part of feeling included and valued in a community is living by that common purpose. When a school community deliberately emphasizes the importance of learning *and* the importance of behaving humanely and responsibly, students have standards of competence and character to live and learn by.

We advocate that these four principles be deliberately factored into educators' planning and decision making about school policy, pedagogy, structure, and content. We believe that these principles need to be embodied in both the explicit and hidden curricula of the school and in the myriad choices that every member of the school staff makes every day.

HOW A SENSE OF COMMUNITY INFLUENCES CHILDREN'S DEVELOPMENT

We postulate along with Connell (1990) and Deci and Ryan (1985) that students have basic psychological needs for belonging, autonomy, and competence, and that their level of engagement with school, or disengagement from it, depends on whether these needs are fulfilled there. When these needs are met through the creation of a school community, students are likely to become affectively bonded with and committed to the school, and therefore inclined to identify with and behave in accordance with its expressed goals and values (Solomon, Battistich, Watson, Schaps, & Lewis, 2000).

It should be noted, however, that others have taken a more critical view of the relative importance of a sense of community, arguing that high expectations ("academic press") play a greater role in boosting academic achievement (e.g., Bryk, Lee, & Holland, 1993; Shouse, 1996; Schaps & Lewis, 1999; Hawkins, Smith, & Catalano, this volume). Most recently, Lee and Smith (1999) found that without an emphasis on academic press, fostering community in school is inadequate for producing achievement gains among low-income, urban students. Lee and Smith concluded, "Only in schools with an organizational thrust toward serious academics does social support (i.e., sense of community) actually influence learning" (p. 937).

We believe that various experiences associated with participation in a caring school community help students not only to satisfy their basic psychological needs, but also to develop their intellectual and sociomoral capacities, including their knowledge of academic subject matter, their reasoning and thinking skills, their conceptual understanding, their empathy with others, their social skills and social understanding, and their understanding of the values of the community. The development of these intellectual and sociomoral capacities also, in turn, contributes to the satisfaction of basic psychological needs, particularly students' sense of efficacy.

According to this model (see Figure 11.1), when students' basic needs are met, they become attached to the school community. This attachment, combined with growing intellectual and sociomoral capacities (including understanding of the community's values), leads students to feel personally committed to the values endorsed in the school. In CDP schools, these include the values of learning, self-motivation, and self-control, as well as ethical and democratic values. Students who develop commitments to these values tend to behave in ways consistent with them. Such behaviors, in turn, help to solidify students' commitments to the community's values, help them to further develop their capacities, and help to reinforce the school conditions that, in combination, constitute a caring community of learners.

Finally, according to the model, children who develop long-term commitments to these values are likely to become adults with constructive intellectual and ethical dispositions. They are likely to become thoughtful and reflective, to make rational and informed decisions, to be self-directing, to maintain and act on democratic values, to be concerned for and respectful of others, to avoid courses of action that are harmful to themselves or others, and to maintain high standards of ethical conduct. These adult dispositions also are influenced by the behavior patterns developed by children, largely indirectly (through the effects of that behavior on solidifying the commitments to community values) but also, to a degree, directly.

THE CDP PROGRAM

The CDP school improvement program focuses on making comprehensive change in the classroom, in the school at large, and in the links between home and school. Until recently revised and streamlined, the CDP program included the following elements:

- A reading and language arts curriculum based on high-quality children's literature drawn from many cultures, designed to help children see that reading can be both fun and informative, encourage them to explore the

Figure 11.1. Model of program effects.

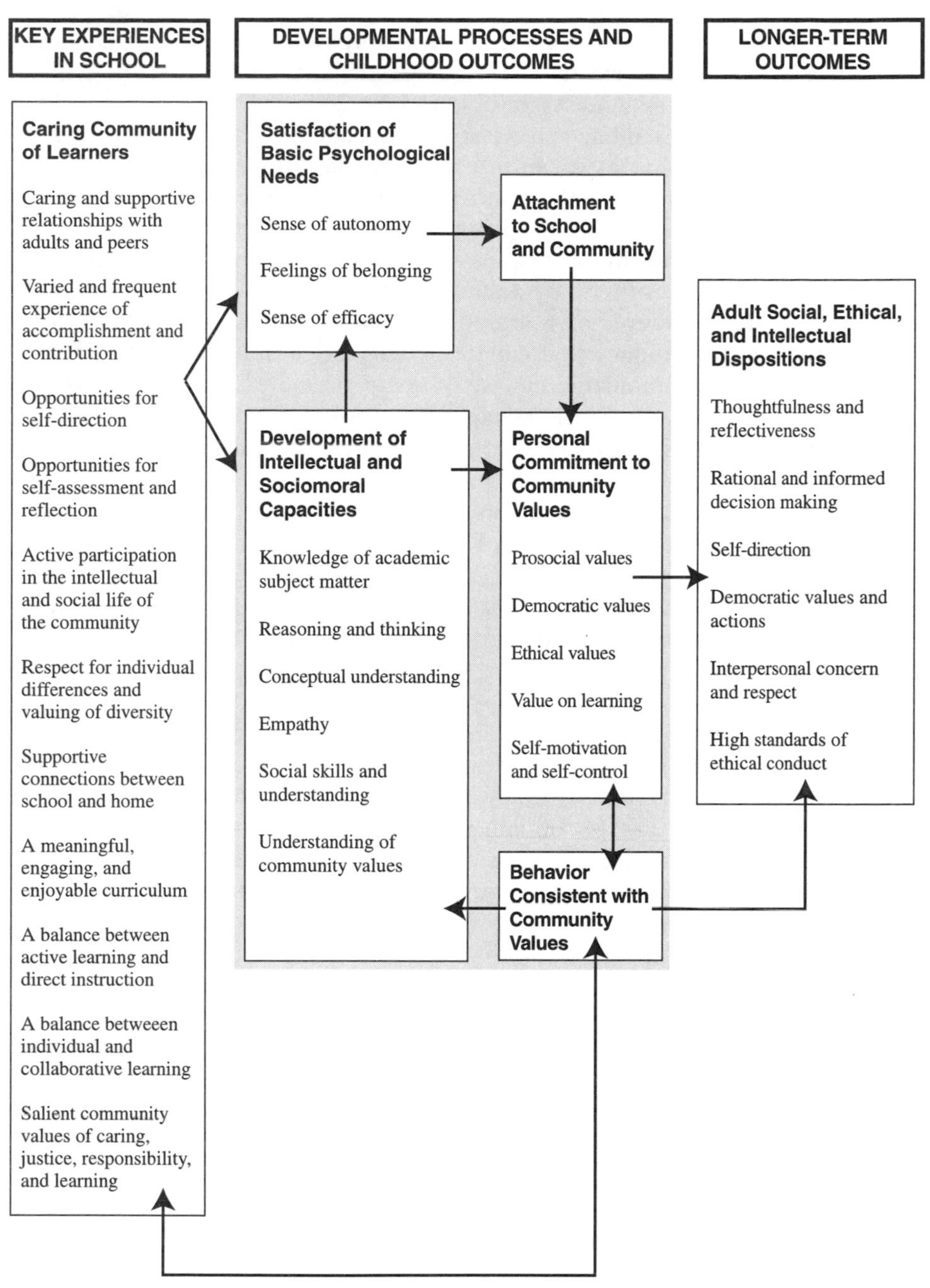

Note: © 1995 Developmental Studies Center.

values and behaviors of characters in a wide variety of fictional situations, and sensitize them to the needs and perspectives of diverse others.

- Cooperative learning, in which students are organized into small collaborative groups, both to master academic material and to learn to work with others in fair, caring, and responsible ways.
- An approach to discipline and classroom management that both engages students in creating a warm and friendly classroom that stimulates learning, and helps strengthen students' capacities to be self-disciplined. This approach focuses on deepening children's bonds with peers and teachers by, for example, helping children understand the effects of their behavior on others, by assuming the best plausible motives, by encouraging children's own search for solutions and restitution, and by avoiding techniques that isolate or stigmatize individual children. It also calls for minimizing the use of coercion and extrinsic incentives and rewards, since extrinsic rewards have been shown in a number of studies to reduce intrinsic motivation (e.g., Deci & Ryan, 1985; Lepper, 1983).
- An extensive menu of home–school activities that invite families to shape and participate in the social life of the school, and share in and support their children's learning at home.
- School service programs, such as a Buddies Program that pairs older and younger students and helps them build caring, helpful relationships with each other.

Beginning in 1982–83, we worked over a 7-year period with teachers at three elementary schools to implement the CDP program. We evaluated the program's effectiveness by following longitudinally a cohort of students in these schools and in three initially very similar schools, from their entry into the schools in kindergarten through their departure after sixth grade. Although the concept of "community" was not explicit in our initial formulation of the program, we came to see, as we refined our program and our thinking during these years, that what integrated the program's elements was the creation of a caring school community—one that met students' basic needs and helped them to understand through direct experience the importance of values of fairness, caring, and responsibility.

We recently have revised CDP to give it a stronger focus on literacy and, especially, the development of early reading skills. CDP now consists of a systematic word decoding program, a tightly focused reading comprehension program, and selected elements of the original community-building program (i.e., class meetings, buddies, parental involvement activities, and school-wide, community-building activities).

CDP'S EFFECTS ON STUDENTS' SENSE OF COMMUNITY—INITIAL RESEARCH

Our initial research on community focused first on whether the CDP program engendered a sense of the classroom as a community among students; and, if so, on how the sense of community was related to students' attitudes, values, motivation, and behavior.

Our initial self-report measure of classroom community tapped two dimensions of students' experience: (1) their perceptions that they and their classmates cared about and were supportive of one another (seven items: e.g., "Students in my class work together to solve problems." "The students in this class really care about one another." "My class is like a family."); and (2) their perceptions that they had an active and important role in classroom norm setting and decision making (ten items: e.g., "In my class the teacher and students plan together what we will do." "In my class the teacher and students decide together what the rules will be." "The teacher in my class asks the students to help decide what the class should do.").

We examined whether the CDP program was effective at enhancing students' sense of classroom community by administering this measure to students when they were in fourth, fifth, and sixth grades. In the initial longitudinal study, program students scored significantly higher than comparison students on the measure each year, with the difference in mean scores ranging between one-third and one-half of a standard deviation (Solomon, Watson, Battistich, Schaps, & Delucchi, 1996). As expected, sense of community was significantly related to many positive student outcomes, either on its own or in combination with the CDP program (Solomon et al., 1996). These included both personal and social qualities (e.g., social competence, conflict resolution skill, empathy, and self-esteem) and some academic variables, such as liking for school, intrinsic academic motivation, and an open-ended measure of reading comprehension. No effects were found, however, on standardized achievement test scores, on which both program and comparison students scored very highly.

These findings from our initial study were limited to a small number of schools in a single suburban school district, with a largely White, middle-class student population. We wondered about the extent to which schools serving more diverse and disadvantaged student populations could be characterized as caring communities and, if so, whether community would be associated with a similarly wide range of positive effects. Theoretically, at least, the more diverse the population, the more difficult it might be to establish a sense of community. Yet doing so could be critical to maintaining social cohesion as our society becomes increasingly diverse. Similarly, the benefits of participating in a caring school community could be particularly great for those students who, traditionally, have not been well served by our schools—the socioeconomically disadvantaged and socially disenfranchised.

SIX-DISTRICT CDP STUDY

A more recent study of CDP conducted in the early and mid-1990s (see Battistich, Solomon, Watson, & Schaps, 1997; Solomon et al., 2000) involved a more extensive examination of the effects of community at 24 elementary schools in six school districts across the United States—three on the West Coast, one in the South, one in the Southeast, and one in the Northeast. The schools in this sample—two program schools and two matched comparison schools from each district—were quite diverse. The schools ranged in size from fewer than 300 students to over 1,000 students. The student populations at these schools also varied greatly, with from 2% to 95% of students receiving free or reduced price lunch, 26% to 100% members of minority groups, 0% to 32% limited- or non-English speaking, and with average achievement from the 24th to the 67th percentile on standardized tests.

Teachers in the two program schools in each district worked to implement CDP. Baseline assessments were conducted in the program and matched comparison schools during the 1991–92 school year, prior to the introduction of CDP in the program schools in Fall 1992. Annual assessments were conducted in each of the subsequent 3 years, during which the program was being implemented gradually. The major assessment procedures included classroom observations, teacher surveys, and student surveys.

We assessed students' sense of community using the measure of student autonomy and influence in the classroom from the original study, an expanded measure of classroom supportiveness, and a new measure of the supportiveness of the school environment at large (e.g., "People care about each other in this school." "I feel that I can talk to the teachers in this school about things that are bothering me."). The overall measure of students' sense of the school as a caring community included all three components.

Our assessment battery was extensive, encompassing school context and student demographic characteristics; classroom practices; classroom and school climate; teacher attitudes, beliefs, and behavior; and student attitudes, motives, behavior, and performance. These data were multilevel, and we examined the effects of school community at multiple levels of analysis (i.e., school, classroom/teacher, student), using various statistical procedures (e.g., multivariate and univariate analysis of variance, multiple regression, covariance structure analysis, and hierarchical linear modeling).

Relationships of Sense of Community to School and Classroom Characteristics at Baseline

One finding from our baseline assessment in the 24 schools was that the higher the poverty level in the community served by a school, the lower the average sense of community among the students in that school. Our data indicate that both students and teachers were less likely to feel themselves members of a cohesive school community as the poverty level increased. The deleterious effects of poverty are well known, and another such effect may be less of a sense of connection and common purpose in school.

When analyzed at the classroom level, the baseline data showed that a number of general teacher characteristics (e.g., teacher warmth and supportiveness) and teaching practices (e.g., promotion of cooperation) were strongly related to students' sense of community and that these relationships were independent of the school's poverty level. Moreover, students' sense of community was strongly associated with numerous measures of student attitudes, motivational orientations, and behaviors. These relationships generally were reduced in magnitude when student poverty level was controlled, but many remained statistically significant. For example, students' sense of community was positively associated with their prosocial attitudes, motives, and behavior (i.e., concern for others, acceptance of outgroups, commitment to democratic values, and altruistic behavior), and conflict resolution skill (see Battistich, Solomon, Kim, Watson, & Schaps, 1995), and was negatively associated with students' drug use and involvement in delinquent behaviors (see Battistich & Hom, 1997).

Most relevant here, students' sense of community at baseline was consistently associated with a positive orientation toward school and learning, including enjoyment of class, liking for school, task orientation toward learning, and educational aspirations.

Program Implementation and Outcomes in the Six-District Study

In the six-district study, we compared program-relevant changes in teachers' classroom practice from baseline to the next 3 years in each of the 12 program schools, as measured against any changes in practice in their respective comparison schools. We found significantly greater changes toward implementing the elements of the CDP program in five of the 12 program schools, with average effect sizes of the differences ranging from .41 to 1.10. We did not find significant movement toward classroom implementation in the other seven program schools as measured against their comparison schools, with average effect sizes ranging from –.06 to .20. Because changes in outcomes can reasonably be attributed to the CDP program only in schools that made progress in implementing the program relative to their comparison schools, we conducted separate analyses for the five schools that showed significant implementation gains and for the seven schools that did not.

Looking across the range of outcomes we assessed, student results were negligible or negative for the seven schools that did not show significant gains in implementation, relative to their comparison schools. In these schools, student attitude, motivation, and classroom behavior measures generally declined relative to their comparison schools, as did some indices of achievement.

For the five high-change program schools, however, over 50% of the student outcome variables showed significant effects favoring program students, including the following:

- *Effects on student attitudes, motives, and inclinations.* A sizable proportion of the measured attitude variables showed positive changes from baseline for the program students (relative to the comparison students) in the five high-change schools, while none showed negative changes. The sociomoral variables showing statistically significant ($p < .05$) effects included *sense of school as community*, *democratic values*, *outgroup acceptance*, *conflict resolution skill*, *intrinsic prosocial motivation*, and *concern for others.* The academic variables showing statistically significant ($p < .05$) effects included *liking for school*, *intrinsic academic motivation*, *task orientation*, *frequency of reading self-chosen books outside school*, and *frequency of reading self-chosen books in school.*
- *Effects on students' classroom behavior.* The observation indices of student behavior did not show significant program effects in the five schools that made progress in implementation.
- *Effects on teacher reports of practices, attitudes, and perceptions.* We examined the effects of participating in the CDP program on teachers' reports of their own classroom practices, attitudes about and commitment to teaching, and their views of the school "climate." Relative to comparison school teachers, program teachers in the five high-change schools reported significantly *greater provision for student autonomy/influence*, *greater student participation in planning*, *reduced use of extrinsic control*, *reduced use of praise*, and *reduced emphasis on control ideology.*
- *Effects on student achievement.* We assessed achievement with district-administered achievement tests, with a revised version of the higher-order reading comprehension assessment we had used earlier, and with a measure of inductive reasoning skill (from the Cornell test; Ennis & Millman, 1985). We encountered problems in handling the district achievement test data because different districts used different tests, three districts changed

their tests during the period of the testing, and districts differed as to the grade levels they assessed (and, in some cases, within a district over time). We therefore found it necessary to examine the standardized achievement test results separately in each district. Because of these limitations, the achievement findings should be interpreted with some caution.

As a group, the five high-change schools showed no significant effects on the DSC measure of *reading comprehension* or the measure of *inductive reasoning*. Three of these five schools showed little effect on district-administered *standardized achievement test scores*, except for a negative effect on math achievement in one. The remaining two schools, however, showed large positive within-year differences from their comparison schools on a high-stakes, state-administered *performance assessment*. Students in one or both of these schools scored higher than those in their comparison school counterparts on *reading, math, social studies, and science performance* in 1, 2, or all 3 years of assessment.

An important contextual factor is worth noting here: We believe that "academic press" in this district—an emphasis on achievement for all children—may have been higher than in the other five districts because of state policies and assessment practices. Of course, this applies to the comparison schools in this district as well.

Modeling Analyses

We looked for additional evidence of the importance of community in school by analyzing the effects of CDP program implementation on student outcomes over time. In these analyses, we combined seven of the observed classroom measures of teacher characteristics with four teacher attitude and belief measures to construct an index of program implementation. We then modeled the linkages between program participation, program implementation, sense of community, and the various student outcomes. Because we were interested in assessing *changes* in practices, behavior, and outcomes that were due to CDP, we controlled for baseline differences on the teacher and student measures.

Using EQS (Bentler, 1992), we tested the effect of program participation by estimating a path from a dichotomous indicator of program status (0 = comparison, 1 = program) to teacher practices in the 3 program years (with baseline scores controlled), and tested the effect on student outcome variables by estimating a path from sense of community to the measured outcome in the program years (with outcome scores at baseline controlled).

A summary of the findings from 13 such analyses is presented in Figure 11.2. For simplicity, the baseline effects are not shown, and paths to all

Figure 11.2. Summary of findings from modeling analyses of program effects.

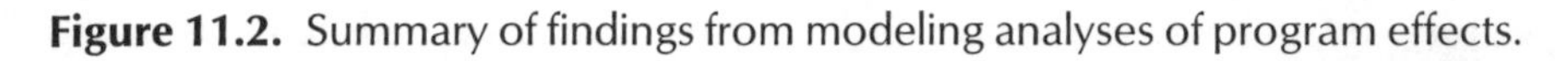

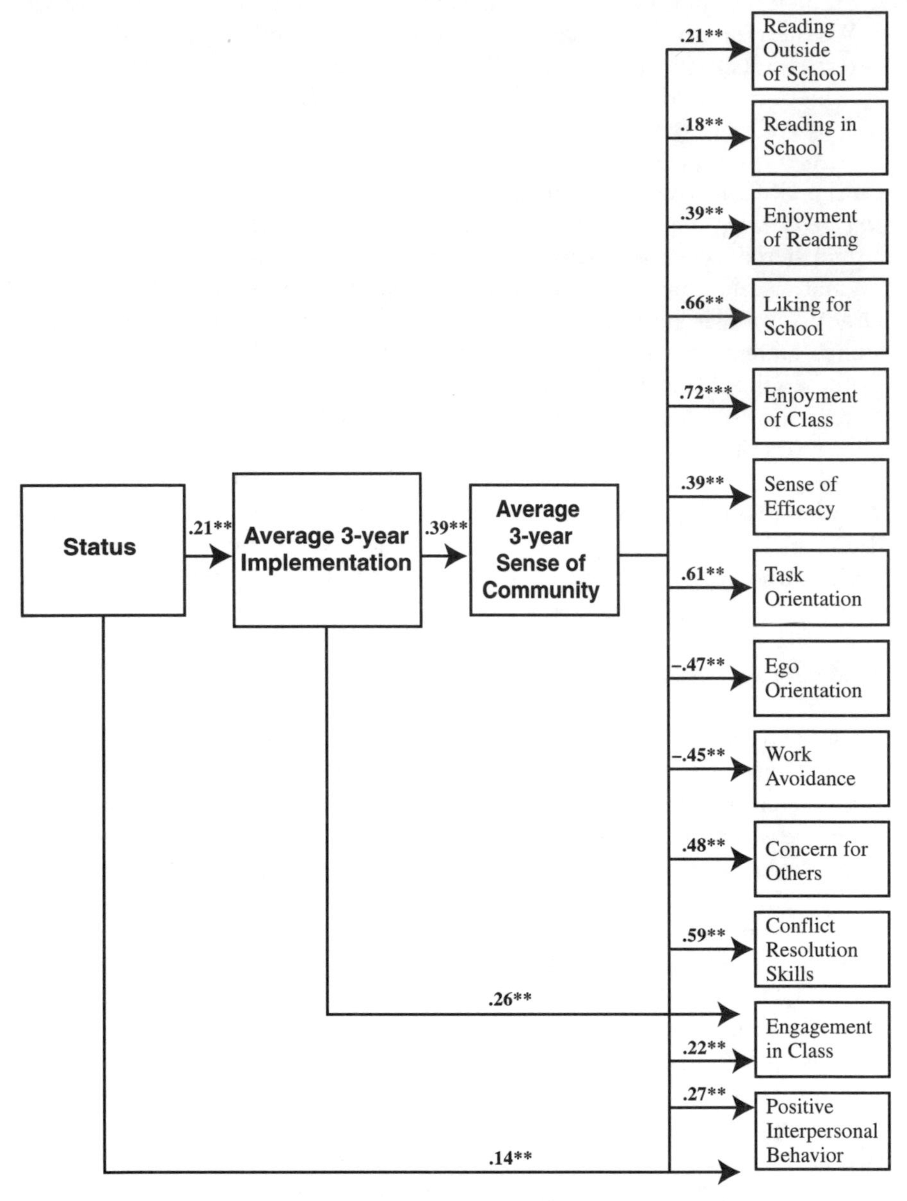

Note: Reprinted with permission from "A Six-District Study of Educational Change: Direct and Mediated Effects of the child Development Project," by D. Solomon, V. Battistich, M. Watson, E. Schaps, and C. Lewis, 2000, *Social Psychology of Education, 4*, pp. 3–51. Copyright © 2000 Kluwer Academic Publishers.
*$p < .05$. **$p < .01$. ***$p < .001$.

13 variables are shown in the figure, although each of these paths actually was estimated in a separate analysis.

The findings shown in Figure 11.2 indicate clearly that participation in CDP had positive effects on teachers' classroom practices, that these practices, in turn, influenced students' sense of community, and that these changes in sense of community brought about desirable changes in a range of student outcomes, including academic attitudes (e.g., liking for school, enjoyment of class, enjoyment of reading), academic motivation (task orientation, engagement in class), and academic behaviors (e.g., reading in school, reading outside of school).

However, we did *not* find a mediating relationship when we used our available achievement data to examine the possible role of sense of community in mediating academic achievement. We examined both the model in Figure 11.2 and additional models in which engagement in class and student motivation were explored as alternative or additional mediating variables. These analyses involved district achievement data aggregated to the class level, which meant relatively small numbers of classrooms because tests were not given at all grade levels in most districts. But when we tested such models with our own measures of reading comprehension and writing quality, and with the measure of inductive reasoning, here too we did not find evidence of mediating relationships.

Middle School Follow-Up Study

In a 4-year, follow-up study, we tracked students from three high-change and three low-change program schools (all characterized as serving "high-risk" student populations) in three of the six districts, along with their comparison school counterparts, as they progressed through middle school. Annual assessments include student and teacher questionnaires, teacher ratings of student characteristics, and data from school records.

Former students from the low-change program schools have fared better during middle school, relative to former comparison students. Analyses of data from the first 3 years of the follow-up study show statistically reliable ($p < .05$) or marginally reliable ($p < .10$) differences favoring students from former low-change program schools on 17% of 42 outcomes assessed, and no differences favoring comparison students. Thus, the negative effects found during the elementary years for these schools did not continue through the middle grades.

Former students from high-change program schools outperformed their respective comparison students on 43% of the 42 outcomes. No differences favored their comparison students. Most interestingly, former program school students outperformed comparison students on two key measures of academic achievement. Their grade point averages were significantly higher—nearly half a grade point on average—and they also scored significantly better than comparison students on district achievement tests. (It should be noted again that two of these high-change schools were in the district where academic press seemed highest because of state-level policies and high-stakes assessment practices.)

CONCLUSIONS AND RECOMMENDATIONS

Overall, our research has shown that the CDP program effectively strengthened students' sense of community in school, which, in turn, fostered academic motivation and aspirations, desirable character-related outcomes, social and emotional learning, and avoidance of problem behaviors. Many of CDP's benefits persisted during middle school, and some new effects materialized, most notably a substantial effect on academic achievement.

But CDP did not consistently promote academic achievement during the elementary years. Because elementary schools are under increasing pressure to show achievement gains quickly, and to reduce the disparities in achievement among various racial, ethnic, and income subgroups, it is not enough for their "graduates" to do well in middle school. Elementary schools must now show achievement gains in third or fourth grade, and sometimes even earlier.

In light of these pressures, we have come to believe that elementary schools that wish to focus on building community also must establish two additional priorities. Specifically, they must establish (1) high expectations for the learning and growth of all students, and (2) important, challenging, engaging learning opportunities for all students. These additional priorities, which sometimes are labeled "academic press" and "academic support," are subject to varying definitions and conceptualizations (as is sense of community). And so we offer our view of what is key to each:

- *High expectations.* Although we advocate setting high expectations for all students across domains (i.e., social, emotional, and ethical as well as academic), we do not expect that every student will progress in the same way, or at the same rate, or even to the same level in each domain. Rather, recognizing that students differ in strengths and abilities, we advocate that schools commit to working for every student's *continuing progress.* This requires a school's staff to come to know each student; to track each student's learning in an ongoing way; and to adjust expectations accordingly in order to support further growth.
- *Important and engaging learning opportunities.* "Important" learning opportunities provide students with the skills and knowledge they need

for effective learning in the various disciplines, and also for beginning to assume adult roles and responsibilities. "Engaging" learning opportunities connect to students' interests and prior experiences—and in this way they tap intrinsic motivation to learn. Making learning both important and engaging involves (1) teaching for both understanding *and* skill development; (2) ensuring that essential content is covered *and* that students can pursue their own interests at times; and (3) balancing and integrating the use of didactic *and* experiential pedagogies.

How complicated is the task of promoting students' academic attainment and also their character and interpersonal and intrapersonal growth? A growing body of research indicates that a relatively focused reform agenda can effectively attain these multiple goals. That agenda—academic press, academic support, and a focus on building community in school—may powerfully meet the needs of both students and society. Of special interest are the indications that this agenda may be particularly beneficial for disadvantaged students. More research is needed on this topic, but challenging, engaging, and caring schools may provide the pivotal support needed by students who traditionally have been least likely to succeed.

Finally we believe that the revised CDP program, with its expanded reading-skills instruction, will be more responsive to students' academic needs and more feasible for a wide range of schools to implement. And we believe it will continue to enhance students' sense of community in school and to yield the wide-ranging, enduring benefits that follow from such a focus.

REFERENCES

Battistich, V., & Hom, A. (1997). The relationship between students' sense of their community and their involvement in problem behaviors. *American Journal of Public Health*, *87*, 1997–2001.

Battistich, V., Solomon, D., Kim, D., Watson, M., & Schaps, E. (1995). Schools as communities, poverty levels of student populations, and students' attitudes, motives, and performance: A multilevel analysis. *American Educational Research Journal*, *32*, 627–658.

Battistich, V., Solomon, D., Watson, M., & Schaps, E. (1997). Caring school communities. *Educational Psychologist*, *32*(3), 137–151.

Bentler, P. M. (1992). *EQS: Structural equations program manual.* Los Angeles: BMDP Statistical Software.

Bryk, A. S., & Driscoll, M. E. (1988). *The school as community: Theoretical foundations, contextual influences, and consequences for students and teachers.* Madison, WI: National Center on Effective Secondary Schools.

Bryk, A. S., Lee, V. E., & Holland, P. B. (1993). *Catholic schools and the common good.* Cambridge, MA: Harvard University Press.

Comer, J. P., & Haynes, N. M. (1999). The dynamics of school change: Response to the article, "Comer's School Development Program in Prince Georges County, Maryland: A theory-based evaluation," by T. D. Cook et al. *American Educational Research Journal, 36*, 599–607.

Connell, J. P. (1990). Context, self, and action: A motivational analysis of self-system processes across the life span. In D. Ciccheti & M. Beeghly (Eds.), *The self in transition: Infancy to childhood* (pp. 61–97). Chicago: University of Chicago Press.

Deci, E. L., & Ryan, R. M. (1985). *Intrinsic motivation and self-determination in human behavior*. New York: Plenum.

DeVries, R., & Zan, B. (1994). *Moral classrooms, moral children: Creating a constructivist atmosphere in early education*. New York: Teachers College Press.

Elias, M. J., Zins, J. E., Weissberg, R. P., Frey, K. S., Greenberg, M. T., Haynes, N. M., Kessler, R., Schwab-Stone, M. E., & Shriver, T. P. (1997). *Promoting social and emotional learning: Guidelines for educators*. Alexandria, VA: Association of Supervision and Curriculum Development.

Elliot, S. (1995). *The Responsive Classroom approach: Its effectiveness and acceptability. Final evaluation report*. Washington, DC: Center for Systemic Educational Change, District of Columbia Public Schools.

Ennis, R. H., & Millman, J. (1985). *Cornell critical thinking tests*. Pacific Grove, CA: Midwest Publications.

Gottfredson, D., Gottfredson, G., & Hybl, L. (1993). Managing adolescent behavior: A multiyear, multischool study. *American Educational Research Journal, 30*, 179–215

Hallinger, P., & Murphy, J. F. (1986). The social context of effective schools. *American Journal of Education, 94*, 328–355.

Hawkins, J. D., Catalano, R. F., Kosterman, R., Abbot, R., & Hill, K. G. (1999). Preventing adolescent health-risk behaviors by strengthening protection during childhood. *Archives of Pediatric and Adolescent Medicine, 153*, 226–234.

Hawkins, J. D., & Weiss, J. G. (1985). The social development model: An integrated approach to delinquency prevention. *Journal of Primary Prevention, 6*, 73–79.

Higgins, A., Power, C., & Kohlberg, L. (1984). The relationship of moral atmosphere to judgments of responsibility. In W. M. Kurtines & J. L. Gewirtz (Eds.), *Morality, moral behavior, and moral development* (pp. 74–106). New York: Wiley.

Lee, V. E., & Smith, J. B. (1999). Social support and achievement for young adolescents in Chicago: The role of school academic press. *American Educational Research Journal, 36*, 907–945.

Lepper, M. R. (1983). Extrinsic reward and intrinsic motivation: Implications for the classroom. In J. M. Levine & M. Wang (Eds.), *Teacher and student perceptions* (pp. 281–317). Hillsdale, NJ: Erlbaum.

Osterman, K. (2000). Students' need for belonging in school. *Review of Educational Research, 70*(3), 323–367.

Resnick, M. D., Bearman, P. S., Blum, R. W., Bauman, K. E., Harris, K. M., Jones, J., Tabor, J., Beuhring, T., Sieving, R. E., Shew, M., Ireland, M., Bearinger, L. H., & Udry, J. R. (1997). Protecting adolescents from harm: Findings from the National Longitudinal Study on Adolescent Health. *Journal of the American Medical Association*, *278*(10), 823–832.

Schaps, E., Battistich, V., & Solomon, D. (1997). School as a caring community: A key to character education. In A. Molnar (Ed.), *The construction of children's character: Part II. 96th Yearbook of the National Society for the Study of Education* (pp. 127–139). Chicago: University of Chicago Press.

Schaps, E., & Lewis, C. (1999). Perils on an essential journey: Building school community. *Phi Delta Kappan*, *81*(3), 215–218.

Shouse, R. (1996). Academic press and sense of community: Conflict and congruence for student achievement. *Social Psychology of Education*, *1*, 47–68.

Solomon, D., Battistich, V., Watson, M., Schaps, E., & Lewis, C. (2000). A six-district study of educational change: Direct and mediated effects of the Child Development Project. *Social Psychology of Education*, *4*, 3–51.

Solomon, D., Watson, M., Battistich, V., Schaps, E., & Delucchi, K. (1996). Creating classrooms that students experience as communities. *American Journal of Community Psychology*, *24*, 719–748.

PART III

Recommendations

CHAPTER 12

Recommendations and Conclusions: Implications for Practice, Training, Research, and Policy

HERBERT J. WALBERG, JOSEPH E. ZINS, AND ROGER P. WEISSBERG

If social and emotional learning (SEL) is to be an essential component of education, it is crucial to establish a compelling conceptual and evidence-based case for linking it to improved school attitudes, behavior, and performance. In the past many SEL efforts did not directly focus on issues related to academics and school success, nor were programs evaluated in terms of such outcomes. Today, however, SEL programs increasingly address practices related to academics and measure the results of these endeavors.

The empirical evidence presented in this book makes a strong case that social-emotional interventions can improve children's success in school and in life. The programs supporting this conclusion primarily result from comprehensive, multiyear, multicomponent approaches that have many of the following characteristics: (a) based on theory and research; (b) teach children to apply SEL skills; (c) build connections to school through establishment of a caring, engaging environment; (d) provide developmentally and culturally appropriate instruction; (e) help schools coordinate and unify SEL efforts; (f) enhance school performance by addressing the affective and social dimensions of learning; (g) engage families and communities as partners; (h) establish organizational supports and policies that foster success; (i) provide high-quality staff development and support; and (j) incorporate continuing evaluation and improvement (CASEL, 2003; Elias et al., 1997; Weissberg, 2000).

SYNTHESIS OF FINDINGS

Contributors to this book provided significant evidence regarding SEL's association with and contributions to student success in school (see Figure 1.4). We recognize, however, that chapters vary with respect to the level of support they provide for the impact of social-emotional interventions on academics. For instance, Johnson and Johnson cite extensive evidence of SEL's positive influence based on hundreds of investigations of cooperative learning conducted over several decades. Other chapters likewise contain substantial documentation of such outcomes. On the other hand, Lopes and Salovey indicate that they found little research support linking what they term emotional intelligence and academic achievement. Others in the field rightfully have raised questions about some of the more extravagant claims made about emotional intelligence and related concepts (e.g., Matthews, Zeidner, & Roberts, 2002). Needless to say, there is a need for additional research on these topics.

Overall, the findings reported in this book suggest a consistent message, which can be summarized as follows:

- Safe, caring, and orderly environments are conducive to learning.
- Caring relations between teachers and students foster a desire to learn and a connection to school.
- Socially engaging teaching strategies, such as cooperative learning and proactive classroom management, focus students on learning tasks.
- When teachers and families work together to encourage and reinforce learning commitment, engagement, and positive behavior, students do better.
- When peer norms support academic performance, students try harder.
- When the instructional content is made more interesting by applying SEL to reflecting on the content, students are more engaged.
- When students are self-aware and more confident about their learning abilities, they try harder.
- When students can self-manage their stress and motivations, and set goals and organize themselves, they do better.
- Students who are aware of the tasks being assigned, make responsible decisions about completing them, and use problem-solving and relationship-management skills to overcome barriers, they perform better and learn more.
- When SEL prevents high-risk behaviors such as drug use and antisocial behavior, these behaviors do not interfere with learning or co-occur with a constellation of other problem behaviors that reduce effective functioning.

When these outcomes are examined collectively, they form the basis of what most parents, educators, and the public want for all children.

CONFERENCE RECOMMENDATIONS FOR PRACTICE, TRAINING, RESEARCH, AND POLICY

As is customary at Laboratory for Student Success book conferences, initial versions of the conference papers that are included as the chapters in this book were precirculated to the chapter authors, other scholars, and educators who attended the conference. In this case, about 100 school teachers, administrators, state and federal education officials, university faculty, researchers, psychologists, and experts in other disciplines first heard discussions of the papers in large plenary sessions that were led by a number of distinguished scholars and then opened up to the large group. Following these sessions, participants discussed the papers in small groups, achieved consensus on recommendations, and reported them in a final plenary session. Although considerable consensus was achieved among the participants, not everyone agreed on all points in their group discussions, nor did all the groups focus on the same topics.

These small-group oral and written reports, nonetheless, echoed several recurring themes and common recommendations based on the discussions, and all of them are included here as they were reported by the conference groups. Within the broad theme of SEL and school success, these are grouped below under several key topics.

Research and Evaluation

As exemplified in the conference papers, investigators have produced much convincing research linking social and emotional learning and school success. This work, however, can be extended and refined in several ways.

The conference papers and other works reveal common SEL elements, although there is less agreement and detail on how they have been implemented and measured. To the extent, moreover, that common ideas and procedures are employed in multiple studies, the research results will become more comparable and useful. Further development and use of assessment tools that measure a broad range of academic outcomes are needed to measure such things as higher-order thinking skills and analytical, creative, and practical skills. Instruments are needed not only for the measurement of SEL outcomes but also for selecting and determining the readiness of teachers, schools, and school districts for SEL programs. They also will be helpful in determining the degree and fidelity of the implementation process and can be used as self-assessment tools for program developers, administrators, teachers, and other end users. Comprehensive and uniform measures employed in future studies would allow greater comparability of effects for various SEL programs. A catalog or handbook of tested measures would serve the field well.

For greater certainty about the magnitude and universality of SEL effects, large-scale randomized field trials, as in medical research, are necessary. The cumulative evidence from small-scale studies, although convincing, has insufficiently established the full magnitude and breadth of the effects of SEL on school and life success. Large-scale studies allow estimates of the effects of SEL under different conditions, in different kinds of schools, and for children of various ages and demographic characteristics.

Because randomized field trials are difficult to conduct, some research must compare groups that have and have not implemented various SEL programs. Such research may incorporate "selection bias," that is, the tendency for schools with inspired leaders, in difficult circumstances and other characteristics, to differ from others. Studies that are designed to eliminate such bias are needed. Randomized experiments may have their own biases such as "Hawthorne" or "hothouse" effects. Therefore, SEL findings that show consistent benefits notwithstanding variations in research methodology will be most convincing.

Moreover, detailed descriptions of the features of SEL programs, how they were implemented, and how they affect school outcomes would enable researchers, policy makers, and educators to better understand the causal mechanisms that link SEL and school outcomes. Meta-analyses of the existing research and future research would allow investigators, educators, and policy makers to estimate the comparative effects for various programs, how the degree or fidelity of program implementation affects outcomes, and how well SEL works for different students on both short- and long-term outcomes.

Vital but often overlooked components of decision making are costs, cost-effectiveness, and cost–benefit considerations. Obviously, school budgets are constrained and, other things being equal, educators rationally should choose less expensive programs. But other things are never equal, and they should raise cost-effectiveness and cost–benefit questions: What is the ratio of outcomes to costs and of monetary benefits to costs? Consumers and firms apply such considerations in everyday decisions such as buying a car or merging firms. Such considerations increasingly apply in litigation and in crucial individual decisions such as undergoing surgery or chemotherapy, even though causation, outcomes, and monetary benefits are difficult to estimate. Policy makers and educators, nonetheless, increasingly want information relevant to such considerations even though the answers may be somewhat uncertain.

Qualitative or case studies are also in order. In particular, it would be desirable to know about barriers to successful program implementation. Why does SEL work in some circumstances and not others? Is principal and superintendent leadership the key, or is teacher "buy in" the crucial factor? Are some pre-existing circumstances inhibitors of successful implementation? What can be done about them? Answers to these and similar questions would reveal the best ways to design SEL programs and how to disseminate and implement them more effectively. In addition, students increasingly are learning in nontraditional circumstances such as on the Internet, in small groups, on field trips, in museums, and in other settings. How can SEL programs and principles be incorporated in such efforts? This is a new challenge for program developers, educators, and researchers.

Professional Preparation

If SEL is to be widely and well implemented, preparation of new and inservice teachers is necessary. Such preparation should include field experience for teachers-to-be and the modeling of positive, supportive classroom environments for new and veteran teachers. These experiences should be thoroughly grounded in the disciplines of psychology, education, and related fields of study. School leaders and other professionals within state departments of education, district central offices, and schools can promote effectiveness in planning, encouraging, and operating SEL programs. These professionals can develop and improve their own effectiveness in such efforts by employing SEL behaviors themselves so they become more successful in their professional and personal lives. State and local school board members should benefit from similar experiences.

In the field, leaders should provide the means and settings for deep dialogue within the community of practice. They can identify, educate, and provide experiences for mentors and coaches. They also should identify exemplary SEL schools in urban, suburban, and rural contexts; videotape them; and share the videos with others as visual models of successful practice. People who led successful SEL efforts can describe the story of change in their schools, what they did to make it happen, and how their practices follow from SEL principles. Case studies, websites, and distance learning afford further means of professional training.

Collaboration with existing professional groups can bring SEL programs and principles into schools. Several groups influence, if not control, preservice teacher education. These include state departments of education; testing agencies; several contending groups that accredit schools, colleges, and departments of education; and state legislators who often determine certification procedures for individual teachers. SEL presentations before these and other groups, such as the Association for Supervision and Curriculum Development, the American Association of School Administrators, and the National Association of Secondary School Principals, are also promising ways of bringing SEL into preservice and inservice educator preparation.

Implementation

It should prove useful to develop selection criteria and assessment of readiness for teachers, schools, and school districts. Similarly, guidelines for quality implementation and self-assessment tools for schools should increase fidelity with SEL programs and principles. To enhance the probability of success, SEL activities should be integrated into curricula and daily instruction. These implementation features are likely to require SEL-trained professional staff, possibly using present school staff. They need skills in bringing SEL programs to scale and developing supportive networks to promote research, implementation, and collaboration. Case studies should be useful in illustrating criteria for successful implementation.

Dissemination

The conferees believed the work of the conference should be continued to accomplish several purposes. Additional policy makers, educational leaders, and teachers should further consider institutional obstacles to SEL implementation. One such obstacle might be the choice of words that name and describe SEL programs, which in the past have been expressed in educational and psychological jargon. SEL ideas will be more appealing to educators and others if they use the language of potential "customers" or at least explain clearly the meaning of technical terms and the need for departing from ordinary language.

Another possible obstacle is the panoply of state and local curriculum requirements. Various federal programs, national groups, and special interests exert strong pressures on what is taught in schools. SEL disseminators need a better understanding of these requirements and pressures. Depending on state and local circumstances, they may need to analyze curriculum and activity requirements to help educators see where SEL programs and principles may fit in best.

Partnerships of educators with other professionals such as mental health providers and organizations can be useful if all keep in mind educators' primary mission of learning in both the academic and broader senses. Educators' attention, time, energies, and budgets, however, are constrained; new programs require these scarce resources. In addition, organizational change imposes psychological and other costs, and teachers play a key role in making new programs successful. SEL should not become just another "reform *du jour*," a term used by educators beleaguered with many outside demands.

SEL leaders also need to understand related efforts. In some respects, for example, SEL shares the goals and means of character education, although SEL draws more on psychological research, and character education derives to a larger extent from religious and humanistic traditions. Greater mutual understanding and linkages between the two efforts may benefit them both.

In explaining SEL, dissemination vehicles should be developed for different audiences that should know about the programs, including not only those mentioned above but parents as well. These should include brochures and short articles that make use of a question-and-answer format. Conferences and books similar to but extending the present work should be useful. It would be desirable for one of the U.S. Department of Education's Regional Educational Laboratories to develop and maintain a focus on SEL, while sharing more broadly the expertise of the other Laboratories and its own. Either this Laboratory or another national center should develop a proposal to carry out further research and development on how caring schools and communities can be integrated with efforts to achieve school success.

How can outreach be extended even more fully? For parent outreach, school–parent–community partnerships seem promising. To reach policy makers, business groups, and others, national and local spokespersons in various fields—including psychology, teaching, administration, and policy—should be recruited to point out the feasibility and benefits of SEL programs. The program might be cast as both solving and preventing chronic and crisis problems and conditions.

A clearly articulated "manifesto" about SEL should be developed and shared with potential "customers." It should explain the research-based principles, supporting structures, practices, and measures of SEL. This manifesto could be a core document for reaching the general public and potential donors, supplemented by a media campaign and dialogues in forums with students and community members about what is needed for SEL and school success. Lobbying state and federal officials and a network of allied parent and professional organizations should be helpful. The SEL message, although carried far and wide, should emphasize quality principles and evidence-based guidelines.

CONCLUSIONS

Schools have a primary mission to develop the academic skills of students. At the same time, as Adelman and Taylor (2000) made abundantly clear, schools must move beyond current school reform efforts that follow a two-component model (i.e., attend only to academic instruction and school management), and simultaneously pay attention to social-emotional issues and the barriers to learning that exist for many students. Large numbers of students cannot focus on learning until these social and emotional needs have been addressed.

From our perspective, much research remains to be done, as we move toward improving and expanding SEL science and practice and going to scale. Developing a common understanding of what constitutes an SEL intervention, or of how SEL interventions might be categorized, is necessary so that the field is not so overly inclusive or disjointed that it is nearly impossible to navigate or to disentangle meaningful results, whether academic, social-emotional, or behavioral. In other words, we need to make certain that we're talking about the same construct. Some of the key research issues involve the evaluation of more multiyear interventions with long-term follow-ups (we have a few trail-blazing studies, but not many); finding out which SEL competencies and social-psychological factors are key mediators for academic performance; determining whether domain-specific instruction (e.g., applying SEL to study skills and academic classwork) would produce stronger effects than more general approaches; considering whether skills, instructional approaches, teacher–children relationships, or SEL skills can independently enhance academic performance, or whether the combined package is needed; learning what can be done to improve quality implementation; determining how to increase commonality in quality measurement across studies; and investigating what factors may affect the broad-scale dissemination and sustainability of SEL programming efforts. Finally, because this is a book about the scientific bases for the field, it is important to emphasize the need to identify ways to improve the science before making the jump to the widespread application to all children in all schools.

In terms of application, we need a better understanding of schools' readiness to implement SEL programming so that those involved are motivated and committed to such change and the organizational climate is receptive to it. Related to this point, effective methods are needed to convince educational leaders and policy makers on a broad level of the merits of evidence-based SEL and of its importance to children's well-being, so that ultimately SEL is not viewed as outside the mandate of the school but rather is integrated into the curriculum. We also need well-developed means to train educators in SEL, and better ways to translate research findings into practice so that effective SEL techniques are found in common use in schools. Furthermore, monitoring and evaluating SEL practices should become routine to ensure their high quality.

Although we realize that social and emotional education clearly cannot solve all the problems facing schools and society, this book establishes the strong relationships between academic achievement and social-emotional development. The contributors provided many examples of how SEL interventions can affect school performance positively. Because social-emotional competence and academic achievement are highly interwoven, they must be integrated and coordinated to maximize the potential for students to succeed now and throughout their lives. We have learned much about methods of classroom instruction, behavior management practices, and climate that can both enhance school success and promote social-emotional competence.

The research-based findings in the book are compelling. The findings are solid enough that we believe the term "social, emotional, and academic learning," or "SEAL," reflects our current conceptualization of the interrelated areas that need to be addressed, and we see the promotion of SEAL as where the future of the most important work in integrated school-wide practice lies. This book helps us chart a future that will advance the science and practice of SEAL. We hope you enjoyed the journey, and we hope you will join us in integrating social, emotional, and academic learning into your professional activities.

REFERENCES

Adelman, H. S., & Taylor, L. (2000). Moving prevention from the fringes into the fabric of school improvement. *Journal of Education and Psychological Consultation*, *11*(1), 7–36.

Collaborative for Academic, Social, and Emotional Learning. (2003). *Safe and sound: An educational leader's guide to evidence-based social and emotional learning programs*. Chicago: Author.

Elias, M. J., Zins, J. E., Weissberg, R. P., Frey, K. S., Greenberg, M. T., Haynes, N. M., Kessler, R., Schwab-Stone, M. E., & Shriver, T. P. (1997). *Promoting social and emotional learning: Guidelines for educators*. Alexandria, VA: Association for Supervision and Curriculum Development.

Matthews, G., Zeidner, M., & Roberts, R. D. (2002). *Emotional intelligence: Science and myth*. Cambridge, MA: MIT Press.

Weissberg, R. P. (2000). Improving the lives of millions of school children. *American Psychologist*, *55*(11), 1360–1372.

About the Editors and the Contributors

THE EDITORS

Joseph E. Zins is a professor in the College of Education at the University of Cincinnati. He is recognized nationally and internationally as an expert on social competence promotion, prevention, and individual and organizational consultation. Professor Zins has over 150 scientific publications, including the books *Promoting Social and Emotional Learning: Guidelines for Educators* (1997), *The Handbook of Prevention and Intervention in Peer Harassment, Victimization, and Bullying* (2004), and *Helping Students Succeed in the Regular Classroom* (1988). He is a Consulting Editor for the *Social-Emotional Learning Book Series* (Teachers College Press), former Editor of the *Journal of Educational and Psychological Consultation*, and a past Secretary of the National Association of School Psychologists. In addition to being a Fellow of the American Psychological Association, Dr. Zins is a member of the Leadership Team of the Collaborative for Academic, Social, and Emotional Learning (CASEL).

Roger P. Weissberg is a Professor of Psychology and Education at the University of Illinois at Chicago (UIC), and Executive Director of the Collaborative for Academic, Social, and Emotional Learning (CASEL). Dr. Weissberg directs an NIMH-funded Predoctoral and Postdoctoral Prevention Research Training Program in Urban Children's Mental Health and AIDS Prevention at UIC and also holds an appointment as Senior Research Associate with the Mid-Atlantic Regional Educational Laboratory for Student Success. Professor Weissberg has published about 150 articles and chapters focusing on preventive interventions with children and adolescents and has co-authored nine curricula on school-based programs to promote social competence and prevent problem behaviors including drug use, high-risk sexual behaviors, and aggression. Recent co-edited books include *Enhancing Children's Wellness* (1997), *Establishing Preventive Services* (1997), *Promoting Positive Outcomes* (1999), *The Promotion of Wellness in Children and Adolescents* (2000), and *Long-Term Trends in the Well-Being of Children and Adolescents* (2003). He also co-authored *Promoting Social and Emotional Learning: Guidelines for Educators* (1997). Dr. Weissberg has been President of the American Psychological Association's Society for Community Research and Action. He co-chaired an American Psychological Association Task Force on "Prevention: Promoting Strength, Resilience, and Health in Young People" from 1997 to 1999. He is a recipient of the William T. Grant Foundation's five-year Faculty Scholars Award in Children's Mental Health, the Connecticut Psychological Association's Award for Distinguished Psychological Contribution in the Public Interest, and the National Mental Health Association's Lela Rowland Prevention Award. He was named a 1997–2000 University Scholar at the University of Illinois. In 2000, he received the American Psychological Association's Distinguished Contribution Award for Applications of Psychology to Education and Training.

Margaret C. Wang was a Professor of Educational Psychology and the founder and Director of the Center for Research in Human Development and Education at Temple University. She established the Center in 1986 as a broad-based interdisciplinary research and development center focusing on human development and education-related fields. Dr. Wang also served as the Executive Director of the Mid-Atlantic Regional Educational Laboratory for Student Success and the National Center on Education in the Inner Cities, both funded by the Office of Educational Research and Improvement of the U.S. Department of Education.

Dr. Wang was recognized nationally and internationally for her research on learner differences and effective school responses to student diversity, student motivation, and implementation and evaluation of innovative school-based intervention programs for students with special needs, including those in special categorical programs such as special education and compensatory or remedial education, and those otherwise considered to be in "at-risk" circumstances.

Dr. Wang published 18 books and over 100 articles. She was the senior editor of the four-volume *Handbook of Special Education* (1987–1991). Books that she wrote or edited include *Adaptive Education Strategies* (1992), *Educational Resilience in Inner-City America* (1994), *Rethinking Policy for At-Risk Students* (1994), *Making a Difference for Students at Risk* (1994), *School/Community Connections* (1995), and *Handbook of Special and Remedial Education* (1995).

Herbert J. Walberg is Principal Investigator at the Mid-Atlantic Regional Educational Laboratory for Student Success; University Scholar, Emeritus Professor of Education and Psychology, and member of the President's Council at the University of Illinois at Chicago; and Distinguished Visiting Fellow at the Stanford University Hoover Institution. Having taught at Harvard and UIC for nearly 40 years, and attained fellow status in four academic organizations, Dr. Walberg now chairs the board of the Heartland Institute, a think tank that has gathered more than 7,000 policy analyses from more than 300 think tanks and provides them on demand to legislators, talk show hosts, and the general public. Dr. Walberg serves on the governing boards of four other not-for-profit organizations that promote children's learning and welfare. He also edits a series of "what works" booklets distributed to educators in 189 countries by the United Nations Educational, Scientific, and Educational Organization. Herb has advised educational leaders in the United States and a dozen other countries and led projects for the Paris-based Organization for Economic Cooperation and Development. Two of his books are *Psychology and Educational Practice* (1997) and *The International Handbook of Education* (1994).

THE CONTRIBUTORS

J. Lawrence Aber is on the faculty at New York University. Since completing his Ph.D. in Clinical Developmental Psychology at Yale University in 1982, Dr. Aber has served on the faculties of Barnard College and Columbia University, directed the Barnard College Center for Toddler Development, co-directed the Columbia University Project on Children and War, co-founded the Columbia Institute for Child and Family Policy, and directed the Columbia National Center for Children in Poverty.

While at Columbia University, Dr. Aber conducted both basic and applied research studies relevant to child and family policy. His basic research focuses on the social, emotional, behavioral, and cognitive development of children and youth at risk due to family and neighborhood poverty, exposure to violence, abuse/neglect, and parental psychopathology. His applied research focuses on rigorous process and outcome evaluations of innovative programs and policies for children and families at risk, including welfare-to-work programs, comprehensive service programs, and violence prevention programs. Dr. Aber is invited frequently to testify before Congress and state legislatures, to provide information to the media, and to consult with foundations and governments on new child and family initiatives.

Victor Battistich is Deputy Director of Research at the Developmental Studies Center. He has conducted research on the Child Development Project for 20 years and has provided consultation and technical assistance to numerous school-based interventions. His research interests are in child development, prevention, school reform, and the social context of schools. He has published numerous articles and book chapters on these topics.

Mary Bay is an Associate Professor of Special Education and Coordinator of the Special Education Teacher Preparation Program at the University of

Illinois at Chicago. Her research interests focus on prospective teacher learning through traditional and nontraditional routes, mentoring, and mentor education. In each of these domains, she situates her work within the challenges and opportunities present in urban school systems.

Michelle R. Bloodworth is a doctoral student in the Community and Prevention Research Division in the Department of Psychology at the University of Illinois at Chicago. Her interests focus on research and policy issues related to influences of social and emotional learning on academic achievement, the promotion of school success for children growing up in urban communities, school and teacher influences on program implementation, and school-based program evaluation. She works on the Partners for Health, Academic, Social, and Emotional Success (PHASES) project, a multicomponent school-based preventive and positive youth development intervention. Ms. Bloodworth is a predoctoral fellow in UIC's NIMH Prevention Research Training Program in Urban Children's Mental Health and AIDS. She completed her B.A. at the University of Illinois at Champaign and received a M.A. from the University of Colorado.

Joshua L. Brown began working as a research associate at the National Center for Children in Poverty at the Joseph L. Mailman School of Public Health at Columbia University in 1993. He has participated in all phases of the design, implementation, and data analytic work related to the evaluation of the Resolving Conflict Creatively Program. His research interests focus on risk and protective factors associated with the development of aggressive and violent behavior among children and adolescents as well as intervention program design and evaluation. He worked for Metis Associates, Inc., and is now on the faculty of New York University. Dr. Brown completed his Ph.D. in Developmental Psychology at Teachers College, Columbia University.

Richard F. Catalano is Professor and Associate Director of the Social Development Research Group at the University of Washington's School of Social Work. For more than 20 years, he has led research and program development to promote positive youth development and prevent problem behavior. Dr. Catalano is the Principal Investigator on a number of federal grants, which include family, school, and community-based prevention approaches to reduce risk while enhancing the protective factors of bonding and promotion of healthy beliefs and clear standards. He is the co-developer of the Social Development Strategy and co-founder of Developmental Research and Programs.

Sandra L. Christenson is a Professor of Educational and Child Psychology at the University of Minnesota. Her research is focused on interventions that enhance student engagement with school and learning, and identification of contextual factors that facilitate student engagement and increase the probability for student success in school. She is particularly interested in populations that are most alienated from traditional schooling practices and/or at highest risk for nonschool completion.

Maurice J. Elias is Professor, Department of Psychology, Rutgers University, and co-developer of the Social Decision Making/Social Problem Solving Project, named as a Promising Program by the U.S. Department of Education Expert Panel on Safe, Disciplined, and Drug-Free Schools. He is Vice Chair of the Leadership Team of the Collaborative for Academic, Social, and Emotional Learning (CASEL) and co-author, with other members of CASEL, of *Promoting Social and Emotional Learning* (1997). His recent books include *Emotionally Intelligent Parenting* (2000), *How to Raise a Self-Disciplined, Responsible, and Socially Skilled Child* (2000) (see www.EQParenting.com), *Engaging the Resistant Child Through Computers* (2001), and *Raising Emotionally Intelligent Teenagers* (2002).

Jane E. Fleming is an Assistant Professor in Teaching and Learning at the University of Missouri–St. Louis. She received her doctorate in Communication Sciences and Disorders at Northwestern University and completed a postdoctoral fellowship at the University of Illinois at Chicago where she was active in the Collaborative for Academic, Social, and Emotional Learning (CASEL). Her current research interests are urban teacher preparation and the promotion of reading success among urban school children.

Mark T. Greenberg, Ph.D., holds the Bennett Endowed Chair in Prevention Research at Penn State's College of Health and Human Development. He is Director of the Prevention Research Center for the Promotion of Human Development. Since 1981, Dr. Greenberg has been examining the effectiveness of school-based curricula (the PATHS Curriculum) and since 1990, he has served as an investigator in FAST TRACK, a comprehensive program that aims to prevent violence and delinquency in families. Dr. Greenberg is the author of more than 150 journal articles and book chapters on child development and understanding aggression, violence, and externalizing disorders.

Lynne H. Havsy, a doctoral candidate in the School Psychology Program, Department of Educational Psychology, at the University of Minnesota, is a school psychologist with the Newark, New Jersey, Public Schools. Her interests include school-based mental health, school–community collaboration, and school-wide prevention and intervention.

J. David Hawkins is Kozmetsky Professor of Prevention, School of Social Work, and Director of the Social Development Research Group, University of Washington, Seattle. He is a co-founder of Developmental Research and

Programs and president-elect of the Society for Prevention Research. His research focuses on understanding and preventing child and adolescent health and behavior problems. Dr. Hawkins is co-author of the "Preparing for the Drug-Free Years" and "Parents Who Care" prevention programs that empower parents to strengthen family bonding and reduce the risks for health and behavior problems in their families. He has co-authored several books and numerous articles on the promotion of social development and the prediction and prevention of health and behavior problems.

David W. Johnson is a Professor of Educational Psychology at the University of Minnesota where he is co-director of the Cooperative Learning Center. He held the Emma M. Birkmaier Professorship in Education Leadership from 1994–1997. He is a past editor of the *American Educational Research Journal*. He received his doctorate from Columbia University.

Roger T. Johnson is a Professor of Education at the University of Minnesota where he is co-director of the Cooperative Learning Center. He received his doctorate from the University of California at Berkeley. He has extensive teaching experience from kindergarten through eighth grade.

Together, Drs. David and Roger Johnson have published over 400 research articles and book chapters and over 40 books in the areas of cooperation–competition and conflict resolution. They have received awards for research and teaching excellence from the American Psychological Association, American Educational Research Association, Association for Supervision and Curriculum Development, National Council for Social Studies, and American Society for Engineering Education. They have consulted with school systems and universities throughout the world.

Carol A. Kusché is a psychoanalyst and clinical psychologist in private practice in Seattle, Washington, where she treats children, adolescents, and adults. She is a faculty member at the Seattle Psychoanalytic Society & Institute and the Northwest Center for Psychoanalysis and is a Clinical Associate Professor in the Department of Psychology at the University of Washington. Dr. Kusché was co-Principal Investigator on the PATHS Project and co-author, with Dr. Mark Greenberg, of the PATHS Curriculum. She is the author of numerous papers and book chapters on prevention, social-emotional learning, cognition, cortical organization, and emotional development.

Linda Lantieri has over 30 years of experience in education as a teacher, administrator, and university professor. She serves as the Founding Director of the Resolving Conflict Creatively Program of Educators for Social Responsibility, which supports the program in 400 schools in the United States. She is also Director of the New York Satellite Office of the Collaborative for Academic, Social, and Emotional Learning (CASEL), whose central offices are at the University of Illinois at Chicago. Ms. Lantieri is co-author of the book *Waging Peace in Our Schools* (1996) and editor of *Schools with Spirit: Nurturing the Inner Lives of Children and Teachers* (2001).

Paulo N. Lopes received a B.A. in economics from Yale University, then worked in business and journalism. He also worked on documentary film and book projects. He obtained an M.S. in psychology and is working toward a doctorate degree, also at Yale University. His research interests include emotional and practical intelligence, positive psychology, and education.

Barbara L. McCombs has a Ph.D. in Educational Psychology from Florida State University and is a Senior Research Scientist at the University of Denver Research Institute. She has more than 25 years of experience directing research and development efforts in a wide range of basic and applied areas. Her current research focuses on applying learner-centered principles to teacher education via emerging e-learning technologies and to violence prevention via school-based professional development strategies. She currently directs a new Human Motivation, Learning and Development Center at the Institute.

Dr. McCombs is the primary author of *Learner-Centered Psychological Principles* (1997). Her concept of a K–20 seamless professional development model is described in her book, co-authored with Jo Sue Whisler, entitled *The Learner-Centered Classroom and School* (1997). A second book, co-edited with Nadine Lambert, is entitled *How Students Learn* (1998).

Nathaniel Riggs recently received his Ph.D. in Human Development and Family Studies from Pennsylvania State University. His research interests are in the relationship between cognition, emotion, and behavior, and the influence of preventive interventions on children and youth.

Tom Roderick is executive director of Educators for Social Responsibility Metropolitan Area (ESR Metro), which implements the Resolving Conflict Creatively Program and an array of other social-emotional learning programs in the New York City public schools. With Linda Lantieri, Mr. Roderick co-founded the Resolving Conflict Creatively Program in 1985 as a collaborative effort of ESR Metro and the New York City Board of Education. He has a bachelor's degree from Yale University and a master's degree from Bank Street College of Education. He is the author of *A School of Our Own* (2001).

Peter Salovey received a Ph.D. in clinical psychology from Yale University in 1986. He now serves as the Chris Argyris Professor of Psychology, Professor of Epidemiology and Public Health, and Dean of the Graduate School of Arts and Sciences at Yale. Professor Salovey is also Director of the Department of Psychology's Health, Emotion, and Behavior Laboratory and

Deputy Director of the Yale Center for Interdisciplinary Research on AIDS. He is co-author, with V. J. D'Andrea, of *Peer Counseling* (1983) and *Peer Counseling: Skills, Ethics, and Perspectives* (1996), and he edited *Reasoning, Inference, and Judgment in Clinical Psychology* (1988) with Dennis C. Turk. Some of his more recent books include *The Psychology of Jealousy and Envy* (1991), *The Remembered Self: Emotions and Memory in Personality* (1993; with Jefferson A. Singer), *Psychology* (1993; with Zick Rubin and Letitia Anne Peplau), *Emotional Development and Emotional Intelligence* (1997; with David Sluyter), *At Play in the Fields of Consciousness* (1999; with Jefferson A. Singer), and *The Wisdom in Feeling* (2002; with Lisa Feldman Barrett). Professor Salovey completed a six-year term as Associate Editor of *Psychological Bulletin*, was named the first Editor of the *Review of General Psychology*, and served as Associate Editor of *Emotion*.

Eric Schaps is founder and president of the Developmental Studies Center (DSC) in Oakland, CA. Established in 1980, DSC specializes in designing educational programs and evaluating their effects on children's academic, ethical, social, and emotional development. Dr. Schaps is the author of three books and 60 book chapters and articles on character education, preventing problem behaviors, and school change.

Brian H. Smith is a Ph.D. student in the School of Social Work and a research assistant at the Social Development Research Group at the University of Washington. He has a background in social work and counseling in schools. His current research interests are in the dissemination of effective prevention interventions for children and youth.

Daniel Solomon, who passed away since collaborating on the writing of his chapter, was formerly Director of Research at the Developmental Studies Center, where he conducted extensive research and published widely in the areas of the social psychology of education, moral education, and children's social development.

Index